NURTURED BY KNOWLEDGE:
Learning to Do
Participatory Action-Research

The Five Friends and Five Enemies

One day while walking with an Indian friend, Malaquías, he told me the story of the five friends and the five enemies.

"The first enemy of human beings is fear. If you live in fear, you will live like a mouse in a dark corner and never see the light. Fear will become your enemy and you will never grow up. But if you are not afraid of the fear you will have, then you can live in light, and fear becomes your friend.

"If fear is your friend, then you are able to look around you with clarity. But if you think that you can see all things clearly, then you are really blind, and clarity becomes your enemy. If, however, you strive to see clearly, then clarity becomes your friend.

"If fear is your friend and you can see clearly, then you will have power. But if you keep power to yourself, you will become weaker and weaker. If, however, you share the power, you will become strong and power will be your friend.

"If fear is your friend, you see clearly, and you share power, then you will be wise. But if you think you have all the wisdom, then in reality you are ignorant, and wisdom will be your enemy. If, however, you admit that you do not know everything, answers will come to you and wisdom will be your friend.

"If fear is your friend, you see clearly, you share power, and you have wisdom, then you will meet old age. But if you sit, doing nothing and denying your history, then old age will be your enemy. If, however, you meet old age with grace, having met fear, seeing with clarity, sharing power, and making wisdom your friend, then you will live forever."

—Mexican popular folklore as told by
Arturo Ornelas

NURTURED BY KNOWLEDGE:
Learning to Do
Participatory Action-Research

Edited by
Susan E. Smith and Dennis G. Willms
with Nancy A. Johnson

Foreword by Paulo Freire
Preface by Budd L. Hall

The Apex Press
New York

International Development Research Centre
Ottawa

Published in the United States by The Apex Press,
New York, and in Canada by the
International Development Research Centre, Ottawa

The Apex Press is an imprint of the
Council on International and Public Affairs,
777 United Nations Plaza, Suite 3C,
New York, NY 10017 (800/316-2739)

Library of Congress Cataloging-in-Publication Data

Nurtured by knowledge : learning to do participatory action-
research / edited by Susan E. Smith and Dennis G. Willms with
Nancy A. Johnson.
    p.   cm.
    Includes bibliographical references and index.
    ISBN 0-945257-82-1 (hardcover). — ISBN 0-945257-81-3 (pbk.).
    1. Social problems—Research. 2. Action research. 3. Action
research—Case studies. 4. Social action. 5. Social participation.
I. Smith, Susan Elizabeth. II. Willms, Dennis George.
III. Johnson, Nancy Arbuthnot.
HN29.N87 1997   97-5888
300' .72—dc21   CIP

ISBN 0-945257-81-3 (softcover, U.S.)
ISBN 0-945257-82-1 (hardcover, U.S.)
ISBN 0-88936-816-3 (softcover, Can.)

Royalties earned through the sale of this book will be put towards
community development and research projects.

Dedicated to our children
Zaina Oman Huhad
Luke Stefan and Mark Walter Willms
and
Malcolm Scott and Mitchell Arbuthnot Johnson

Contents

List of Figures and Tables ix

Foreword, by Paulo Freire xi

Preface, by Budd L. Hall xiii

Acknowledgements and Explanations xvii

INTRODUCTION 1
    Participatory Action-Research within the
       Global Context, by Susan E. Smith 1
    "You Start Your Research on Your Being,"
       by Dennis G. Willms 7

1. COWS FOR *CAMPESINOS*,
    by Gerald Debbink and Arturo Ornelas 13

2. CHANGING DISABLING ENVIRONMENTS
    THROUGH PARTICIPATORY ACTION-
    RESEARCH: A CANADIAN EXPERIENCE,
    by Mary Law 34

3. DOCTORS, *DAIS*, AND NURSE-MIDWIVES:
    WOMEN'S HEALTH SERVICE UTILIZATION
    IN NORTHERN INDIA, by Patricia Seymour 59

4. "WE ARE DYING. IT IS FINISHED!": LINKING AN
    ETHNOGRAPHIC RESEARCH DESIGN TO AN
    HIV/AIDS PARTICIPATORY APPROACH IN
    UGANDA, by Patricia Spittal, Janette Nakuti,
    Nelson Sewankambo, and Dennis G. Willms 86

5. GROUNDING A LONG-TERM IDEAL:
    WORKING WITH THE AYMARA FOR
    COMMUNITY DEVELOPMENT,
    by Maria-Ines Arratia and Isabel de la Maza 111

6. *PASANTÍAS* AND SOCIAL PARTICIPATION:
    PARTICIPATORY ACTION-RESEARCH
    AS A WAY OF LIFE, by Arturo Ornelas 138

7. DEEPENING PARTICIPATORY
    ACTION-RESEARCH, by Susan E. Smith 173

About the Contributors 265

Index   271

List of Figures and Tables

Figure 1: Communicative Analysis during the
Research Process 43
Figure 2: Map of Region of Tarapaca 117
Figure 3: Schema #1 — Communitarian Hospital 152
Figure 4: Schema #2 — Methodological Proposal
for the Establishment of a
Communitarian Hospital 154
Figure 5: Schema #3 — Formation of the
Community Councils 155
Figure 6: Sistema de referencia 159
Figure 7: El hospital en la comunidad/La
comunidad en el hospital 163
Figure 8: Radio salud/Health on Radio 165
Figure 9: The Total Reality of the People
Is the Point of Departure 167
Figure 10: Framework for Participatory
Action-Research Praxiology 198
Figure 11: Fernandes and Tandon Model of
"Ideal" PAR (1981) with addition
by Maguire (1987) 254

Table 1: Forms of Research 180

Foreword

Nurtured by Knowledge: Learning to Do Participatory Action-Research is a book about people searching for the beauty of knowledge, recognizing that true knowledge is full of politics and dreams and actually arises from rebellious struggles to change the world and ourselves. Those promoting participatory action-research believe that people have a universal right to participate in the production of knowledge which is a disciplined process of personal and social transformation. In this process, people rupture their existing attitudes of silence, accommodation and passivity, and gain confidence and abilities to alter unjust conditions and structures. This is an authentic power for liberation that ultimately destroys a passive awaiting of fate.

When people are the masters of inquiry—the owners of the questions under study—their research becomes a means of taking risks, of expelling visible and invisible oppressors, and of producing actions for transformation. The authors of this book celebrate the human potential to imagine, learn, and create, but also admit that the efforts required to communicate, understand, and work together are disturbing and sometimes painful. It is both difficult and joyful to see patterns of domination that result in internal and external forms of violence, and then to construct practices that strengthen hope and the growth of human protest and spirit.

Nurtured by Knowledge reflects people's experiences in learning actively and consciously to pursue research as a form of liberation. We are indeed nurtured by the construction of meaningful knowledge and thereby give rise to its emergence.

Paulo Freire

Preface

Susan Smith, Dennis Willms, and Nancy Johnson have assembled a most important set of ideas and papers for this book. Their work builds on ideas and feelings about different ways of creating knowledge and different relations between knowledge and power. Reading this manuscript drew me back to 1970 in Tanzania. It was a time when Tanzanian and non-Tanzanian academics were being pushed and pulled to reflect on the political implications of our own research methods. Julius Nyerere, the first President of Tanzania and an intellectual of deep substance, had drawn our attention to the ways in which colonial patterns of education had created dependencies in Tanzania. He spoke of the ways that all imperial powers in Africa and elsewhere had used ideas and knowledge as the most powerful of weapons in the struggles for resource domination and control. Arms, guns, jails, and more were present in the histories of colonialism, but the dominant powers in the world soon found that schooling, administrative procedures, and carefully done research were more effective. When people control themselves, outside coercive forces are not needed.

In Latin America, during the 1970s, Paulo Friere was writing about "thematic investigation," a new way to do social research, which he described in his classic *Pedagogy of the Oppressed*. Many researchers in Tanzania, elsewhere in Africa, and in other parts of the former colonial world were beginning to object to the epistemological assumptions in much of the dominant research methodology of the day. Research that started

xiv NURTURED BY KNOWLEDGE

with an idea in the head of a university-based or outside researcher, and that had as its goal the discovery of information about "others," began to feel contradictory to the goals of increased participation and democracy being called for on the political front. "Participatory Research" was the label that Marja Lissa Swantz, a Finnish researcher in Tanzania, first coined to denote an approach that she and a team of Tanzanian researchers brought forward.

At the same time, Orlando Fals-Borda and many in Colombia and elsewhere in Latin America were stretching the boundaries of sociology with practices that drew on the capacity of ordinary people to create transformative and action-oriented knowledge. They called their work "participatory action research." These two streams of work and other similar streams came together in the Cartagena Conference on Action Research in Cartagena, Colombia, in 1977. The International Council for Adult Education (ICAE), based in Toronto, Ontario, Canada, took up the challenge as well under the leadership of such persons as Rajesh Tandon of India; Yusuf Kassam and Kemal Mustapha of Tanzania; Francisco Vio Grossi of Chile; and Ted Jackson, Deborah Barndt, and Dian Marino of Canada. The ICAE financed an international participatory action-research network that linked activist scholars from all parts of the world.

This book can trace its heritage directly from the rich and diverse challenges that participatory action-research represents: challenges to "Western" or "colonial" patterns of research for domination; challenges to academia to become engaged in the struggles for justice in all fields; challenges to notions of philosophy and the value of ideas; challenges to patterns of patriarchy and race domination; and challenges to false ideals of detachment and objectivity.

Some of the chapters in this book deal with the practical difficulties, the ethical dilemmas, and the frustrations experienced when academically trained researchers confront issues in their lives and communities. These chapters offer us a rare insight into what are the real questions that face us as researchers—not topics that we find in most journal articles or research

books. Other chapters provide us with rich details about doing participatory action-research in a variety of settings. The
"Cows for *Campesinos*" piece, which allows an Alberta dairy
farmer and a Latin American popular educator to dialogue, is
a good example here. But all the case studies have poignancy
and purpose. The final chapter by Susan Smith weaves together
an extensive and complex theory that will be immediately valuable to students and veterans alike.

This book does not attempt to represent all the tendencies
or strands of participatory action-research. There are far too
many profound ways in which we are beginning to understand
indigenous ways of knowing, environmental ways of knowing,
or Third World women's ways of knowing to be able to cover
all that in one book.

The most powerful contribution that *Nurtured by Knowledge*
makes is from the dimension of the spirit. The text offers insight into the thoughts of a group of democratically minded
and sensitive people as they try to understand and give meaning to their own lives and the lives of others. These writings
suggest that the persons who engage in participatory action-
research from dominant or privileged positions are at least as
deeply transformed as those with whom they work. This is an
intimate work, a work that must be read over and over again.

Budd L. Hall, Ontario Institute for Studies
in Education, University of Toronto, Canada

Acknowledgements and Explanations

On separate hunches, we attended the Celebrating People's Knowledge Conference held in Calgary, Alberta, Canada, in July 1989. Athough we did not know it at the time, we plunged into unknown but captivating water and eventually this book emerged.

While still in Calgary, Murray Dickson, a good friend from Saskatchewan, provoked us over coffee to organize a follow-up workshop that would sustain a growing interest in participatory action-research (PAR) in Canada. Ready for a challenge, we teamed up and planned a retreat at the Regina Mundi Centre in Ontario for October 1990. We wanted to engage participants in a smaller event with few case studies (three) in order to deepen our understanding of PAR. Rather than concentrate on abstract "ideal" models, we sought out people with grounded experiences in PAR.

After deliberating with others and obtaining financial support generously provided by the International Development and Research Centre (IDRC) and the Canadian International Development Agency (CIDA), we invited the following resource people to Regina Mundi: Maria-Ines Arratia (Canada-Chile); Isabel de la Maza (Chile); Reg and Rose Crowshoe (Alberta, Canada); Alfred Jean-Baptiste and Greg Conchelos (Toronto, Canada); Dan Kaseje (Kenya); Helen Lewis (Virginia, USA); and Arturo Ornelas (Cuernavaca, Mexico). Fifty people attended the four-day workshop.

Toying with the idea of a book for a year, we finally decided to compile detailed examples of participatory action-research that would include the ones presented at Regina Mundi. These case studies would help elucidate the difficulties in undertaking PAR. Why was this important? Sometimes, individuals interpret the language of PAR in mixed ways: idealistic but intimidating, captivating but overwhelming. In this respect, the challenge of doing research for social justice can seem daunting, constrained by personal misgivings or predictions of failure. We wanted the book to contain real life experiences about social change and the attainment of knowledge, ones that would explore the journey itself. In some instances, the cases would exemplify PAR; others would reflect the frustrations of traditional approaches and the difficulties of crossing the threshold to doing genuine PAR. Hence, the subtitle of this book: *Learning to Do Participatory Action-Research*. (Some of these frustrations and difficulties are amplified on pages 8-9 of the book.)

We also recognized that the experiences on which the book would be based would draw on a rich legacy of past efforts by marginalized peoples and social scientists in the Third World to fashion fresh approaches to creating knowledge and improving lives. This legacy is further described on pages 175-176.

From the first moment that we heard Arturo Ornelas speak, he stepped into our lives and became a friend and critic. He is a concrete manifestation of this legacy. We are indebted to Arturo for his faith in us and for the development of certain ideas about research and knowledge found in this book.

The authors of the six case studies continuously demonstrated their commitment and hard work. We acknowledge with gratitude the contributions of Maria-Ines Arratia, Gerald Debbink, Isabel de la Maza, Mary Law, Janette Nakuti, Arturo Ornelas, Nelson Sewankambo, Patricia Seymour, and Patricia Spittal. Their vulnerability and honesty, evidenced in personal revelations and lessons learned, can only help others to engage in participatory action-research.

Preserving the uniqueness of each case study while, at the

same time, ensuring the use of a clear, personal voice, true to the actual experience in the field, was in some cases a delicate balancing act. Our intention was to draw out the type and depth of internal commitment and motivation; the nature of people's questions, processes, and actions; and the moral dilemmas—all part-and-parcel of conducting PAR. The writing, editing, and rewriting had predictable tensions so that, at times, we were certain that authors wanted to step away from the project with its numerous demands. We are immeasurably grateful for the authors' willingness to persist and to share of themselves in their writing.

Nancy Arbuthnot Johnson, our research associate, worked closely with us and the case study authors. Quite frankly, this book might not have happened without her. An anthropologist with years of experience in discourse analysis and editing, Nancy was able to interpret meanings, the "said in the saying," identify gaps where readers might be confused, and critically question the content, structure, and sense of the book. We benefited greatly from her kind and gentle heart, her "patient impatience" that prodded and encouraged, and her active, green pen—many, many "thank yous" for all of it, Nancy.

Finally, we acknowledge with appreciation the funding contributions of IDRC and CIDA. Both agencies repeatedly extended deadlines during the slow process of communicating with nine authors in multiple countries and carrying out our own responsibilities. Warm thanks also to Rolande (Rollie) O'Brien and Marc Hyndman at the Canadian Society for International Health in Ottawa for managing the finances and supporting *Nurtured by Knowledge* during all phases of its evolution—from the initial idea of a workshop at Regina Mundi through to publication. Views expressed in this book may not be shared by our funders and administrative supporters. That responsibility is, of course, ours.

The Editors

Susan: Unpredictably, particular instances seem to "still," captured in my inner eye, impressed fully onto my heart (although I am not always aware of this happening at the time). These instances tend to resurface later, pushing me to re-see, re-feel, and mull over the experience and its vital meaning.

Several moments of this vivid stillness occurred during the writing of *Nurtured by Knowledge* and the (related) production of "From the Field," a film about participatory action-research created by a small group of friends here in Calgary and in Mexico. Each instance helped me to understand better the potential of participatory action-research as a way of knowing and being in the world. I recall Orlando Fals-Borda, of graceful wisdom, saying, "I do not try and convince others, I only pile up the evidence," at the 1992 Struggling for Strategies workshop held at the foot of the Rocky Mountains; conducting a dialogue-drawing of participants' comments with Lorne Jaques at the 1993 Participatory Action-Research as a Way of Life conference in Calgary; sudden recognition of a broad pattern to personal involvement in PAR while listening to Gerald and Arturo talk (sometimes haltingly) in response to probing and, at times, troublesome questions posed by Val Wiebe and myself; and sitting with the group of community health nurses (you know who you are) in talking circles, passing the stone, coming to know ourselves, each other, our work, and our worlds. I am grateful to all of you.

Recently, after intensely reviewing the Uganda case study, poignant, tearful feelings from a running river of deeply layered memories broke to the surface—a river formed ten years ago when I was living in the midst of thousands of famine refugees, people with absolute courage stranded in hellish misery. Sometimes, people's stories, when truly fixed to an experience, have unexpected effects on both the reader and the writer. When the words touch the hidden or the unknown, they can evoke the fortitude to look and renew the strength to try. We "lose fear of the fear we will have." This is why it is so important to express what happened clearly, with feelings and depth, and without muddying the telling for the sake of reputation, funding, or deadlines. The case studies hopefully do that.

While *Nurtured by Knowledge* was being put together, I moved back to Calgary to begin graduate studies under the able guidance of Mathew Zachariah in the Faculty of Education at the University of Calgary. My family, now within driving distance, helped me immensely with the ins and outs of everyday living. I was assisted greatly by a research fellowship from the Ministry of Health of Ontario, Canada, and by moral and administrative support from dear colleagues at the School of Nursing, McMaster University, Ontario. (Again, views expressed in this book may not be shared by the Ministry of Health nor by McMaster or Calgary universities.)

Dennis: What happens to one, happens for a reason! Meaningful events, significant relationships, unexpected insights that have influenced my life at different times: these have happened for a reason. This is what I believe!

There are a number of ways to interpret such happenings: some call it fate, chance, accident, Spirit. What I do know is that the friendships, family, and freedom that have come my way have seemed both providential and unexpected.

I have come to learn that it is all right to be vulnerable, and human (ultimately, humane) to embrace the Mystery, as yet, not fully understanding why things are as they are. I am still learning how to respond to these truths in a way that sustains, strengthens, and silences the fear.

For me, this monograph is a testament to the human spirit and evidence of a deeper, more encompassing logic. The persons represented here have taught me much more than a theoretical understanding of participatory action research (PAR); rather, they have taught me about accountability, nurturance, and that making even a small difference matters. This is a moral logic and fundamental to all other forms of reasoning and explanation.

Appreciating the "lessons learned," I am extremely grateful to family, friends, and colleagues who have nurtured me along the way. Rita, my wife, has been an invaluable support to me and to our work in so many ways. For one thing, she has made it easy, relaxing, and enjoyable for friends to come home. It is a gift she has. More importantly, she has been a constant and loving presence for Luke and Mark when work takes me away. They and I are indeed fortunate.

INTRODUCTION

Participatory Action-Research
within the Global Context

Susan E. Smith

Stretching as far as the eye could see across the barren land, makeshift straw mats sheltered broken families from the vicious sun. The people themselves, 100,000 in total, provided the only relief to the tediousness of the virtual moonscape, unbroken by any hint of green. Two refugees, both men dressed in near rags, approached and spoke to me quietly, hesitantly, through an interpreter. Having just come from the weekly food distribution, they explained that for the past three weeks, their family wheat ration had been only two-thirds of the allocated amount. They held open their cotton sacks so I could see the contents—unappetizing, grey-looking flour ("A Gift From The People Of The United States of America" printed on the outside of the bag). Hardly something to get excited about. But without this allocation, their children, with skin visibly stretched over bone, would get almost nothing to eat. All of us standing there in the hot, shifting sand knew that.

Annoyed, I reacted quickly, "Get into the truck. We'll speak to the camp coordinator." The coordinator glanced inside the sacks and spoke rapidly to the two men. As they stood stiffly without response, he turned to me, switched to English, and smoothly said, "Please don't worry, Susan. I will look after it." Relieved at having one less problem in the midst of this chaos, I thanked him.

*Later, Oman translated what the coordinator had said to the refu-
gees: "You will get what you are given. If you dare complain to the
Canadian again, I will see that you are severely punished." Angry
tears smarted. Damn, once again—a simplistic response on my part
and a thoughtless acceptance of patronizing and false reassurances,
with potentially serious repercussions.*

*The multiple meanings of something so basic to human survival:
food as sustenance for landless people escaping famine and war, living out the consequences of political decisions made by distant, powerful others; food in the guise of charitable foreign aid, arriving too
little and too late; food as greedy corruption; food as effective means
for punishment and control. Desperately needing food, we were chok-
ing on the dust of that grimy flour.*

I cried for the people. And for my naivete.

—Personal recollection, 1985

When a contradiction appears in flesh and blood—when
we live it—we are never the same again. The disturbance cuts
deep, making an open wound. When the contradictions start
to accumulate, piling up one on one, oozing slowly, not healing, they become intolerable. As a privileged person with
countless opportunities but wrestling with nagging doubts
and no longer willing to coast or conform, I began to search,
increasingly driven by desire for meaningful purpose.

GLOBAL CONTEXT OF CRISIS

Four crises characterize our global context, both in the
North and South: poverty, war and militarization, ecological
destruction of life forms, and repression of human beings.
Threatening the continuation of life on Earth, each of these
four world crises actively reinforces the other in a convoluted
"global problematique."

Paul Ekins elaborated on these four crises and their causation at length in *A New World Order: Grassroots Movements for*

Global Change (1992). He also provided multiple profiles and examples of individuals and people's organizations that promote new movement for social change based on democratization of knowledge, development, and the state. These were characterized by "cultural diversity within a global perspective"; an ecocentric perception, that places "humanity within and as part of nature"; the "development of people in the round"; and, a "mode of governance which promotes autonomy, initiative and capability."

The refugees in the story above were engulfed in the vortex of these four crises—living within poverty and war in a spreading desert, often receiving degrading treatment. Certain images typify the reality of people living in long-term poverty: the nauseating smell of acute destitution; the cracked, hardened palms of the prematurely aged father; the resilient woman's sigh of survival or silent defeat; the cocky, defiant eyes of youth, clouded with fear.

Other overt signs of crisis vary in combination from region to region: poor food, landlessness, inadequate housing and green space; high rates of underemployment and disease; physical exhaustion from overwork; and attacks on self or others that release an inner violence. This is a context of raw existence, permeated by fatigue and sometimes despair.

The majority of the world's populations contend with day-to-day survival and, over time, acquire multiple symptoms of poor health and encounter few life opportunities. With little control over their lives and destinies, they are caught in down-spiralling cycles that result in tangled webs of deprivation that are characterized by disorganized vulnerability, powerlessness, isolation, physical weakness, and insecurity (Chambers, 1983: 112).

There is another type of poverty, one rampant in the urban, industrialized world. Cities grow too big with little sense of community; people are increasingly mobile, focussed on individual competition and consumerism, and are bombarded with media messages. The ties that compassionately bond human relationships are disturbingly weak. Too many people are

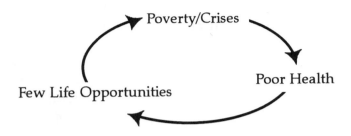

Cycle of Economic or Spiritual Poverty

vaguely discontent or living on the edge of anger. Rising rates of addictions to drugs and alcohol, child and sexual abuse, battery, family violence, loneliness, obesity, depression, and suicide attest to widespread confusion and emptiness. This is a poverty of spirit. It also is cyclical, revealing symptoms of poor health that also lead to limited opportunities in life.

DOMINATING FORCES

When we critically examine these poverties and crises, digging deep for their root causes and consequences, a more complete picture appears. Problems and strengths are studied within a totality—within the social, political, economic, and spiritual context. We can examine the specific forces that ultimately determine health and circumstances in relation to the civic and personal responsibilities held by individuals and groups in the local setting and beyond. This type of structural analysis allows us to better understand the opportunities and choices held by people in different circumstances.

> By the end of the century, the defining characteristics of modern Western society were in place—centrality of the economic and technology-centered institutions, rising demand for democracy and equity, unbridled national sovereignty, and "reality" defined by science. These characteristics account for the astounding successes of modern society; they are also the source of the global dilemmas we all now face (Harman, 1988: 19).

Ekins summarized three dominating forces that are causing and maintaining the current cyclical crises of poverty, war,
ecological destruction, and denial of human rights (1992: 203-
205). The first is "scientism," a prevailing attitude among scientists, academics, policymakers, and others that maintains the
hegemony (authority) of modern technocratic science—the scientific method—and attempts to monopolize the definition of
knowledge. Those holding this world view, certain of its successful achievements in prediction and manipulation of the
physical environment, continue to devalue the "ideas, experiences and accumulated wisdom of the majority of human-
kind" (*ibid*.: 203).

A second, related force is "developmentalism" which de-
fines consumption and accumulation as major goals for all
countries. Actions are justified with arguments of wealth creation and economic efficiency. Participation in competitive
economic markets is enforced; and too often "resources and
social structures that give independence or relief from the
market are ruthlessly assaulted or sequestered; families and
communities are ruptured; and water and biomass expropri-
ated" (*ibid*.: 205). Self-reliance and small-scale production for
local consumption are eroded.

"Statism" is the third major force causing global crisis. This
is the sovereignty of the state governments which have legiti-
mized command over people's lives and obtained frequent oppressive, "penetrating power" through the use of controlling
technologies and information (*ibid*.: 205-206). There are numerous examples of outrageous irresponsibility by individuals
in various governments that have resulted in massive public
debts, terrifying patterns of attack and torture, gross environmental degradation, and opulent lifestyles for an elite few, ultimately financed by the poor.

These three predominate forces are converging, bringing
about an unprecedented, volatile state on Earth. Over the
past decade, many have warned that prevailing societal patterns seriously threaten the planet: human beings are at a
critical juncture.

FIRE OF HOPE

Countering the ultimate death within life—the death of dreams—is the inspiration of hope. A search for hope can start with a single question and lead people on a path of discovery. Vital flashes of learning can deepen analysis, build passionate understanding, and strengthen the will to respond to fundamental human needs. Humanizing life experiences that touch the inner self give courage to face dehumanizing situations.

Nurtured by Knowledge is about an approach to research and social change called participatory action-research (PAR). Engagement in PAR is a journey of development, permitting people to rediscover the realities of their lives and their potential capabilities. Prompted by diverse questions and tensions, individuals enter into a fluid process, searching for difference, encountering problems and doubts, and joining forces with others in the complex struggle to build self-reliance and re-humanize their worlds.

When people form a group with a common purpose, investigate their situation, and make decisions to take actions that re-form power and create justice, their reality is transformed. In so doing, they also are transformed—losing fear, gaining confidence, self-esteem, and direction. This process of participatory action-research produces knowledge based on experience: the wisdom of the people.

References

Chambers, R. 1983. *Rural Development: Putting the Last First.* London: Longman Scientific and Technical.

Ekins, P. 1992. *A New World Order Grassroots Movements for Global Change.* New York: Routledge, Chapman & Hall.

Harman, W. 1988. The transpersonal challenge to the scientific paradigm. *Revision* 11(2): 13-21.

"You Start Your Research on Your Being"

Dennis G. Willms

. . . [T]here was research going on in my own mind, research
in Arturo's mind, research in all the campesinos' *minds. We*
were all researching what we were doing.
—Gerald Debbink

REDISCOVERING RESEARCH

When we think about "research," often what comes to mind are images of technicians in white lab coats hunched over microscopes, ivory tower professors absorbed in stacks of books, flickering computer screens, and assistants filling in survey questionnaires or conducting interviews and focus groups. Generally, research is perceived to be the domain of scientists, academics, and universities. To do research is to collect, analyze, and interpret data by means of certain accepted and well-defined procedures and protocols.

Our meaning of research, however, is broader. Research should be understood as a process of rediscovering and recreating personal and social realities—a definition which recalls the etymology of the word. The word "research" derives from the verb "recerchier" in Old French ("rechercher" in modern French), meaning "to look at again." When so understood, it gains a new legitimacy: a legitimacy of liberation. Doing research encompasses an Alberta dairy farmer questioning, "Why do some people 'have' and others 'have not'?" while working with Mexican *campesinos* to find potable water and grow new crops; health personnel and community members in Honduras rethinking the purpose of a community hospital; or parents of disabled children in a small Canadian city looking at the "sorts of things" that make it easier or harder for their children to participate in everyday activities.

Participatory action-research is based on this liberating understanding of the nature of inquiry. It is about individuals and groups researching their personal beings, social-cultural settings, and experiences. They reflect on their values, shared realities, political resistances, and collective meanings, needs, and goals. The group remembers what has been dismembered: the capacities to think, explore, love, participate, resist, decide, and act. Knowledge is generated: a way of knowing with the mind and heart that incorporates personal and social understandings and authenticates experiences. The recovery of personal and social histories, reexamination of realities, and regaining of power through deliberate actions leads to the production of knowledge that can nurture, empower, and liberate persons and groups to achieve a more humane and equitable world.

PAR as a Journey

Doing PAR means taking a journey because PAR is about movement—movement from the way things are to the way things could be. It is about transformation on both personal and social levels. At the heart of this transformation is a research process which involves investigating the circumstances of place; reflecting on the needs, resources, and constraints of the present reality; examining the possible paths to be taken; and consciously moving in new directions.

Finding one's way can be a fearful experience. Individuals and groups have to be open to learning, growing, and taking risks. In questioning the status quo—institutional or bureaucratic systems, unfair distributions, conventional research methodologies, or family heritage—people risk criticism, loss of position or status, and sometimes even their lives. Initially and at different points in the process, persons and groups, plagued by doubts and uncertainties, may fear "stepping out" of what is familiar. Doing PAR takes time and patience; the pace of the journey varies, sometimes quick and at other times agonizingly slow. Usually, people require opportunities to "talk it through" in a critical dialogue of authentic listening and speaking. Others draw nearer, joining forces to undertake chosen actions and eliminate or avoid obstacles in their path. People living within a sense of community transform their ways of reasoning and acting. Others then also respond differently.

The authors of the six case studies in *Nurtured by Knowledge* give voice to their journeys, demonstrating a breadth of experiences in social investigation. Writing in the first person and placing themselves in the picture, the authors of four case studies (Honduras, Mexico, Canada, and Chile), speak about PAR as lived experience. The authors of two chapters relate their experiences and frustrations with more conventional research methods—their rich descriptions allow readers to come to the threshold of PAR while the other cases demonstrate the complex dimensions of PAR as a process of social change and knowledge production. Later, after the case studies were written, all authors again reflected on the nature of their experiences and lessons learned, relating these to their present purposes and situations. These retrospective considerations are postscripts to each chapter, reflecting continued movement and the reshaping of emotion, thought, and action.

In "Cows for *Campesinos*," Gerald Debbink, a Canadian dairy farmer, tells of his ongoing journey towards a deeper and more intimate understanding of himself, his privilege, and tradition, and the suffering and inequities experienced by Mexican *campesinos* (subsistence farmers). His is the personal voice in the chapter. A second voice is that of Arturo Ornelas who guided Gerald as they worked together in the small villages during Gerald's first years in Mexico. Arturo, a Mexican educator and community activist, comments on participatory action-research, linking methodological ideas to Gerald's account.

"Changing Disabling Environments through Participatory Action Research: A Canadian Experience" documents the work of a university-based research team led by Mary Law with parents of children with disabilities in Cambridge, Ontario. It is also about Mary's first experience in organizing group-controlled, action-oriented research and her efforts to step out of her "ingrained positivistic, quantitative world view." The group breaks down stereotypes of children with disabilities, creates a sense of solidarity between families with children with disabilities, and eventually forms a parents' organization to address the problems encountered by their children.

In "Doctors, *Dais*, and Nurse-Midwives: Women's Health Service Utilization in Northern India," Patricia Seymour, a primary care physician with an interest in women's health, describes her desire to "go into the community, learn something, and give back to the people" during a year-long stay in northern India. It is a wrenchingly honest and often humorous personal account of her experience—a time of questioning and "intense learning" as she examined her own assumptions about the priorities of the rural women, and grappled constantly with different expectations about local participation in research.

Patricia Spittal and three other members of an ethnographic research team interweave two major threads in "'We Are Dying. It Is Finished!' Linking an Ethnographic Research Design to an HIV/AIDS Participatory Intervention in Uganda." The first thread reflects their desire to document the life experiences of women "who fear and suffer the consequences of HIV/AIDS" in a small Ugandan town. The second thread is about the research team itself. After achieving a deeper and broader understanding of the complexity of a situation characterized by "hopelessness and despair," they began to doubt their work and underlying assumptions, and acknowledged feelings of guilt and uncertainty. Now the research team is wrestling with the question of how to begin a PAR process in a community that is so seriously demoralized.

In "Grounding a Long-Term Ideal: Working with the Aymara for Community Development," Maria-Ines Arratia and Isabel de la Maza describe work done by an non-governmental organization (Taller de Estudios Aymara), among Aymara women of the remote highlands of northern Chile. Their case study recognizes how knowledge and social change are produced in many different ways, and demonstrates the dialectical relationship between participatory development and participatory action-research. Both women approach PAR as a way of life. They are committed to "a certain way of being in the world"—a way that values just, democratic participation and a "love of other human beings," that is "in tune with the 'other'" and trustfully "gives back."

"*Pasantías* and Social Participation: Participatory Action-Research as a Way of Life" tells of Arturo Ornelas' experience in organizing, together with a facilitation team, a series of *pasantías* for health personnel and community members to rediscover the purpose of a community hospital in the small Honduran town of La Esperanza. Broadly translated, *pasantía* means "passing through" a social experience with a critical eye and a sense of personal fulfilment. Arturo's personal reflections on PAR as a transforming process that can move people from oppressive alienation to liberation are interspersed with his descriptions of the *pasantías* and the actions taken by the various communities.

In the final chapter, "Deepening Participatory-Action Research," Susan Smith proposes a holistic framework for PAR methodology where "spiralling moments within an individual and for the group" constitute potential movement for social change. The case study authors entered "inside the spiral" when they spoke of their personal transformations and involvement in group actions and decisions. Research can lead to redirection of self, others, and society. Yet, "the intention to do PAR, while perhaps establishing important groundwork for individual or team transformation, does not constitute PAR itself. In situations of disturbing struggle for social participation and change, people come face-to-face with themselves: these are probably the most difficult moments of all."

A PAR journey is marked with signposts: shifting questions and doubts, points of critical awareness, moments of celebration, and connections that demonstrate a deepening understanding of lived and transformed realities. For many readers, the narratives may recall familiar circumstances and times—signposts on our own journeys of rediscovery and recreation.

The hardest thing to do is to step out of what you are comfortable with. The unknown is always there once you step out. Then you have to take everything that comes at you. You have to answer for yourself and that's how you learn.
                                        —Gerald Debbink

1

COWS FOR *CAMPESINOS*

Gerald Debbink and Arturo Ornelas

ဢ Editors' Note: Throughout this case, two voices alternate. One voice is that of Gerald Debbink, a Canadian dairy farmer. He talks about his recent experiences in Mexico and an emerging life commitment. His story actually highlights five smaller stories that focus on some cows, leftover chicken bones, the value of salt, a water truck, and the use of a tractor. Building on the other, each story demonstrates Gerald's continued struggle to learn and his subsequent shifts in perception.

The second voice is of a more abstract, philosophical nature. Arturo Ornelas, a Mexican educator and community activist, comments on participatory action-research, linking methodological ideas to Gerald's lessons. Arturo's own struggle for meaning, fraught with tensions similar to Gerald's, lies behind his comment: "This chapter contains many of the conclusions I reached after years of living through both alienation and success."

Working together with local Mexican *campesinos*, their experiences were complex—full of twists, questions, doubts, as well as moments of joy. "Cows for *Campesinos*" moves from an initial act of charity to the creation of a bridge of solidarity.

Nancy was instrumental in the development of the chapter. Following extensive interviews with both Gerald and Arturo, conducted by Dennis and later Susan, Nancy reviewed the interview transcripts, and, recognizing the fit between the practical and philosophical voices, constructed the alternating voices in the dialogue. ဢ

Getting Started

Gerald: In 1988, Christian Farmers Federation of Alberta organized a study tour to Mexico. I joined the tour group. Upon arrival we went to a place called the Cuernavaca Centre for Intercultural Dialogue on Development (CCIDD). We asked the organizers of CCIDD to invite somebody from the rural cooperatives—somebody who was working with the *campesinos*—to speak to us about their problems. We heard lectures, visited families, and learned about the history and struggles of Latin America. This, by the way, is how I first met Arturo. He was one of the people who came to speak to us.

The tour really opened our minds and our eyes to how people in the Third World live. Throughout the next year, the Alberta farmers who went got together to talk about our experience. My wife Mary Anna and I prepared a slide presentation, speaking to churches, schools, and a number of different groups. This generated interest in organizing another tour, and so the following year Mary Anna and I put one together. This time there was more emphasis on agriculture in the rural setting, the cooperatives, and how we as Canadian farmers could build a solidarity with farmers in Mexico—farmer-to-farmer solidarity. During the tour, I decided to spend three days with Arturo in the villages in the municipality of Tepoztlan. The group was very moved by the two-week experience and wanted to help.

Shortly after we returned to Canada, people from both tours met near Millet, Alberta. We shared our experiences and talked about how we could support the Mexican *campesinos*. Many wanted to give money, but I said, "If we give money, it's very cold. You give them money and you don't remember; you forget. Why don't we do something more concrete, something that we can always remember these people by and they can always remember us." Since the majority were dairy farmers, I asked, "Why don't we see if we can get some cows together and give the cows?" Although a little hesitant, they felt perhaps there was something to it. We decided that we would explore the idea first to see if people were willing to contribute. A notice was sent out through two organizations: Christian Farmers Federation (now called Earthkeeping) and Change for Children. In a matter of a month, we had 36 cows and two bulls— 34 Holsteins, two Jersey heifers, a Jersey bull, and a Holstein bull. Altogether, 38 were collected to go to Mexico. In this way, more than 25 Canadian families were involved in the effort.

I contacted Arturo and he asked the *campesinos* if they wanted the cows. They said yes and set about deciding how to distribute the cows when they arrived. At the time, the *campesinos* were reluctant to work together; they were divided.

Arturo: In their desire to dominate and control the people, the Latin American governments have worked to make us believe that we are separated and cannot work together. They would have us believe that we cannot establish common goals and objectives, make use of common resources, or do common work. The governments have worked to destroy "community." Community means common unity, common goals, common work.

I do not deny the importance of individual values, individual desires, or individual progress, but what has happened is that we no longer talk with our neighbour or enjoy being a part of our community or *barrio*. We no longer work together even as a family. We tend to live our lives at the level of ideas, creating fantasies, sometimes being anguished by fantasies, sometimes trying to achieve unattainable dreams—a big house, a big car, a big job. It is the same for peasants in Mexico as it is for Canadians. We are seldom happy or content with what we have. Living by these values, we have become alienated from one another and in the social sense are weak. There is no community. We cannot struggle together easily.

Participatory action-research permits us, little by little, to discover the reality of our lives. I use the word "discover" because even if we think we know this reality, many times we are misled. Our alienation makes us believe that our reality is a fantasy, and that fantasy is reality. Participatory action-research is about really knowing a reality, and in knowing that reality, taking action in order to transform the reality for the better. Through the act of transforming reality, we are transformed ourselves.

Gerald: I went along on the truck carrying the cows and met Arturo at the Mexican/U.S. border. We hired a Mexican trucker to take the cows the rest of the way. When we arrived at the cooperative, Arturo and I invited the peasants to help with the unloading of the cows. Forty *campesinos* were there to help unload the cows and take them to a corralled area. In a meeting, we talked about how to distribute them; it was decided among the people that they would distribute the cows on the basis of which families were capable of taking care of them. The cows were the property of the cooperative until the first heifer calf was one year of age. At that point, the family had to give the calf to another family poorer than themselves within the village or return it to the cooperative, and the cooperative would decide who would receive it.

Shortly after the cows arrived, I went home to Canada for two weeks. During several meetings with Canadian people in different parts of Alberta, I explained what had happened to the cows after they left Canada, all the troubles we had had, and everything that went on. It was a definite miracle that the cows got there. The Alberta farmers were excited and continually wanted to know more about the cows and how they were doing.

At that time also, Mary Anna and I decided to move our family to Mexico. We sold our dairy cows and rented out our farm in Millet. We wanted to work with the village *campesinos*. For the first year we visited the villages; I went with Arturo to the weekly and monthly meetings of the different cooperatives. The cows were just one part of the whole *campesino* movement. There were projects involving mushrooms, chickens, and a corn grinder for the women to make tortillas; there were different water projects; there was a group of farmers working on transportation to deliver their tomatoes to market; there was a goat cooperative. In any village, there may have been four different projects, not all happening at the same time but over a matter of eight years and affecting different people. One group of people would work with the cows; another grew mushrooms. Yet another was in charge of the corn grinder. Within a village, depending on the number of projects, up to approximately one-half of the adults in the community were involved in one way or another. The people worked together—organizing, planning, participating, recognizing the barriers, and accepting the rewards.

Arturo: As individuals engaged in participatory action-research, we must live with the people, walk with them, work with them, be with them. We must learn with them to read their reality, to read the context of their lives. This is not the type of research done in laboratories or in universities where you read texts. What is important is reading the context of peoples' lives. Of course, it is possible to read books in order to gain an understanding of the context, but not to create more ideas coming from ideas. We must let go of the myth of the separation of manual work and intellectual work: the two are intertwined. When a peasant goes to do his work, he needs to think, analyze, and prepare a plan in his mind. When an intellectual needs to take action, he must engage in manual work. There exists a theoretical practice and also a practical practice—I'm talking about a practical practice, not an academic one.

Manual work is the only real link between an intellectual and the community. If you do not work alongside the people in the community, they will not believe you. You create a moral value among the people—a belief in their reality. If you do not do manual work then you cannot be transformed yourself. Work is a source of transformation; it is also a source of knowledge. There is a sense of community when a group of people come together to do work.

So the first question is, "How can I, as an outsider, really be in touch with the internal rationality of the people with whom I am working?" I must begin by trying to gain a moral value vis-à-vis these people. How do I gain this moral value? I gain it by working with them, living with them, being with them. I begin internalizing the intimate threads of their lives—of their reality. To do so, however, I must start with the idea that I am an ignorant. I must go, not with the conventional idea that I am somebody who knows and who will teach, but as someone who is ignorant and needs to learn. If I go as an outsider who knows and who will teach, what happens is that I teach nothing and learn nothing. I will live in a vacuum. That vacuum is very dangerous because it can lead outsiders to impose authoritarian ways. We end up teaching our ideas because we need to see a concretization of them. We become tyrants.

Chicken Bones and Salt Licks

Gerald: The first year I did not know much. The only thing that I knew was that these cows had to eat. The most important thing for me was the cows. Now I know better, but for me at that time the important thing was that the cows not suffer. I did not understand the hardships of the families there. I knew they were poor. I could see that they were poor. They lived in these cardboard shacks but I didn't *know* hardship.

After two years in Mexico, Samuel said to me, "You don't know the poverty in my village." And I answered, "How can I not know? I've been with you for two years. I've eaten in your house. I've slept in your house. I've gone with you to many functions. I've talked to you a lot. What do you mean I don't know?"

He said, "You come for a fiesta, or whenever you come to the village a meal is prepared for you and you eat with the owner of that house. If you watch next time, you will notice that he will not finish his plate. He will not eat all his chicken and sauce. You know why?"

Samuel said that people know that North Americans never finish their plate. Because they are so well nourished, they do not need everything on their plate. "People want to show you in their way that they are well nourished and don't have to finish everything on their plate. After you leave, what you don't see is that they literally lick the bones of the chicken that you ate." Samuel added, "You'll never see that because you're a foreigner."

Arturo: You begin by recognizing a need and knowing it well. Then you start taking action. Reflecting on that action with the others, maybe every day for a half an hour or more, a dialogue starts about the need and about the action. The intention of the dialogue is to discover the intimacy of the subject about which you are concerned. Intimacy is a type of soup made with honesty, sincerity, deepness, emotion, feelings, thoughts, utopias—everything. It nourishes you. You discover or learn when you eat this soup. The Spanish word for knowledge, "saber," comes from the Latin "sabor," meaning flavour. In order to know, you need to taste, to eat. In my culture, you cannot separate these two things. You eat knowledge. You are nourished by knowledge. You achieve intimacy by doing a deep analysis of your inner being and celebrating that analysis by dialoguing with others. It is an act of creation and re-creation.

Gerald: Every week I went with Arturo to visit the villages and I remember that my main concern was the well-being of the cows. Every week I noticed that the cows were not getting salt. I explained to Arturo that the cows needed salt if they were going to be healthy and strong. At that time, I do not think I realized that the people weren't even healthy and strong, let alone the cows. During a meeting, I mentioned the importance of the cows having salt. Arturo and I went home. The next week we came back and there was no salt. I said to Arturo, "Look, these cows have to have salt. They've been without for four months now." At the next meeting, I stressed more strongly that cows must have salt. We went back home.

The next week there was still no salt. I said to Arturo, "Tomorrow I'm going to go and buy the salt." He said, "Good. Go. You buy the salt but understand what you're doing." On the way home I asked him what he meant by "understand what you're doing." He said, "Just think through what you're doing." I thought about it and didn't get the salt because I didn't know what he meant. We went back the next week and the *campesinos* still didn't have salt. I said to Arturo, "Tomorrow, for sure, I'm going to do it because the cows need salt." He explained to me that I could go and get the salt tomorrow and the *campesinos* would have salt until the salt was gone. Then I would have to get them more salt because they would not have done it themselves. He said that it might take time for the *campesinos* to understand that they needed the salt, but when they did, they would go about getting it forever. I said, "Well, okay. I'll give them another week to do it."

The next week the *campesinos* had salt. We had given them all the information. We had found out where it could be bought, the cost, the colour. Everything. But the *campesinos* had to take the step and get it. They cared very much about the cows, but they cared more about their own families and even their own families did not have salt. Why should they spend money to buy salt for a cow when the families were struggling themselves?

One day a group of five *campesinos* decided among themselves to go and collectively get a load of feed for the cows as it was a lot cheaper than if they did it individually. When they went to cut the corn in the field and load it on the truck, they said, "We are already close to town. Why don't we pool our money and buy a block of salt." And so they got the salt.

Arturo: You facilitate the reflection, the action, the reflection, the action and reflection. You become part of them at the moment when the people open their hearts and their minds to you. When the people recognize that you are not an agent of domination, that you are not an agent of the church or the government, that you are not an agent of such and such institution that has come to experiment with them, they begin to recognize you as a person. At that moment, they open their hearts. At that moment, you can start working with them and facilitate different techniques or methods to examine reality and transform it. It is a long process—quite, quite long. It is not easy. You need to be very critical and help to demystify the situation. The group then starts to see the social quest. People start knowing, being organized, and working together. We as researchers start knowing and being part of their process. It is in this sense that we become part of the group and the concern becomes socialized.

The Water Truck

Gerald: In December of 1990, a group of farmers in Alberta organized a visit to Tepoztlan to see their cows. Individual farmers lived with a *campesino* family for two or three days in several of the villages. They each worked for a couple of days on a community project, such as widening a road or renovating the church. It was not hard work, but the Canadians and the *campesinos* worked together. As a group, they talked about why the *campesinos* are poor. The Canadians tried to understand that reality. Asking questions about living conditions, they could see clearly that politics keep the people poor.

Back in Canada, the farmers put together a new slide show for people in their area. Shortly after, one of the farmers phoned me in Mexico and asked, "What do you think of the idea of more cows?" I said, "Well, let me see. It's not my decision. It's the decision of the people."

In each village, I asked what people thought about Alberta farmers giving them more cows. They said, "In these villages we don't have water. We don't have food for the cows. We have to work eight or ten hours a day and after that we have to go three hours into the mountains to get water for ourselves as well as for the cow. We have to transport feed to the village. It's too much."

I said, "Does that mean you don't want the cows?" They replied, "No, no, no. We're not trying to say that. What we're trying to say is that we have to do it differently. Maybe we have to put the cows where the feed and water is, and where there's a market for the milk. Keep them all together." When I heard that I jumped! I thought, "This is what we have been trying to do for the last year and a half."

I told the people in Alberta that the *campesinos* were willing to receive the cows. Two weeks later they phoned me to say they had 55 cows. Two weeks! Unbelievable. They could only put 42 on the truck; the rest were sold and the money forwarded to the *campesinos*. All the arrangements were made to bring them to Mexico.

Everyone knew that more water was needed. The *campesinos* started looking around for a water truck. When they found one, five *campesinos* invited me to come along to see if it was any good. They kept asking, "Do you think it's a good truck to buy?" I asked if it ran. They said they didn't know. Getting the key, we started it up and drove it. They said, "We think it's a good truck, but what if something happens with it?" I answered, "We'll fix it. If the truck doesn't work, then the next time we'll know what to check." They bought the truck. The motor was very dirty. The next day the men had the whole motor torn apart; every nut and bolt was spread out over the ground because I said the motor needed to be cleaned.

I had trained as a mechanic for five years but I did not do anything to help them. Instead, I concentrated on the paperwork for the cows. Several days before the cows were to arrive, the motor was still apart—all apart. I worried, "Look, the cows are across the border now and a truck is on its way to bring them the rest of the distance. They're going to be here in four days."

They responded, "Ah, don't get excited." I said, "Yeah, but the cows need water when they arrive." Two days later some parts were reassembled. I repeated, "The cows are going to be thirsty. They have to have water." "Don't worry," they said. The cows arrived Christmas Eve.

In Mexico, Christmas Eve is an important celebration. Nine days before, taking a little doll from the church, a family and their friends form a procession called a *posada*. They walk with candles and sing in the street. Arriving at a neighbour's house, they ask in song, "Do you have room in the inn?" The family inside sings a reply, "No, there's no room in the inn." The people at the door continue, "Please let us in. Mary is expecting a child. She will give birth tonight. We must find a room." Eventually the family inside opens the door and receives the "baby." This *posada* is reenacted for nine consecutive nights with the people going from house to house.

On Christmas Eve, everyone gets together and moves in a procession to bring the doll to the church. And on Christmas Eve, the truck carrying the cows arrived, pulling in right behind the *posada*. It was absolutely beautiful. The people led these cows to the church—the cows became part of the *posada*.

When it was over, the cattle truck backed up to the homemade loading chute; everyone was about to help unload the cows and herd them to the nearby field. As the truck backed up, I questioned a friend, "Where's the water truck?" He replied, "I don't know. They left at 11 o'clock this morning." It was then 11 p.m. and they weren't back yet. "Well, we've got to get water somehow."

As we were lifting up the door of the truck, up drives the water truck. The men got out. They walked up to us and said, "Huh! We're early. The cows aren't even off the truck yet!"

The leading team of *campesinos* organized the people to work with the cows—milking, feeding, growing feed, bringing the milk to the village, and selling it. They had to explore how to work together—their differences, their strengths, their likes, and dislikes.

Arturo: Participatory action-research enables people to explore in a democratic way what are the best decisions to make and to retake power for themselves. Changes happen not because people become "educated" and therefore transformed, but rather because their needs drive transformation.

Taking the Tractor

Gerald: Throughout the three years that my family and I were
in Mexico, I was thinking about what was going on. I heard a
lot of talk about humanization, democratization, solidarity, retaking power, and so on. I was trying to piece together in my
mind what all these words meant.

During my first year, I worked on a project in one village.
Now, much later, I understand what happened. This story
shows some of the similarities between life in communities in
Canada and in Mexico. It illustrates how the structure of society limits our thinking. As a community, as a group of people,
we live in fear—the fear of confrontation, the fear of stepping
out of where we are.

Walking in a small village one day, I saw a tractor sitting in
a field with a flat tire, surrounded by weeds. I asked some
people in the community what had happened to this tractor
and why they did not use it. They said it was not theirs. I asked,
"Who owns this tractor?" One person explained that it belonged to the village leader who had used it for only one year
and then let it sit idle. Another thought it belonged to all of
them. I asked what was meant by "it belongs to all of us." The
man explained that five years ago the Ministry of Agriculture
donated it to the community just before the elections. It belonged to the community but because the leader of the village
was the only person who knew how to drive the tractor at that
time, he took it for himself. He then sold the services of the
tractor to the people at a rate they couldn't afford.

This was interesting. I gave Arturo the serial number, asking him to find out about this tractor. Through his contacts,
Arturo found a letter stating that the tractor was for the use of
the community. The next week I brought a photocopy of the
letter to a village meeting. One man read the letter aloud.

I asked the group, "What does this mean?" One person replied, "It means that the tractor is here in this community but
it doesn't say that it is for us."

I said that to me it meant that this tractor was for everybody in the community and we, as a group, had a right to take the tractor and make it available for everyone's use. I asked, "What's wrong with it anyway? Is the motor gone?"

"No," they said. They recalled that an official of the Ministry of Agriculture drove it to the field, therefore, the motor must have been good.

I said, "Well, take the tractor." To me the matter was very simple, but for them it was not. They said that they could not do that. They were afraid to act—they were afraid of confrontation. They didn't want to take the tractor because it would bring a confrontation. They did not want to break their relationship with the village leader. They all lived together. It is easy to break but very hard to rebuild relationships among members of any community.

For the first half hour of every weekly meeting we would discuss this tractor, but they refused to go and take it. They thought about it for months. After a while I wrote the tractor off, thinking the people were not going to do anything.

One afternoon there was a knock on the door of my house. Five *campesinos* wanted to take the tractor and asked me if I would go with them. They had talked about it among themselves all the while. Three months had passed during which people learned together what the tractor was for, why it was there, who gave it, and so lost their fear. They were clear about how this tractor was to benefit the community so that the previous pattern of one family controlling it would not happen again. At that moment, the group had all the answers; they knew exactly what they were going to do. This afternoon they decided to take the tractor—to take power for themselves.

Arturo: When people make a decision to take power for themselves, they transform their reality. In so doing, they become transformed. They lose fear. They gain self-esteem. They gain internal forces as individuals. As a group, they can see in a very concrete way that they can transform their world.

Gerald: Squeezing into our Volkswagen, eight or nine of us drove to the village. We walked into the leader's yard. He sensed what was going on. He came out with a shotgun and told us to get off his property. The *campesinos* said, "No, all we want to do is talk to you." He agreed after a few minutes and put away his gun. They talked and talked and talked. I didn't understand the discussion because it was in Nahuatl, their indigenous language. But, they clearly explained to him their plans for the tractor and, in the end, he gave them the tractor.

The next day we returned with a battery, a big rope, oil, and some filters. We replaced the battery. The engine turned over very slowly. After pulling it 100 feet with the truck, the tractor ran perfectly. For two years it had not had a battery and that is why it did not run.

Each one of the group had gained power. They had the option at that time to keep this power, or to share it with the larger community. If they had kept the power and only used the tractor within the small group, they would have failed.

The group organized fees for the use of the tractor so that costs of fuel and repairs could be recovered. They asked me to train two people to operate the tractor, which I did. Those two people decided that they did not like driving the tractor and did not want the job. The group discussed what to do. Since nobody wanted to drive the tractor, they asked the village leader if he would. The community could have asked several other people, but they approached this man specifically because they didn't want to break solidarity with him. They wanted to demonstrate that they were not taking the tractor away from him, just making it available to everybody. They were not keeping power but rather sharing power. The village leader accepted. There is now a bond with no hostility; the village is happy. The leader now drives this tractor, having had it for years before, and experiences ownership of it but in a different sense—in a communal sense.

The tractor project is a good example of the difference between the individual struggle and the larger social struggle. The village leader was struggling as an individual; when the tractor broke down after one year, he did not have the community behind him to help fix it. That was his problem. Perhaps the tractor had to sit idle for several years before the community was able, as a group, to take the tractor and make it available to everyone. No one could have done it alone.

The *campesino* movement is enabling people to participate in their own reality—to determine their own reality. We, as outsiders, are assisting them to investigate their own realities and in the end to take action as a result of their research, to act consciously in their own reality. Not all the people are at the same level in the process. Some are very advanced in understanding their own social reality and consciousness; others are at the beginning stages of understanding. But, the important point is that we all must determine our own reality and not have it predetermined for us by others.

Arturo: The word "development" has come to have many meanings—some good, some bad. When development means outsiders imposing their own notions of what it means to be "developed," with planning from the top down and without an understanding of the people or culture, it is a bad thing. Development can be a good thing when it is the creation of the people, when it uses their thinking, their decision-making powers, their resources, and their knowledge. Development must be the transformation of reality in harmony with the population's dreams.

Epilogue: The Importance of the Cows

Gerald: Even though I do not want to believe that sending the cows to Mexico was a charitable act originally, I know it was. In the beginning, deep down, I don't think I knew any different because of my traditional upbringing. All my adult life I had worked for myself, and what I didn't need, I could give away. That is charity. Although this is not the true way of sharing, it was all I knew.

My inner being was changed by living and working with

the Mexican *campesinos*. I discovered how to give to others because I love people and want to share in the struggle, not because I feel guilty or want something in return.

I now see charity as an act of giving, usually out of a feeling of guilt—guilt about seeing people live with too little. The act of stepping back and reflecting on *why* people are living with less does not happen. What began as an act of charity by me and other Alberta farmers is becoming an act of solidarity. Solidarity is an act, not of giving, but of common struggle—a fight for a common goal of social justice. Solidarity demands that you are one with the people. This requires constantly stepping out of a situation, looking at it, and reflecting on it.

Many of the Alberta farmers asked me, "How's my cow doing? How's the family who has my cow doing? What are the crops like? Did they have enough rain?" These questions focussed on events in Mexico, and the farmers began to ask other questions such as, "Why is the price of corn so low that the *campesinos* cannot support themselves?" The deeper questions of "why" emerged. They built a link between the low price of grain in Alberta and the low price of corn or beans in Mexico. Our awareness as farmers expanded beyond our own borders. The Mexican *campesinos* wondered about the people in Alberta who donated the cows. "People bridges" started. Farmers from Mexico went to Alberta, farmers from Alberta went to Mexico, and an interchange began, creating connections between the two groups.

I quickly understood that the purpose of sending the cows was not so the Mexican farmers would have 30 litres of milk produced per cow per day. The cows allowed the farmers in Mexico to know that there were farmers in Alberta who cared for them, who loved them, and who wanted to share with them.

Arturo: For the *campesinos*, the cows were never the important point. From the beginning, the *campesinos* had decided that if the cows died, they were going to eat them. For me, personally, receiving this Canadian was a burden. In fact, I didn't want to receive any more charitable things from any white man of the North to the "underdeveloped" people of the South. I created many obstacles to show Gerald that it was close to impossible to bring these cows. But he was so stubborn. I could see by his stubbornness that he had decided to do it. At that point, I understood also that it was not a charitable act but a personal decision to be in solidarity with us.

Most of the cows survived. But, the important thing was that we increased our organization as a region, thanks to these cows. We could strengthen our understanding of people living in Canada. Many Canadians, more than 100, passed through the houses of the *campesinos*. They experienced the conditions of the *campesinos*. They became more aware and more enlightened about the meaning of poverty, ignorance, social oppression, and social injustice.

In that sense, the cows became an excuse to let our hearts grow as human beings. That is the beauty of the cows. At the beginning, the Canadians came to see their cows, and later the Canadians only spoke of the people of Mexico.

When the first truckload of cows arrived in Mexico, *campesinos* were there waiting for them. That day a calf was born. It was a good omen for us all. In fact, it was not a calf that was born but a beautiful friendship between two different cultures and countries. We learned that we are not two very different people—we share many values and the same heart.

The cows were not a "project." The cows arrived in Mexico thanks to the audacity of two Canadians, Gerald and Mary Anna Debbink. The cows joined the flow of the river of *campesino* life. At the same time, these cows disturbed that life and created distractions, causing divisions within the community. Some families received a cow and other families received nothing. The cows became a political event because the families that received a cow would tell other families, "You need to join our organization in order to receive a cow." In one community, the *campesinos* were compelled to reflect on existing corruption in local government when an official from the Ministry of Health urged the *campesinos* to exchange the Canadian cows for a local variety. In another village, the men decided that they could not handle the cows; instead, the women could do it. These women gained a critical role in their families and began having more status.

Some *campesinos* wanted to sell the milk to other areas in order to buy feed for the cows. Others said, "No. Why should we sell the milk only to buy feed for the cows? We need to improve our own nutrition." A critical tension arose. People began asking themselves vital questions related to the health of their communities. Many of the *campesinos* do not take care of their health. Because they feel their lives have little value, they place little value on their health. But when some cows became sick, they spent money on treatment because the health of the cows was important. In the process, they learned that human health also is valuable.

The monotony in the daily lives of the *campesinos* creates a certain security. How is escape possible? How can one emerge from that monotony to grow and to go beyond? It is difficult because people follow the cycles, the cycle of the rain, of the sun, of eternity. Escape, or growth, can happen when certain opportunities happen that, in turn, create movement. The cows came into the life of these *campesinos* and created movement—movements of cutting the grass, planting alfalfa and oats, carrying water, and caring for the cows. The cows necessitated physical movement. They also provoked organizational, intellectual, and cultural movement. People reacted by thinking, questioning, being curious about their situation, and transforming their reality.

Gerald: Curiosity, in part, prompted me to seek personal change, to pick up and move with my family to Mexico. I was looking for answers to such questions as: "Why do some people 'have' and others 'have not'?" In order to satisfy that curiosity, I had to go and find out what the injustice was and where it was happening.

I became a farmer because my father was a farmer. I followed in his footsteps: I farmed land, grew crops, and milked cows. That is how I supported my family. But I was doing the same job over and over again and not completing a cycle of production. This made me look for something more in life.

On the one hand, this routine gave me a sense of security. On the other hand, it gave me a sense of insecurity—of not having sufficient purpose or meaning in life. The seeds of discontent had been there for a long time. They grew and made me decide that I must break from the traditional ways in order to reach out and understand a more holistic approach to "being."

My search for the seeds of "content," replacing those of discontent, has led me to connect with like-minded people. This growth is producing a new tradition, one that includes developing work-study programs for learning. This is giving me a true sense of self and security.

El Senor Fermine milks the cooperatively owned Holstein herd twice a day in Morelos, Mexico.

Canadian Val Wiebe learns to make tortillas with La Senora Ramirez in Morelos.

El Senor Fermine sells milk house to house, contributing to local consumption of dairy products.

Canadian farmer, Barry Schorr, milks one of the donated cows in Morelos while on a 1994 study tour organized by Earthkeeping (Edmonton, Alberta).

El Senor Julio, a member of the small cooperative, also provides care for the dairy cows in Morelos.

2

CHANGING DISABLING ENVIRONMENTS THROUGH PARTICIPATORY ACTION-RESEARCH: A CANADIAN EXPERIENCE

Mary Law

ℰ EDITORS' NOTE: Mary Law realized "how ingrained [her] positivistic, quantitative world view" was while writing and rewriting the chapter: the academic style of reporting facts and observations using the third person and passive voice was almost entrenched. Finally, to capture her own feelings and reactions to ideas and events, Mary talked out loud to herself while pacing her living room with a tape recorder running. She then had the tape transcribed into notes and used those as a reference for writing. Much later, when the chapter was approaching final form, Dennis and Nancy spoke with Mary about her views on participatory action-research over lunch and taped the conversation. This became the basis for the Epilogue: "A Bit of a Rebel" section, where Mary as a person is forcefully revealed. Her experience in writing this chapter points to the value of using multiple means of expression, such as conversation or talking-to-self in combination with fieldnotes and data, to develop a fuller, often more creative documentation.

The first phase of the study clearly drew on the external research team's familiarity with qualitative methods and procedures. The team pinpointed their research question: to identify important themes about "the 'sorts of things' that made it easier or harder for disabled children to participate in everyday activities." They collected and analyzed data from parents of disabled children through small focus

34

groups organized by the research team, followed by individual interviews. Then the second, more open, participatory phase began with the first group meeting of parents. During this phase, parents decided to form an ongoing support group which one participant described as "launching a ship."

The case study is detailed. Perhaps because of Mary's academic background and setting, she carefully specifies the planned phases and steps, the facts, and her observations. It is relatively easy to determine what the external research team did, how they did it, why and when as well as the team's perceptions about parents' reactions and their actions. Her language reflects standard terms of conventional research as well as phrases more closely associated with PAR. For example, "study findings," "trustworthiness of data," and "interpretative, qualitative analysis of transcripts of focus groups" are mixed in with "we remained actively involved . . . but as supporters and resource people rather than active facilitators," and "later, I became comfortable with these uncertainties [of not knowing where the process would lead]."

Unconventionally, at different points throughout the chapter, Mary brings in her feelings (of surprise, disappointment, amazement); her questions ("I was unsure how to conduct the study so that participants would have a stake in and actively control the direction"); and her concerns ("the PAR process would be ineffective if I, as a researcher, unduly pushed or influenced any decision-making"). She outlines the external team's considered and cautious use of suggestions and techniques. She summarizes the shifts in people's roles, her decreasing control over process and decisions as parental involvement increased over time, and lessons that she personally learned about research, participation, and knowledge. Reflecting on the group's success and her own satisfaction with what happened, Mary describes this experience as "using the right process at the right time with people who were ready to take on these challenges," adding that PAR philosophy "fits very comfortably" with her personal and professional views.

This chapter documents the work of a university-based research team with parents of disabled children in Cambridge, Ontario. But it also is about Mary's first step into organizing group-controlled, action-oriented research. Balancing between the familiar realm of conventional biomedical research and the unknown sphere of participation and (reformist) social change, she kept a foot in both worlds. Using a PAR approach was an instrumental means for bringing together people with a shared concern for their disabled children and assisting the group to take deliberate actions. ∞

Studying Disabling Environments
from a New Perspective

Children with disabilities frequently have little control over their day-to-day activities. They spend more time in self-care and passive activities in their home environment than in activities in the community (Brown and Gordon, 1987). This is reflected in differences in activity patterns between children with and without disabilities (Brown and Gordon, 1987; Hewett, Newson, and Newson, 1970; Margalit, 1981; Statistics Canada, 1986). These differences are minor at a young age but increase as the child grows. These studies have not identified the range of environmental factors outside the child's immediate family that constrain activities. Brown and Gordon (1987) and Hewett, Newson, and Newson (1970) discuss the uniqueness of each family's experience and the considerable variance in activity patterns between families.

Significant environmental constraints hinder their participation in the everyday activities of childhood and adolescence. These environmental constraints include physical, social, institutional, economic, and cultural factors in a child's home, neighbourhood, or community. During the past decade, disability advocates have stressed that disability is a problem in the relationship between the individual and the environment (Hahn, 1984; Jongbloed and Crichton, 1990). If our environments foster dependency and poor solutions to the problems of disability, then solutions would exist predominantly in planning and social policies aimed at the modification of the environment. The fundamental principle of this approach is the recognition of the ecological nature of disability, that the problems of disability are caused by the interactions of a disabled child with the environment, not by the disability itself.

However, the substantial effect that environments have on the activities of a child with a disability is not well understood. Knowledge about the interactions between disability and the environment for children is scant. Disability, activity, and environmental factors have rarely been examined together in the past. Rather, the practice has been to examine these factors independently.

As an occupational therapist working with children and their families, I had explored how children spend their time and the sorts of things which influence their day-to-day activities. Increasingly concerned about child rehabilitation services, I noticed that most rehabilitation efforts focused on changing the child to fit the environment, rather than on changing the environment. When the issue of changing disabling environments was addressed, the emphasis was most often on only the physical environment.

A literature search on the daily activities of children with disabilities revealed a few studies, mainly of a descriptive or survey nature. Most of these studies did not examine changes in the daily activity patterns of the child and family or the influence of environmental factors. The studies lost meaning because of the statistical averaging of the many different responses from children and their families. Knowledge about the relationships between activities and the environment was scant.

My research training was in epidemiology and biostatistics with experience in conducting experimental research studies. I wondered if cross-sectional surveys were able to elicit the needed information and began to search for a different research methodology to chronicle the experiences of children with disabilities. After extensive reading and discussion with others, a qualitative perspective that would identify trends and themes about activities and environmental supports and barriers seemed to be a more appropriate approach. I was interested in the participants being actively involved in the research process, and the possibility of affecting change through the research—both tenets of participatory action-research.

The process of designing and carrying out a participatory action-research project would be challenging, as the health field has not viewed participatory and qualitative methods positively. But my background as an occupational therapist (OT) was helpful in exploring an alternate methodology. As an OT, I practice from a client-centred perspective, believing that the client's values and goals are most important in determining the focus of any occupational therapy intervention. A dichotomy existed between how I viewed people as a therapist and as a researcher. Involvement in participatory action-research potentially could reduce the discrepancy between a person as a "subject" in experimental research and as a valued participant.

Participatory action-research would enable me as a researcher to work closely with participants to define problems, explore alternate solutions, and facilitate change. I was intrigued by a type of research that was qualitative in nature, action-oriented, and enabled participants to themselves make changes to improve their future. Participants' ideas and experiences could be central to defining and conducting the research study.

Goals for the Study

The primary goal was to identify environmental factors that had an important influence on the daily activities of children with physical disabilities. Together with parents, I wanted to discover the environmental situations which presented the most substantial challenges to their children. A second goal was to examine the use of participatory action-research in a disability-related community context: parents would be the principal architects of the study-action process. A final aim of the research was to plan strategies with parents that could alter activity patterns and enhance participation.

Participants shared common concerns but did not know each other. The process of bringing together participants and their involvement during the study were as important as the research outcomes.

Contacting the Study Participants

The study took place in the city of Cambridge, a manufacturing centre in southwestern Ontario, Canada, with a population of 92,000 people. The location of the study has been indicated at the request of the study participants, who stated that they want others to know what they have accomplished in Cambridge. Cambridge is located 75 kilometres west of Toronto, the capital of Ontario. It is part of the Regional Municipality of Waterloo, which includes the cities of Cambridge, Kitchener, and Waterloo, and the Townships of North Dumfries and Woolwich. People from Cambridge often travel to Kitchener or Waterloo for health or social services. I chose Cambridge for this study for a number of reasons: I live there; current services for children were similar to most populated areas of the province; and it was large enough to have a complexity of relevant environmental factors.

No organized group of parents of children with physical disabilities existed in the Cambridge area. I realized then that families would probably not know each other, and was unsure how to conduct the study so that participants would have a stake in and actively control the direction and findings of the project. The first challenge, however, was to find people who were interested in participating in the study.

The local children's treatment centre was willing to send out a letter to all parents who had a child with a physical disability between the ages of three to 12 years. Letters were mailed to 36 families explaining the nature of the study and asking parents to return their consent to participate in a stamped, addressed envelope.

Two weeks later only three parents had returned the form. I was surprised and disappointed; I wondered if the letter was too impersonal or just one more form to complete. The director of the children's treatment centre agreed to allow a staff member to telephone the families. Confidentiality did not permit me to contact parents directly. A physical therapist contacted the remaining 33 families, explaining the study and answering their questions.

This more personal process was successful. Twenty-four families agreed to participate, and 22 remained involved in the research process until the end of the study. The reasons for the 12 refusals included: parents too busy (1), child's disability too mild (4), language barrier (1), research-"shy" (2), not interested (3), and no reason (1). The participating and non-participating families were similar in terms of the parents' marital status, culture, and the child's type of disability. Over the course of the study, two families dropped out. One was no longer interested. The other had a language barrier and the research team had problems obtaining translation services.

Envisioning the Process

I understood participatory action-research to be a cyclical, iterative process. I initially envisioned this process to involve the following: establishing focus groups, exploring issues that affect activity patterns, determining how to study these issues, collecting data, discussing this data, determining actions based on the groups' perceptions and the data, performing actions, and evaluating results.

Defining the Problem

I invited parents to attend the first of a series of four focus groups. Participants were to identify and discuss significant factors that supported or hindered the daily activities of their children. In this way, I could ensure that participants' concerns formed the basis for individual interviews with all 24 families.

Twelve people agreed to be part of a focus group. A research assistant and I had considerable difficulty developing an approach for facilitating the focus group discussions. The most difficult task was finding the appropriate non-academic words to describe relevant issues. For example, we were interested in talking to parents about environmental factors that affected their child's daily activities. After trying various word combinations, we decided to use the phrase "sorts of things" to represent environmental factors.

The group discussions centred on the "sorts of things" that made it easier or harder for their children to participate in everyday activities in a variety of environmental settings, including the home, neighbourhood, school or nursery, and community. Cultural, economic, institutional, physical, and social environmental factors were considered. All focus groups were audio-taped and later transcribed for analysis. Participants identified issues of social attitudes, lack of integration, and bureaucratic procedures as the most important barriers to participation. All 12 participants received a summary of each focus group discussion. We asked participants to check the summaries for accuracy and what they wanted to do with the information gathered. Most participants looked briefly at the focus group summaries and stated that they did not have revisions or additions.

As this was early in the study, I was not surprised. I hoped that, as we proceeded, participants would comment more on the summaries. When the participants did get back together, they used these summaries as a basis for their discussions.

Analyzing Information from Focus Groups

Interpretative, qualitative analysis of the transcripts of the focus groups identified significant themes related to barriers and dilemmas, current strategies, and suggestions for change. The primary method of data analysis was the textual analysis of the investigator's fieldnotes, interview records, and focus group proceedings, supplemented by the quantitative analysis of activity patterns. The textual analysis was used to develop understandings and find meanings in the actions and words of participants (Miller and Crabtree, 1992).

An initial textual coding scheme was developed after reading and studying the focus group transcripts. The initial coding scheme was developed by myself and the research assistant, in consultation with a medical anthropologist. The next step in the process involved re-examining the focus groups transcripts from a more global perspective, recording what was observed, what was thought, and other issues in the transcripts. Using this information, a second coding scheme was developed. As data collection and analysis proceeded, the coding scheme was revised to include new information or issues. In all, the coding scheme underwent nine revisions. Discussion and comparison of observations were used to achieve consensus about emerging concepts from which themes were developed. The texts and interpretations were coded in a database for easy retrieval using the Ethnograph software (Seidel and Clark, 1984).

Analysis of data took place throughout the study and was shared continually with the participants and all members of the research team (see Figure 1: Communicative Analysis During the Research Process). "Participants" were the parents involved. The research team consisted of "interpreters" (myself and a research assistant) who were most involved in the analysis process, and four academic colleagues ("co-investigators") who contributed by reading and commenting on significant sections of text. We met regularly to discuss any concerns in the study process, to assist with coding the themes emerging from the data, and to check coding accuracy. As more data were collected and analyzed, these themes and ideas were re-coded and refined.

Interviewing the Participants

Emerging ideas and themes identified from analysis of the focus group discussions formed the basis for individual interviews with each family. These interviews could potentially elicit more information about participants' views, as well as involve participants who had not attended a focus group. During the summer and fall of 1991, 22 families were interviewed. When possible, both parents were interviewed. It was at this point that two families dropped out. Six appointments

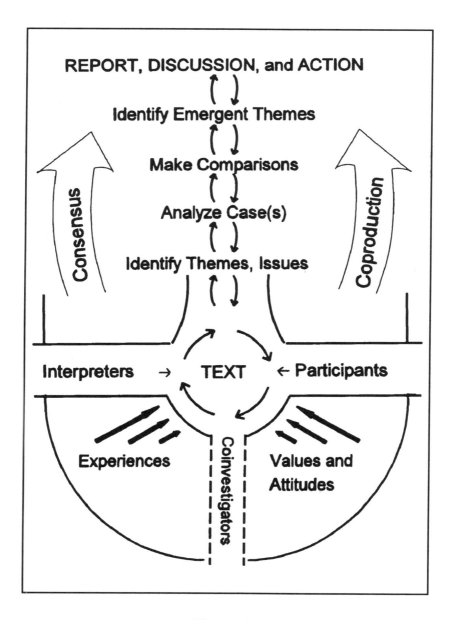

Figure 1:
Communicative Analysis during the Research Process

were cancelled by one family. The other family spoke only Portuguese; it was not possible to interview them because of difficulties in arranging interpretive services.

Interviews were audiotaped and transcribed. All families interviewed received copies of their interview text and were asked if it accurately reflected their thoughts and experiences. Participants were told: ". . . it was very important for everyone to be a part of this, and we want to accurately reflect what you say and move along together, so that's why we're giving all this information back." This process, called member-checking, helped to assure the trustworthiness of the data (Patton, 1990). The data was very similar to that obtained from the focus groups. In most cases, participants said that reading their transcripts was interesting, but they did not have much information to add.

All participants stated that it was important to get back together in some way to discuss the information. In fact, several emphasized that without getting back together this research process would be similar to other research where they had completed questionnaires but had never received the results. These experiences had been very frustrating. They did not want it repeated during this study.

Inviting, Involving, and Empowering Participants

Several methods ensured that the research process was as participatory as possible and that the parents controlled the directions of the research. When introducing the study during a focus group or individual interview, I emphasized the flexible and participatory nature of this research. I described the project as different from other research because the participants would determine the direction of the process. I explained that we wanted to explore ideas and make recommendations with parents—we wanted to learn from parents' experiences. As I stated at the beginning of a focus group:

> We really want all your ideas. We feel we can really learn
> from you. . . . We haven't come up with any set ideas . . .
> sort of very general questions that we'll use, but anything you
> think about or anything you want to say is great. We're not
> looking for anything specific so you just speak up. We
> thought we might start by having each of you just talk a bit
> about your child and what sorts of activities he or she enjoys
> doing.

Intentional Nudging

"Intentional nudging" was the principal method used to encourage participants to take control of the research process. The
term intentional nudging grew out of discussions in research
team meetings. We believed it aptly described a process by
which we would bring participants together to listen to each
other, learn from each other, and decide for themselves what
action they wanted to take. Throughout the research process,
we tried to ensure that participants were relaxed and comfortable. We actively listened to what they said, often asking questions to probe further into their experiences and ideas. We followed their lead in determining the direction of the interviews.
When issues about barriers were raised, we asked for suggestions to change that situation. As well, we often told participants about suggestions already made by other parents.

The challenge in using intentional nudging was to talk
about issues with participants clearly and fairly. It was important for us, as the initial link between participants during interviews, to share participants' suggestions about possible actions, although it was tempting to manipulate the research process by relating participants' suggestions in a way which
favoured our ideas.

For example, in the first focus group, one participant suggested that it would be a good idea for everyone to meet again.
She had enjoyed talking to other parents during that evening
and felt that a parent support group should be established in
Cambridge. However, it seemed premature on the basis of one
person's suggestion to tell parents that a parent support group

might be formed. We decided that if another participant made the same suggestion, then we would state that other participants also had suggested that idea. This approach encouraged participants to suggest actions and allowed us to share information without manipulating people's ideas for potential actions.

As a researcher, I found this aspect to be one of the most difficult. Once a participant had suggested that a parent support group be formed, I recognized that this would be an exciting result of the study process. For such a group to be successful, it had to be suggested and supported by a number of participants. The participatory action-research process would be ineffective if I, as a researcher, unduly pushed or influenced any decision-making about organizing a support group.

We highlighted the action component of the project in each focus group and interview by asking participants what should be done with the information being collected. When participants made suggestions, we asked more specific questions to clarify the ideas. For example, after members of the first focus group suggested that it would be useful to get together again, the following discussion occurred:

Researcher: ". . . Do you think it would be helpful to get back together as (this) group or maybe a larger group or . . .?"

Participant: ". . . Have people, parents of disabled kids band together, sort of demand something, some changes, especially if there's certain areas that would help to have a group meet. . . ."

Participant: ". . . It was interesting just the three of us, it would be interesting to see what other people would have. . . ."

Participant: ". . . Perhaps all of us together could help in some way, which would be nice to be part of the solving. . . ."

Researcher: "Well, exactly . . . this is a shared process."

In one of the last interviews, after a number of parents had suggested that they should work together to use the study information and make changes, I sought feedback about this idea:

Participant: "... I would like to see Cambridge get its fair share of things for our kids."

Researcher: "What do you think would be the best way to go about that? Do you think that the best thing would be some sort of working group, or advocacy group, or something like that?"

Participant: "I think so, yeah. There's more power in a group and you are supportive of each other. . . ."

When it became clear that most participants wanted to get back together, we sent a complete summary of the information collected to all participants along with an invitation to attend a scheduled meeting to discuss the results. The summary was organized as a workbook with information about important concerns and suggestions for the future identified by the participants.

Working Together to Change Barriers

Twelve participants from eight families attended the meeting held on November 25, 1991. Eight other families did not attend but stated that they wanted to continue to receive information about the study and action decisions. I began the meeting by briefly summarizing the process of the study and the work done together so far. Participants wanted more information about who had been involved in the study. Once this was described, a participant stated that there were probably more families who had children with special needs in Cambridge and that a "lobby group" of parents could help change the community.

Participants then reviewed their written information. They discussed several issues related to attitudes and physical barriers in the community, schools, and recreational programs. A common concern was that parents had to search for information and fight the "system" on their own. As one participant said:

> It's also the fact that you have the fighting or the advocating or the lobbying to do on your own, like you really feel like you are on your own. There is no opportunity really to talk to other parents that have been through it or that type of thing. . . .

In considering what to do next, participants asked if the researchers would remain involved. I answered:

> In terms of this study, the research isn't necessarily over. Certainly this has to be written up and that kind of stuff, but we are committed to follow along with whatever you folks want to do. We don't feel that it would be best if we went alone and said to the City, well, I think we should change this. . . . But we are committed to . . . help in whatever you want to do.

Participants discussed forming a parents' group to work on the identified barriers. They believed that proactive effort was necessary but were unsure about how to begin. As one participant noted:

> I think the point is most of us would be willing to get involved in something like that but we don't know how to get started. We don't know where to go and what roads to take, who to contact. And really, what's the most important issue. Like we have so many in front of us, which one do we take and start with?

One participant asked if it was the researchers' goal to develop a group once the grant was finished. I replied:

> I think if that is your goal, that's what I would like to do. As

> I said at the beginning, this research is different. We are do-
> ing it in a different way than other research is done. Normally
> research would be done, we would have a meeting and say
> here's all the information, fine, we're done. That's all. But we
> would like to go further. But we would like to be directed by
> you. Say what you want to do and we will help you do it.

I told them about an organization called Participating Families–Ontario (PF–Ontario) which helps parents of children with
special needs set up parent support networks. After further discussion, participants decided to contact PF–Ontario for more
information.

On December 9, 1991, a parent from PF–Ontario met with
the participants. A provincial organization, founded in 1987,
its purpose is to provide information, education, and training
for parents of children with special needs. At that time, PF–
Ontario had funding to set up four family support networks
in various regions in Ontario. Participants talked about how
they could link up with Participating Families. They decided
to form a group and draw up plans for the coming year. They
also wanted to expand their group to include parents of children who were older or had other disabilities.

On January 20, 1992, participants formed a parent support
and advocacy group called Participating Families–Cambridge.
The goals for the group included advocacy, information gathering and sharing, and parent training. The group was open
to all parents of children or adolescents with special needs. Participants decided that the group would meet monthly, hold a
community awareness meeting in May to introduce themselves
to other community agencies, publish a newsletter, and develop
a resource library. Different people volunteered for various responsibilities—contact person, resource librarian, treasurer, and
newsletter committee member.

Since January 1992, Participating Families–Cambridge has
met monthly. Five newsletters have been published and distributed to many families in Cambridge. Fifteen new members
have joined the group. The group has advocated successfully
for the development of improved swimming programs from the

City of Cambridge as well as for subsidization of private swimming lessons. They appeared before the Region of Waterloo Health and Social Services Committee to advocate against decreased funding for the Infant Development Program. Although this lobby effort was not successful, members gained experience. Information sharing has continued at and between meetings.

Since the formation of Participating Families–Cambridge, parents have planned and led all group meetings. As researchers, we remained actively involved for the first six months, but as supporters and resource people rather than active facilitators. For example, I was asked to help one parent write a letter to the City of Cambridge about their aquatics programs. During this time, we were simply two members of Participating Families–Cambridge.

Evaluating What Had Been Done

At the June 1992 meeting of Participating Families-Cambridge, I discussed with the participants their perceptions about being involved in this participatory action-research project. The following probes guided the discussion:

- Tell me what it has been like to be part of this research.

- Was there a point when you felt involved and wanted to continue to meet with the other participants?

Participants felt very positively about the research experience. They stated that the research process, with the focus groups and interviews, had allowed them to express their feelings so they could then move on to facilitate change on behalf of their children. They discovered that others had similar issues and difficulties to face, even if their children had different impairments. As a result, they were no longer as isolated.

Participants stated that the actual mechanics of the research process did not feel like a research study—it was not just a questionnaire to complete. As one participant said: "... we've been in research before, filled out forms, etc., and that's been fine, but we've never benefitted from it. I guess others have but not us—so that's the difference; we've got something from this research, we have benefitted. ..."

They enjoyed being a part of the research. In fact, as one participant explained: "I know this is a research project, but it never felt like a research project; it was very informal, even when you came to my house, it was just like chatting about my child and family, so it hasn't felt like research, it's been great!"

The point at which individuals felt committed and wanted to stay involved varied from person to person. For some parents, the first group meeting when the study results were shared was important. At that meeting, they realized that all the parents had common experiences and concerns. Others stated that they began to feel committed to the parent group and the process of action when the same people kept coming to the second, third, and fourth meetings. It was at this point that they realized that together the parent group could "make things happen." As well, the contribution of Participating Families–Ontario was cited as critical because it provided ongoing support and connected the parents with support groups in other communities. This helped ensure continuity of the group.

During the first few months after Participating Families–Cambridge was formed, I observed changes in the parents' participation in the group: participants assumed greater control of the meetings and decisions. My role altered to being more of a support person than a facilitator. As their personal control increased, participants gained confidence in their ability as a group to help each other and make changes in the community. J. Lord identified a similar process of gaining awareness, control, and competence among people with disabilities as they experienced personal empowerment. He defined empowerment as "processes whereby individuals achieve increasing control of various aspects of their lives and participate in the community with dignity" (1991: 7).

Through the formation of Participating Families–Cambridge, parents have increased their personal control. They are using their understanding of their community as the basis for actions to change barriers to participation in school, play, and recreation activities. Participants believe that they are making "slow but sure" progress. As one parent stated, "It's like we've launched a ship." They view Participating Families–Cambridge as their own creation.

Learning from Our Experience

The findings of this study chronicle the experiences of certain families who have a child with a disability in a city in southwestern Ontario. The findings reflect the participatory process of bringing people with a common concern together to generate solutions to difficulties facing them and their children. As these people talked and shared experiences, they came to know each other and realized that they had much in common. They experienced a sense of community and decided to work together to facilitate change. The approach supported active involvement and control by participants, empowerment of participants, a commitment to action, and the researchers learning with participants (Brown, 1986; Hall, 1981).

This study illustrates the process of participatory action-research without a pre-formed citizen group. A key characteristic was the use of "intentional nudging." Through ongoing discussion and questioning, participants' visions and values became apparent, providing an effective basis for suggesting policy changes and action. The process was effective in dealing with the complexities of disabling environments because we examined concerns in an iterative manner.

There were some constraints in doing participatory action-research in this context; it took a great deal of time and involvement. But we were able to achieve consensus over time because people were involved from the beginning. In previous research, I was accustomed to having control over the research process and study results. Using a participatory action-research approach, my control over data collection and analysis was less, particularly as the study progressed. Because this study group was not pre-formed, I had more control at the beginning of the research. After January 1992, participants controlled the agenda and direction of the project.

My role as a researcher was initially to be a facilitator rather than a technician. The greatest problem in assuming this role was to listen, understand the participants' stories, and accurately use their ideas as the basis for further discussion. I struggled at times not to allow my own thoughts to bias the action decisions. Not knowing where the research process would lead was difficult, as was avoiding the temptation to push things too quickly before the intentions of the participants became clear. Later, I became comfortable with these uncertainties and intrigued by what might happen when the participants got back together. The suspending of judgment and a non-directive approach are quite different from the technical, expert role that many researchers currently assume. In the end, my roles as a facilitator and group member were more satisfying personally than if I had worked from an expert-based framework.

This study brought parents and myself together to examine the "sorts of things" which helped or hindered children with physical disabilities in participating in the everyday activities of childhood. Important social, attitudinal, and institutional factors were identified as the most significant barriers to participation. Policy suggestions to change these barriers were recommended and sent to the local municipal government, service agencies, and school boards.

Through the participatory action-research process, parents acted to change disabling environments. They described barriers and supports, recommended policy, and began to work together to facilitate change in their community. They assumed control of the research process, formed a citizens group, and are continuing to strive for improvements in their community for their children.

Epilogue: "A Bit of a Rebel"—Reflections on Participatory Action-Research

I found the writing of the case study to be a very painful process. Over the years, I have developed a style of writing and a very set way of expressing my opinions. The editors asked me to adopt a new style of writing—to "put myself into the story." As an academic, I am not encouraged to do that elsewhere, because then I open myself up to questions about my objectivity. The writing process made me realize how ingrained the positivistic, quantitative world view was, in some respects, still in me.

I entered my Ph.D. program fully prepared to do a large cross-sectional survey. Looking at environmental issues for children with disabilities, I discovered that we do not know a great deal and spent a year searching for a research methodology that would allow exploring these issues in depth and working with families to change things. I decided to approach the research in first a qualitative and then a qualitative, participatory way. A participatory approach was the most appropriate one, I felt, and the most challenging.

Participatory action-research fits very comfortably with the way I am personally and professionally. As an occupational therapist, I value the experiences that people bring to a situation, and am only a good therapist if they can help me define what their needs are. Working from the perspective of how I can help solve problems, I do not identify the problems and tell people what they need. I am able to make people feel comfortable in a situation so that they open up and talk about their experiences, and thus can reflect ideas, thoughts, and feelings back to them.

Both occupational therapy and participatory action-research demand a great deal of flexibility. There is also a similarity in terms of how I would look for and create a partnership. The main difference between the two approaches is that the therapist does act as an expert, but as an expert facilitating solutions to problems that are identified by clients. I did not experience that nor did I feel an "expert" role was useful within the participatory action-research process.

The bottom line is that participatory action-research takes a certain kind of individual—someone who fundamentally respects the world view of others and really knows how to listen. It also takes a person who likes bucking the system, a person who is a bit of a rebel. I am like that. I do not like someone telling me what to do. The sure way to get me to do something is to tell me that I can't or shouldn't do it. Having a sceptical attitude is healthy because it lets me look at things differently, so that I am not always accepting the status quo. Participatory action-research demands that we look for new avenues of doing things and solving problems.

When I look back on the whole process, I do not have any regrets. Maybe I have a couple of minor ones, but nothing that stands out as something I definitely should have done differently. The work evolved in a way that was the best that it could be—this always amazed me. I was constantly surprised that things went as well as they did. I can remember doing some of the interviews and thinking to myself that it did not feel like research. The participants, at the end, said the same thing—that it did not feel like a research project.

A certain amount of the success was the result of using the right process at the right time with people who were ready to take on these challenges. Most of the people we talked to wanted to work together with us as researchers and look at these issues.

I found it tremendously hard initially to not know where things would go or what would happen. From the very first focus group, people started talking about how parents should get together, about how they should form a group. This idea had the potential of shared group experiences and of group action. I could see possible directions. It is important that the people who participate in the research feel that we have genuine respect for them and their experiences, that we value their opinion, and perceive them as partners in the process. It is very easy to say that I want to be a partner in the process but I could still control the situation, albeit in a very subtle way. If a person has a very set view of the world, if he/she really needs control and answers all the way along, that person is going to have tremendous difficulty doing participatory action-research.

What developed for all of us is that we came to know each other in a way that got rid of some of our myths—myths that families held about each other and myths that I held about families with children with disabilities. We developed a real sense of community looking at the commonalities that we shared. With greater respect, we saw that we could achieve more by working together as partners rather than alone as individuals.

Knowing when to "disengage" was very difficult. The group has continued and I maintain informal contact with the members. New people have come in and others have dropped out. I used to ask myself, "What if the group stops? What if it disbands?" I now realize that perhaps this is not bad if the group has accomplished what it needed to do at that point in time.

From this experience with participatory action-research, I gained a much broader notion about what research is and how we generate knowledge. In using an experimental approach to research, I have always tried to include the therapists and parents by feeding back information and involving them in the process. What my experience in participatory action-research has made me think about is the nature of participation and the need to do more than just give back information. We needed to be partners in looking at what needs to be researched. I have changed what I study and how I do it.

I now believe that the choice of research method should depend on what is being studied. Some questions are best addressed using participatory methods; there are others that are best looked at using qualitative methods; there are still others that are probably best examined using experimental methods.

References

Brown, L.D. 1986. Participatory research and community planning. In: B. Checkoway (Ed.) *Strategic Perspectives on Planning Practice.* Toronto: Lexington Books.

Brown, M. and Gordon, W.A. 1987. Impact of impairment on activity patterns of children. *Archives of Physical Medicine and Rehabilitation* 68: 828-832.

Hahn, H. 1984. Reconceptualizing disability: A political science perspective. *Rehabilitation Literature* 45: 362-365.

Hall, B.L. 1981. Participatory research, popular knowledge and power: A personal reflection. *Convergence* 14(3): 6-17.

Hewett, S., Newson, J., and Newson, E. 1970. *The Family and the Handicapped Child.* Chicago: Aldine Publishing.

Jongbloed, L. and Crichton, A. 1990. Difficulties in shifting from individualistic to socio-political policy regarding disability in Canada. *Disability, Handicap and Society* 5(1): 25-36.

Lord, J. 1991. *Lives in Transition: The Process of Personal Empowerment.* Ottawa: Secretary of State.

Margalit, M. 1981. Leisure activities of cerebral palsied children. *Israel Journal of Psychiatry and Relational Science* 18: 209-214.

Miller, W.L. and Crabtree, B.F. 1992. Primary care research: A multimethod typology and qualitative road map. In: B.F. Crabtree and W.L. Miller (Eds.) *Doing Qualitative Research.* Newbury Park, California: Sage Publications (pp. 3-28).

Patton, M.Q. 1990. *Qualitative Evaluation and Research Methods.* (2nd ed.) Newbury Park, California: Sage Publications.

Seidel, J.V. and Clark, J.A. 1984. The ethnograph: A computer program for the analysis of qualitative data. *Qualitative Sociology* 7(1): 110-125.

Statistics Canada. 1986. *The Canadian Activity Limitation Survey*. Ottawa: Statistics Canada.

3

DOCTORS, *DAIS*, AND NURSE-MIDWIVES: WOMEN'S HEALTH SERVICE UTILIZATION IN NORTHERN INDIA

Patricia Seymour

ᗄ EDITORS' NOTE: In "Doctors, *Dais*, and Nurse-Midwives," Patricia Seymour, a Canadian physician and novice researcher, describes her experience of doing research with participation during a year's stay in northern India. This is a strikingly honest personal account, one that is truly fixed to her perceptions and actions at the time.

Soon after her arrival in India, Patricia experienced the stress caused by constant adaptation to a distant culture: "The first three weeks in Banaras were probably the most stressful weeks of my life; I felt guilty and doomed for failure. These feelings, waxing and waning over the following ten months, became my guiding force." Learning by doing, she began to understand that, "[w]orking through an interpreter *and* across cultures *and* across socio-economic strata made [her] task complex and frustrating." Her words reveal an emotional roller coaster: repeated feelings of confusing uncertainty ("I could physically get myself to the village but whose door would I knock on first?") are coupled with her "small successes" and humourous portrayals of her own actions ("I had, by this point, become completely swept away by it all and watched the proceedings as if they were a bizarre dream.")

Patricia repeatedly notes the pressure of insufficient time, "I felt trapped by time, allowing it to dictate my approach and expectations."

She received what appears as conflicting advice about an appropriate research process, and tried to sort out conventional biomedical-epidemiological procedures, as distinct from a social science perspective, while striving to incorporate active participation by local people in the research.

Some readers will question Patricia's purpose or process, but perhaps no more than Patricia did herself. She continuously asked herself if she was doing the right thing, so that by the time of her departure: "I again ruminated about what, exactly, had I done in this project, if not participatory action-research? What, if anything, had I accomplished?" Patricia anxiously concluded, "I was yet another in a stream of unidentified health workers who enter [the village women's] lives for a brief moment and then vanish forever."

Three years later, Patricia feels better about her time in India. She has been able to "reframe [her] work and accomplishments, legitimizing an incredibly valuable, intense learning experience," and to recognize the "real obstacles as [her] pre-set goals and expectations."

When people are confronted with strong, almost overwhelming, challenges, subsequent doubts and conflicting feelings create a crucial, internal vulnerability. Vulnerability can result in weakness and feelings of failure, but can also lead to a greater openness and a growing humility when personal limitations are recognized and there is a committed willingness to learn. This unusually rich case study identifies the value of working within a team or with an accessible, experienced mentor who is able to provide supportive guidance. Readers recalling their efforts at social participation and research across cultures, class, or language may see themselves in this chapter, and say: "I've been there."ᵇ

In the fall of 1989, I started jotting down ideas for a proposal to work with village women in northern India. I was in my first year of the Family Medicine residency program at McMaster University. My husband and I were preparing to spend a year in Banaras, a holy city in the northern state of Uttar Pradesh; he was to do his anthropology Ph.D. fieldwork and I would do some kind of health-oriented work. My main interest as a budding primary health care physician was women's health.

My background in international development was limited. As a child, I had lived and travelled in Asia owing to my father's job, and I remained captivated by the magic and mysticism of India. Also, in my last year of medical school, I had gone to Papua New Guinea for a three-month elective, doing a small survey on child growth and development. When I began writing my proposal, I had never heard of participatory action-research (PAR). I just knew that I wanted to go into a community, learn something, and give back to the people. I shared my ideas with a woman who worked at McMaster University and was also interested in PAR. She suggested that my ideas embodied certain elements of participatory action-research and directed me to the PAR literature. The concept of PAR immediately appealed to me because it was action-oriented, community-based, and emphasized empowerment of the community to control and sustain its own development.

I applied to the Canadian International Development Agency (CIDA) for an educational grant, proposing to study if and how village women use nearby government health services. I wanted first to discover the main factors that either promoted or inhibited this use. Then, through an interactive process of interviews and discussion with village women, I hoped to improve their use of services and planned to involve in the discussions primary health care workers, such as auxiliary nurse midwives (ANMs) as well as the traditional village birth attendants (*dais*).

CIDA awarded me the grant, but I greeted my success with mixed feelings of amazement and trepidation—trepidation at the thought of undertaking such a major project on my own. As required by CIDA, I found a supervisor in India, a woman I had fortuitously met in the winter of 1989 at McMaster while she was presenting her work on women's health in rural India—the Director of the Centre for Women's Studies and Development at Banaras Hindu University (B.H.U.). Taking my meeting with her in Canada as a good omen, I felt readier to confront my destiny in India.

My background reading about Uttar Pradesh (U.P.) revealed that it is a densely populated state in India with the highest rates of infant and maternal mortality. Women in U.P., as in most of India, are socially and domestically oppressed, a situation which severely limits their access to education and health care. Women's health, when viewed within the sociocultural context in which women in rural U.P. live, is a complex and sensitive issue. The fact that women occupy positions of low status within social and domestic hierarchies—that they are devalued by virtue of gender alone—has health implications at several successive life cycle stages. Female infants may be deprived of adequate nutrition and health care as more attention is often given to male children. Female children are less likely than their brothers to be sent to school, and therefore less likely to benefit from school health programs and meals; they are engaged in domestic labour at an early childhood age and are married in early adolescence. After marriage, most young girls must go and live with their husbands in the houses of their parents-in-law. The youngest daughter-in-law (*bahu*) has the lowest status in the household and must defer to her in-laws, including any older *bahus*.

With this information, I set off for India with my husband. In the 11 months that followed, I underwent a process of intense learning, constantly questioning what I was doing and whether or not it was valid within the framework of international development. PAR was my research paradigm. As the project evolved, however, I also questioned whether my approach remained true to the principles of PAR.

Settling In and Making Contacts

The first three weeks in Banaras were probably the most stressful weeks of my life. Although fascinating, the environment alone was overwhelming—a chaotic mosaic of bizarre noises, sights, and smells. My existence had a surreal, dreamlike quality over which I had no control. I fluctuated between enjoying these strange new experiences and being immobilized by anxiety at the thought of carrying out the project. I felt my funding agency had seriously misguided me: by legitimizing the project, I had been falsely led to believe that it could realistically be done. I had no idea how or where to start. The seemingly impossible task of making contacts and finding a village in which to work loomed ahead of me; it was obvious that it would take the entire year just to find my supervisor at B.H.U.!

Despite my feelings of having been misled by CIDA, I also felt an enormous burden of responsibility towards the agency. I had to *do* something productive with the grant. I felt guilty and doomed for failure. These feelings, waxing and waning over the following 10 months, became my guiding force. In fact, as project work began in the village, I assumed added guilt, feeling that participating women would gain nothing from the project. I would become yet another researcher floating into their lives for a fleeting moment and then floating out again.

Having major responsibilities, my supervisor at B.H.U. did not have time to take me by the hand and guide me through the project as I had secretly hoped. Since we had never actually discussed what her supervisory role would be, my expectations of her involvement were faulty. Her primary role, as it turned out, was to direct me to appropriate contacts; this in itself was of great value. She introduced me to my first research assistant, and to one of her project workers who became a close friend and whose sister was my second assistant/interpreter. Through another of these contacts, I met a male health supervisor, Mr. Pande, who became a source of constant guidance and support in the early phases of the project.

I discovered that establishing contacts is an essential process that takes a lot of time. This was especially true when trying to find an interpreter who would become my ears and voice, thus influencing, knowingly or unknowingly, how people understood and perceived me, and how I understood and perceived them.

After two months in Banaras, my husband and I were well established in a small, downtown flat. I had hired an interpreter through the Centre for Women's Studies, found my way to the Primary Health Care Block Centre (the secondary-level health centre which serves approximately 100,000 people from 90-100 villages), met and spoken with the Deputy Chief Medical Officer and a number of medical doctors, met and interviewed many ANMs and *dais*, and visited a number of health subcentres in the area around Banaras. I had even learned how to navigate an ancient bicycle through the narrow, cobbled, crowded streets of Banaras while wearing a sari. These were all small successes that did not seem, in my anxious state of mind at the time, to add to the success of the project as a whole.

Understanding the Workings of the PHC System

After about three months in Banaras, I had a good grasp of the structural elements of the regional PHC system and believed the programs to be conceptually sound. The Maternal and Child Health (MCH) program, for example, covered areas such as immunizations for mothers and children, antenatal and post-partum care, family planning, sanitation and hygiene, and general health education. The extent to which these programs are

ANM delivering immunization on one of her village rounds. Infant is held by his father.

implemented, however, was limited as a result of numerous bureaucratic problems, which ultimately led to understaffing of PHC centres and limited or no resources.

The front line PHC workers were the auxiliary nurse mid-wives (ANMs) who were women with two years of post-secondary nursing training. They worked with the traditional village birth attendants called *dais,* some of whom have received sporadic training from the government in antenatal care and childbirthing. An ANM was expected to deliver care to 5,000 or more people in two or three villages; she worked out of a small rural PHC subcentre which supposedly was accessible to those villages.

I visited about half of the 20-odd subcentres in the PHC block around Banaras, most of these lacking both electricity and running water. At the time of my visit, only one subcentre was stocked with condoms, oral contraceptive pills, or intrauterine devices (IUDs). Despite these inadequacies, most of the ANMs seemed resigned to the challenges of their work. They commented that they could not possibly care for so many people distributed over such large areas, but that they did what they could under the circumstances.

Revising Goals and Preparing for the Pilot Study

I originally had planned to conduct a comparative study in two villages, one close to Banaras and one further removed. The desire to do a comparison study probably reflected the quantitative scientist in me (and perhaps also the fact that my Canadian supervisor was an epidemiologist). After two months in Banaras, I chuckled on re-reading this goal, realizing how unrealistic and impossible this was, having already learned the importance of revising goals and expectations as a project evolves.

Rather than a comparative study, I decided to do a pilot study in a nearby village in order to test my interview techniques and questions, become comfortable with approaching village women, and raise questions for further study in the next village. After four months in Banaras, I was ready to begin the pilot study.

Mr. Pande suggested a small village three to four kilometres outside Banaras. I was quite dependent on his guidance in terms of how I should approach the village and recruit women to be interviewed. The way to "enter" a village still eluded me somewhat: I could physically get myself to the village but whose door would I knock on first?

On one of my first visits to this village, I was walking with a young university student recruited by Mr. Pande to help us. Extremely self-conscious, I walked past the stares of many people while wearing a sari that I was afraid might fall off at any moment. I said "hello" in Hindi to each and every person with whom I made eye contact, raising my hands, palms together, in the Indian gesture of greeting. The student, noticeably embarrassed, leaned over and whispered to me that it was not really necessary to greet everyone in the village. Later, thinking of the situation in reverse, a young Indian woman walking through a Canadian town saying "hello" very sweetly to everyone she met, I realized how ridiculous this must have seemed.

Originally, I had planned to conduct semi-structured, audiotaped interviews using open-ended questions. Mr. Pande convinced me that women might feel intimidated by the tape recorder and would not respond well to open-ended questions. He also thought more women could be interviewed in a shorter period of time if a questionnaire with only close-ended questions was used.

With Mr. Pande's help, I devised a questionnaire consisting mostly of yes-no questions. I would conduct the main body of the interviews with the help of the university student and Mr. Pande would collect the demographic data and childbearing histories from each woman.

I had several concerns about Mr. Pande's involvement in the pilot study: his status as a high-caste male and as a member of the PHC system could influence women's responses to questions about their health or the PHC system. However, more in-

Mr. Pande explains the importance of immunization to a village man whose wife sits on the ground, her head covered by a sari.

terested in learning how to interview women in a rural village than in the actual content of the interviews, I needed his guidance despite the potential limitations stemming from his involvement. I hoped that valuable information would emerge from the pilot study for consideration in the focus village.

The following fieldnote entry describes an interview with a very young Muslim mother of one infant. This anecdote reveals our interviewing process as well as the women's lack of familiarity with the PHC system in general:

> We sat outside, the student and I on chairs and the young woman on a low, twine bed. She was shy and nervous. She was probably the youngest woman we had interviewed so far; most young mothers are probably either too shy to participate in the interviews or are not allowed to do so by their mothers-in-law. This frustrates me because I very much want to be able to speak to the youngest mothers in each hamlet. This particular woman had listened to the previous interview. There was a crowd of women and children around us, including the young woman's mother-in-law.

The student and I began to ask her questions concerning what she knew about the PHC system. Despite her shyness, the young woman was surprisingly talkative and added comments in between her responses to the yes-no questions. It was an extremely frustrating experience for me not to be able to interact directly with her and to guide the interview myself. The student, I could see, was not really interested in the interviewing process.

Half-way through the interview, the ANM for this village and one of the trained *dais* appeared on the scene, having just done some rounds in the village. The only person who could not see the ANM and the *dai* was the young woman we were interviewing. While the ANM and *dai* stood behind her, listening in on the proceedings, the young woman told us that she had never seen or heard of the ANM in her village, nor had she ever seen the *dai*. The ANM burst into a fit of giggles, followed by the other women sitting around us who realized what was happening. The young woman smiled shyly, also realizing that this was the ANM standing behind her. In fact, many women that we had interviewed claimed that they did not know who or what the ANM was and had never seen her in the village. The fact that this ANM was in the village today is proof that she does make an appearance from time to time. I hope that this was not a special appearance on my account, requested by Mr. Pande.

Following the pilot study, women's perceptions of the PHC system remained somewhat of a mystery. The ANM's visits to the village probably were infrequent, although I believed that most village women had seen the ANM but had simply not understood her role; they had not associated her with the state PHC system. Amazed that many women did not know about the existence of a PHC subcentre in their village, I later discovered that this subcentre had, in fact, been closed for months. Perhaps the problem of underutilization of government services was related to a lack of information on the part of village women.

Questions of accessibility and availability of services also needed to be explored. Many women, for example, stated a preference for private village doctors who were known, trusted, and accessible. This was the first time I even considered private doctors as an important source of health care for the women.

The pilot study revealed the inadequacies of the yes-no questionnaire format. The close-ended questions were leading and wrought with assumptions about the participants' experiences, knowledge, and priorities. For example, I asked each participant if they knew what and who the ANM was and most women stated that they did not know. This response effectively closed this line of questioning about PHC services in the village. Women probably did know the ANM but, perhaps, not by this title.

I decided to stick to my original idea of doing audiotaped interviews using open-ended questions, which would allow me to tailor the interview to the participants' individual experiences and to capture all the commentary and lessen the problem of built-in assumptions. Having discovered how talkative the women were, I was sure that they would respond well to open-ended questions. This approach would require a female interpreter interested in the research process and able to direct the interview and to nurture women's interest.

I was also bothered by the lack of privacy during an interview. Perhaps the responses of women would not have reflected their own thoughts but the general group opinion. They might also have felt inhibited to respond honestly when their mothers-in-law were present. Watching how women responded during private interviews, I wondered whether the importance I placed on privacy was a Western-based assumption. The concept of privacy to women who led totally communal lives was probably quite foreign; perhaps the group opinion was what really mattered.

Launching the Participatory Study

Following the pilot study and feeling ready to strike out on my own, I looked forward to working independently in the next phase of the project. I still had two problems: no interpreter and no village. Both were solved by a new Banarsi friend who suggested that her younger sister, Usha, work with me in a village called Akhri about 12 kilometres outside Banaras. My friend had visited the village as part of an initial survey for my supervisor's upcoming project.

Five months into the project, I visited Akhri for the first time, escorted by my friend. We walked around the village explaining to women who I was and what I would be doing over the next few months. I was received warmly. The rural location suited my purposes very well as the villagers did not go to the city hospitals for primary health care.

Typical of villages in the region, Akhri was divided according to caste into a number of different hamlets, each consisting of about 20 households. There was a small school in the central hamlet. The economy was agriculturally based, although many men commuted to Banaras to work as labourers. Akhri was situated equidistant from three PHC subcentres, all about six kilometres away. At least six private doctors lived and practiced in Akhri, but only one was legitimately trained in ayurvedic medicine and legally registered to practice in the village. The others were all self-trained doctors of various disciplines.

One week later, Usha and I again made our way out to Akhri. I had spent the previous week discussing my objectives in detail with Usha and concentrating on the participatory nature of the project. We talked about her role and I encouraged her to take responsibility in the project—to see herself as my partner, not just as an assistant. I hoped that she would naturally assume the role of facilitator. Usha seemed interested and receptive.

Over the next few months, I watched Usha with interest and was most impressed with her ability to build rapport with the village women. She had a confident, outgoing nature and could humour even the shyest young women into sharing their thoughts with us. She was very skilled at nurturing open-ended, unstructured interviews and did so with little input from me. She later proved herself to be incredibly competent at handling group situations. As Usha was unmarried and childless, I was afraid she might not be convincing while soliciting information from women about childbearing and family planning. Perhaps more significant in terms of power relationships in a hierarchical society was the fact that Usha came from a high-caste, Brahmin family, while we were working primarily with women of the lowest or "untouchable" castes. Early on, Usha refused outright to interact with women of one particular caste. She seemed at ease with other low-caste women, however, as they did with her. But, I was never sure if her caste position would influence the ways that the women responded to questions or participated in the project.

Usha and I spent considerable time discussing the need to remain "neutral" in the village. She was quick to form what could be perceived as alliances with, for example, the Brahmin landlord of the village. She also became allied with a trained village *dai* who was very unpopular with most women, even those in her own caste. These alliances might inhibit the village women from speaking freely with us if they feared that their information might reach the wrong ears.

At times, Usha made some disparaging comments to women in one hamlet about the lower-caste women from another hamlet. The point, as I explained to her, was to bring these women together and emphasize their commonalities, not their differences. Forming alliances with certain people could influence the way that women reacted towards us; any group process could also be jeopardized if women of different hamlets refused to meet because of our comments. It was difficult to read Usha's reactions to my commentary; she neither agreed nor disagreed. Again, I was uncertain if I was imposing upon Usha my Western values about how to relate effectively to people.

I was preoccupied with the problem of working through an interpreter throughout the Akhri study; it was hard not to be, as Usha was my main link with the village people. It was most frustrating when Usha answered questions directed to me rather than translating the question and allowing me to respond.

I had thought that participatory methods would help me
overcome the problem of communicating with people through
an interpreter. My reading had suggested that a community
member could be directly responsible for overseeing a project
within a community and the external researcher or "outsider"
would play a more facilitative role, liaising with the community
member. As I learned, this certainly requires that the facilitator/
researcher and community-based worker communicate effectively and have a common interest in the project. Working
through an interpreter *and* across cultures *and* across socio-economic strata made my task complex and frustrating. In terms
of background and life experience, Usha was almost as much
of a cultural outsider to Akhri as I was; the main difference
between the two of us was that she spoke Bojpuri, the local dialect. Expecting that Usha would naturally assume the role of discussion leader and village "insider" was unrealistic and unfair.

Over the next four to six weeks, we made our rounds
through the village, recruiting and getting acquainted with
participants from three different hamlets. We did this by talking to a senior woman in each household and diagramming the
occupants based on her information. Through these diagrams,
we discovered the whereabouts of the youngest mothers and
got permission to talk to them. All of these activities went re-
markably smoothly: the women seemed interested, friendly,
and talkative.

Far from deterring women, the tape recorder proved very
valuable as a means of enticing women to speak, as they enjoyed listening to themselves with the earphones. The tape recorder also enabled us to enforce some privacy during the interviews. We told the women that in order to hear themselves
on the tape, the room had to be quiet; in fact, some older
women ordered everyone out of their houses and shut the door
against the usual mob of children so that they could speak with
us. Others were not as concerned about a quiet environment.
Most of the young mothers wanted at least one other village
woman with her and, often, the mother-in-law insisted on being present.

A mother from the Rajbhar hamlet massaging her baby girl.

On the whole, the interviews went well. They usually took place in the home of the participant and each interview lasted about 45 minutes and focussed on the childbearing and illness experiences of the participant. I had learned in the pilot study that women seemed more comfortable and animated when telling stories about their own experiences, rather than answering hypothetical questions about illness such as, "If you became ill, where would you go for treatment?"

Major Themes from Interview Analysis

It took just over a month to complete 18 interviews, translate and transcribe the tapes, and analyze the data. What follows is an overview of how women in Akhri perceive and utilize the PHC system.

It was clear that PHC services, particularly MCH services, were underused by women in Akhri. The main reason for this was that women lacked the necessary information for making decisions about when to seek health care and where to go to get it. Basic health information would help women recognize if their health or their children's health was at risk: usually by the time medical services were sought, it was already too late. Many women did not know of the existence of subcentres, and so opted for another source of care.

The limited availability and accessibility of existing services were also deterrents to women seeking those services. Women commented that, upon arrival at the PHC subcentre, either the ANM was not there or no supplies were available. Women preferred a private village doctor because, even though they had to pay for his services, they knew who he was, where he was, that he was available to help them, and that he would make house calls at night if necessary.

Originally, I had thought that the low status of women in Indian society would play a significant role in women's ability to access health care services. In Akhri, this was true, but not because young women were not valued and thus were denied adequate care. It was more likely true because a young *bahu's* mother-in-law or husband was not adequately informed and was unable to make appropriate decisions regarding her health care. Any campaigns to increase women's awareness about health and health care services must include the husband and mother-in-law.

The extent to which women were informed about PHC services was dependent on their own health priorities as well as the health priorities of the state government. Women prioritized their children's health. They were best informed about children's immunizations and wanted to know more. Half of the women had had some or all of their children at least partially immunized through the subcentre, by visiting immunization camps, or through private village doctors.

Women were also well informed about one method of family planning—sterilization. Sterilization was a state government priority and had been promoted to the extent that women knew only about sterilization and not about other reversible contraceptive options. They wanted to know more about these other options and were unwilling to discuss sterilization.

There was general confusion amongst women about who
was who in the health care system. The village was sporadically
visited by a variety of people: B.H.U. researchers, Red Cross
workers, government doctors, as well as the ANM. Most often,
women did not know who these people were or where they
had come from. The ANM was just one of this undefined group
of health care workers, often not associated with the state PHC
system or with any place of work or hospital. When associated
with the state, she was viewed as an agent of family planning
with the sole purpose of recruiting candidates for sterilization.
No association was made between the village *dais* and the ANM.

The issue of private doctoring was interesting. I spoke to the
legally registered ayurvedic doctor as well as several illegitimate
doctors practicing allopathic or Western medicine. It is safe to
say that this latter group presented some risk to patients, dis-
pensing injections and advice with little knowledge and no
training. The ayurvedic doctor in Akhri, however, provided
what seemed to be a legitimate source of health care, as he prac-
tised traditional ayurvedic healing based on herbal remedies as
well as allopathic medicine. Among other things, he dispensed
all the necessary immunizations for a small fee. Most women
preferred his services over all the other village doctors' services.
These registered private doctors could play an important role
providing women with accessible services.

Preparing for Group Meetings

Having completed the interview phase, I now understood
the complexity of PHC service delivery and its use by village
women. Given my time limitations, I wanted the next phase of
the project to have well-defined, simple, short-term objectives.
I concentrated on group sessions which would: (1) bring women
together in an atmosphere of sharing and solidarity; (2) introduce women in Akhri to members of the PHC system, specifically the ANMs and *dais* who work in Akhri; and (3) dissemi-
nate information on topics in which women had expressed an

interest.

The first group session was held near the end of my seventh month in India; the meeting was open to all other women in the community. I hoped the session would create a sense of commonality amongst women and enable a two-way exchange between the ANMs and the women regarding women's health needs, PHC workers' roles, and service availability. The ANMs agreed to act as resource persons provided that I obtain their supervisor's permission and arrange transportation to and from the village. Usha would facilitate the discussion.

About one week before the meeting, Usha and I walked through the village informing people of the meeting and slide show. The prospect of a slide show was exciting to all the women, providing us with an excellent way of drawing them out to the meeting. Over the next few days, a meeting time was established: women agreed that noon was the best time as it was too hot work outside. The Brahmin landowner in the Central hamlet gave us permission to use the schoolhouse as a meeting place. All the participants knew of its location which was within easy walking distance. I hired an electrician to operate the generator for the slide projector, and the day before the meeting, Usha and I revisited all the households to remind everyone of the meeting time and place.

The meeting was to proceed in a fairly structured way, although the discussion itself would be open. I wrote out a full script for Usha, outlining how to approach the meeting and promote discussion. We spent several days together discussing the script and other possible approaches.

In the first 15 to 20 minutes, we planned to introduce the ANMs and village *dais* and explain our presence in the village. The slide show would visually introduce women of the different village hamlets to each other. A 20- to 25-minute discussion would follow during which women could ask questions of the ANMs or share experiences of illness and health care. In the remaining 15 to 20 minutes, the ANMs and *dais* would talk about their work in the village and describe MCH services. An hour seemed to be enough time to accomplish our objectives without impinging on the women's work time.

The following is an excerpt of my fieldnotes, describing the scene at the schoolroom:

> Shortly after we arrived, a small crowd had already gathered outside the school—mostly children. They watched me set up inside the school house. A young girl belonging to the Brahmin family who owns the school helped me organize things. Meanwhile, Usha had gone in the rickshaw to get the two ANMs who had agreed to attend the meeting and help us explain the workings of the PHC system.
>
> The school is a shabby brick-plaster building with small, shuttered windows along the front wall facing into a courtyard. It sits in the shade of a huge tree. There are two small rooms inside, joined by a door in the dividing wall. Each room has a separate entrance doorway. The doors and windows provide some light and ventilation but not much. There is no electricity so, of course, no fan or lights. The room that we were using was, at the most, 20 by 20 feet.
>
> Within 20 minutes, everything was set up and ready to go. By this time, the room was packed with noisy kids and adolescents. There was only one participant there with her mother-in-law from the Harijan *basti*. It was still only 12 o'clock, the time that I had planned to start, so I decided to wait a few minutes. More kids kept crowding in so that, even if the participants came, there was no room for them to sit. I had thought that there would be kids there and my plan was to show the slides to whomever wanted to see them and then kick the kids out for the group discussion. I began to revise my plan.
>
> As time wore on—10, 15 minutes—the kids became more restless. Some were demanding to see the slides. The one participant's mother-in-law was threatening to leave if I didn't start the show. There was still no sign of Usha. I initiated my contingency plan made up on the spot. I explained to the crowd that I would show the slides once to the kids and then they would all have to leave to make room for the participants and other interested women. I asked one young teenager from the Rajbhar *basti* where all the Rajbhar participants were.

She told me they all had work to do despite the fact that I had visited all the participants twice in the previous week and painstakingly had arranged a time when they would all be free. I sent the girl to get the participants and sent another messenger to the Harijan *basti*.

Then I had my first showing. There were roars of approval from the children. Half-way through the presentation, I looked up and caught sight of Usha swimming through the crowd, the two ANMs in tow. Usha gave me a despairing look. I tried to look apologetically at the ANMs but I had a feeling they had lived through many similar experiences before in their village work. They seemed to take it all in stride, waded their way towards two chairs in the back of the room, and sat down. I was sure they were thinking I was absolutely crazy.

By now, the temperature in the airless room had reached about 45 degrees Celsius. The first viewing was over. Usha and I started ordering the kids outside. They would not budge. I was bodily picking them up off the floor and hurling them towards the door. The ANMs also got into the act. There was a self-appointed bouncer standing guard outside the door, a man whom we had met before who had been working in Akhri on a family planning survey. We managed to clear all the kids from the room. Slowly, women were filing in and sitting down. But none of them were women I had ever seen before. Still, not a single participant had shown up. The one who had come had been dragged out of the room by her mother-in-law after the slide show. I told Usha to hold the boat on course. I would go and get the women myself. So much for voluntary participation! Oh well.

When I arrived at the Rajbhar *basti*, many of the participants had started mobilizing themselves to come to the school. I encouraged them along. I could see a line of women filing through the fields on their way to the school from the Harijan *basti*. By the time I returned to the school, the room was again packed. There must have been about 60 women seated or standing in the room. There was almost no floor space left. Each woman had brought one or two small infants along, the ones that were too small to leave outside. In all there must have been about 120 people in that small, dark, hot room. Usha fretted around like a tiny, caged mouse, yelling her introduction to the crowd, using a script she had prepared from my outline. Every few minutes she would look at me with an expression which I would describe as a mixture of panic, hysteria, and disbelief. She would yell at me "Oh God, Patricia, God!" in her wonderful Hindi accent, implying, "What the hell are we doing?!" I had, by this point, become completely swept away by it all and watched the proceedings as if they were a bizarre dream. The foremost thought on my mind was how I was going to get from the door to the slide projector through the swamp of bodies on the floor.

It did not take long for Usha to abandon her script. She barked an order at me, "Okay Patricia, show the slides, show the slides!" I could not think of a better idea. The slide show seemed to settle the crowd a little. It was extremely gratifying for me to listen to the laughter and watch the faces of the women, completely overcome with amusement and pleasure at seeing themselves, larger than life, on the screen.

After the show, a number of women left, including, unfortunately, several young participants who were forced to leave by their mothers-in-law. About 40 women remained. Usha raised some questions for discussion, but the women were more interested in asking the ANMs questions and the ANMs proceeded to talk about MCH issues.

Fifteen minutes later, the group decided to move outside under a tree; the unventilated room was, by this time, unbearably hot. The presentation resumed outside with the women expressing a great deal of interest in the ANMs. One older woman wanted to know more about how to get children immunized; the ANMs suggested that the village hold an immunization camp. The ANMs reviewed aspects of antenatal care and actually dispensed iron tablets to certain women. Pushpa, a young and smartly dressed, educated mother, wanted to know how to become an ANM and work in the village. Following the meeting, she joined the group of ANMs and *dais* for refreshments that I provided.

I could not even begin to evaluate the meeting until several days later and wandered around in a strange state of revelation and exhaustion. During the meeting, I experienced an un-

defined sensation which later slowly formed itself into the revealing question, "What did you expect?" Usha was certainly
speechless.

Clearly, there were several problems with this first group
session—primarily my expectation that the imposed agenda
would work. This was the first meeting of its kind in Akhri, and
certainly the first slide show ever seen by the villagers. Women
from the different village hamlets had never met together before. I was naive to think that women from differing castes and
religions could immediately engage in group discussion or even
be interested in meeting and talking to each other. In my
supervisor's project, I had watched a diverse group of village
women from various hamlets discussing water sanitation. But
that group session had emerged out of many months of work
in the village, beginning with small groups in individual hamlets.

The group and I had completely different objectives: I was
there for a group discussion; they had come to watch slides. To
some extent, the session nurtured interest in MCH issues, but
there were too many people in the school room and the situation was over-charged with excitement about the slide show.
Perhaps the kind of group process I had envisioned could have
emerged out of smaller meetings in individual hamlets over a
period of months. I had taken a premature shortcut and was
still reeling from the effects.

I now more fully appreciated the logistical difficulties associated with such a meeting. For example, "noon" does not happen at the same time for everyone in the village; it is difficult
for women to commit themselves in advance to a prescribed
meeting time, given their household and other work; and
women need to bring their small children. The large turnout
was a surprise. So was the fact that men, of course, also wanted
to watch the slide show.

Despite these problems, the question and answer period
was encouraging. For the first time, the women had interacted
with the ANMs, knowing who the ANMs were and where they
worked. I decided to pursue the group sessions but in a differ-

ent way—the way I should have probably started. Small group meetings in two individual hamlets would more easily allow an interactive process and an assessment of each hamlet's priorities. Thus, women could become more familiar with maternal and child health topics and more easily encouraged to share their thoughts in a group situation. Perhaps then women would be better prepared to meet with women from other hamlets in a larger group.

Revising Plans for Group Sessions

My approach to presenting information to the small groups of women was direct, almost didactic. During the interviews, women had repeatedly expressed their desire for more information, but my time was running out. I felt that if I did not take this rather unilateral approach, the information would not be disseminated and nothing would be accomplished. The decision left me feeling somewhat unsatisfied, realizing that this approach was far from a participatory one. I felt trapped by time, allowing it to dictate my approach and expectations.

I organized two presentations. The first one was on family planning options, as women seemed most interested in this subject; some had actively sought more information about reversible methods of birth control. The second session was on antenatal care; the women were least informed about this subject but it is of great importance in preparing mother and infant for a safe delivery.

The main messages were presented in several ways. I wrote two stories based on the information accumulated in my interviews and observations of village life. One story addressed the issue of family planning; the other, antenatal care. The stories contained very clear messages about the consequences of not seeking antenatal care and not limiting family size, reflecting my attempt to change women's behaviour. Stories with particular morals or teachings are often used in India to deliver messages and to effect change; Mr. Pande and my supervisor both agreed that the story approach was very good. I, however, felt dissatisfied, preferring a more interactive model of disseminating information but realizing that there was just not enough time.

Usha translated the stories from English to Hindi but was not interested in ensuring an accurate representation of a rural, Indian life. Instead, a man who had spent many years living and teaching in villages helped me to find an appropriate writing style and convincing dialogue. I illustrated the family planning story with a series of black and white drawings, and commissioned an artist to paint pictures for the antenatal story.

Five or six questions for group discussion followed each story. I then planned to present a few main points using another series of pictures. The women would be able to see real samples of condoms, oral contraceptive pills, and IUDs. Each session would take a maximum of one hour.

Usha and I spent several days preparing for the presentations. I had written a few prompters on the backs of pictures to help her with the main points and she led the sessions with little help from me. Each presentation was held twice, once in each hamlet.

The turnout was good in both hamlets—almost all the participants attended the sessions as well as other interested women. The family planning session was more popular than the antenatal session. Most of Usha's questions after the stories were answered by two or three older women in the groups; the younger women remained quiet but attentive. There was not a lot of spontaneous discussion or questions from the group. Women were content to listen. This did not surprise me given that the topics were new to these women. But I wondered what would have happened if the women had chosen the discussion topic themselves.

This idea led me to rethink my assumption that health was a priority for these women. After reading about the high rates of maternal and infant mortality in this part of rural India, I had concluded that health was a priority for villagers. This might not have been the case; my whole project may have been based

Young mothers and other participants in the small group sessions

on a false assumption. I had not actually asked women what were the priorities in their community. I again ruminated about what, exactly, had I done in this project, if not research involving the participation of local people? What, if anything, had I accomplished?

Rajeev Ghandi was assassinated shortly before I was to leave India. Resulting curfews prevented me from visiting Akhri in the last two weeks before my departure. Generally disappointed and fed up with the project, I felt as if I had cheated the village women out of an opportunity to make positive changes in their lives. I was yet another in a stream of unidentified health workers who enter their lives for a brief moment and then vanish forever.

Epilogue: Reframing My Experience

Now, three years later, I feel better about my work in Akhri village. When I first returned from India, I could only think about the project in terms of what I had *not* done, and felt so

dissatisfied that I could not face the task of writing about it until
10 or 12 months had passed. Then slowly and reluctantly I
sorted through the data and wrote a report and this chapter.
Over time, I was able to reframe my work and accomplishments,
legitimizing an incredibly valuable, intense learning experience.

A recurring theme in my original report was my struggle
with time. The project I had planned to do would take years.
Working with people effectively and interactively to elicit
change means building trust and developing rapport over time.
This is true even in a familiar culture and environment where
no language barrier exists. After working in a hospital in
Ontario for almost a year, I am just now becoming involved in
a PAR-like process of identifying problems and priorities and
initiating change. It has taken me 10 months to get to that point.

While time was a major problem, the real obstacles were my
pre-set goals and expectations—I needed to realize that these
could be adapted to the situation. Rather than being a failure,
the use of stories was a legitimate, acceptable approach given
the circumstances. I do not know if the stories influenced the
women in any way, but they may have been a springboard to
change. The process of discovery and change was really just
beginning for the women and myself as I left Akhri.

I would not tackle a community-based project in the same
way again. First, I would get involved with a project that was
under way, or hook up with a non-governmental organization
and get started that way. Secondly, I would begin by living and
working in a village to gain a better understanding of what is
going on around me and what the community's priorities are.
At one point, I put down on paper all the necessary steps that
lead up to an actual participatory project. One step was to understand the geographical area itself which could take a year
or longer. I would have to start small and get a grounding of
what the area is like and what things could be possible. Otherwise, I would again find myself throwing darts, hoping to hit
something important.

During the project, I often questioned my role as a foreigner
doing development work. I still do. At my most cynical, I felt I

had no business working in India at all. Most of the successful, sustainable community-based projects in India have been carried out by Indians using PAR principles. While in Akhri, the language and cultural barriers between the villagers and me seemed too great for effective work with PAR. I have since changed my mind about this. What I did not acknowledge about the Indian PAR projects was that they also evolved over years. I could, with time, become comfortable in a community, get to know people, and learn the language, much as I have had to do in the hospital where I now work.

I now understand the term "participatory action-research" as a label for a broad approach to problem-solving and communicating. PAR appeals to me because of its cooperative, interactive, egalitarian qualities—qualities that are innate in my approach to people and life in general. As I carried out the project, I questioned whether I was incorporating local participation and evaluated my work, not in terms of what I had accomplished, but how it fit a loosely defined PAR methodology. Perhaps PAR is not as well-defined as I had thought. I now think of my work as an interactive, community-oriented project, informed by elements of participatory action-research. This is what it was.

4

"WE ARE DYING. IT IS FINISHED!": LINKING AN ETHNOGRAPHIC RESEARCH DESIGN TO AN HIV/AIDS PARTICIPATORY APPROACH IN UGANDA

Patricia Spittal with Janette Nakuti,
Nelson Sewankambo, and Dennis G. Willms

ଔ EDITORS' NOTE: The four authors, all members of an ethnographic research team in an ongoing study, interweave two major threads in "We Are Dying. It Is Finished!" The first thread reflects their desire to document the life experiences of women in a small Ugandan town, "women who fear and suffer the consequences of HIV/AIDS." As readers, we catch telling glimpses of the everyday lives of Maama Mally, Juliette, and Josie—glimpses that reveal tragically courageous people situated in "a troubling place."

The second thread is about the research team itself. During a mid-point retreat, literally surrounded by ethnographic data attesting to the depths of people's suffering, they admitted their emotional exhaustion and realized a transforming moment: a dead silence of grief. The team members began to question their work, acknowledging doubts about their underlying assumptions, feelings of guilt, embarrassment, and naivety, as well as an uncertainty of what to do next. They intimately touched knowledge and, in the process, came face-to-face with themselves. With deeper understanding of the complexity of a despairing context, they now encounter the difficulties of incorporating participation by community people. Their statements, "Our intent had always been participatory, but so far our process had not been" and "It would seem like we have exploited them just to collect information," capture the team's current moral and practical tensions. "No longer strangers," they have gained commitment to the creation of enabling opportunities but do not know how to do this.

This chapter speaks to the *intention* of doing participatory action-research: it documents the work of a research team using standard ethnographic methods but preparing themselves to do more. Its double richness lies in the Ugandan women's stories and in the team's emerging courage to disclose their personal struggles to understand and respond. Readers resisting the temptation to sweep strong, personal emotions or ethical doubts under an academic carpet may see themselves reflected here.cs

This disease is everywhere. There is nobody who does not have HIV. Even if you are alright, this disease is in our bodies. There is no way people can prevent it from entering. We are all going to die. We are dying. It is finished!

—Maama Mally

As a Canadian doctoral student in anthropology and one of two non-Ugandan members of the ethnographic research team, I lived and worked for 14 months in a small Ugandan town. I worked closely with Janette Nakuti, a friend, colleague, and confidant. While my voice is presented in this chapter, I speak on behalf of all the members of our research team in Uganda: Nelson, Addison, Godfrey, and Dennis, but primarily Janette. As women, we wanted to capture the life experiences of women in this town—women who fear and suffer the consequences of HIV/AIDS.   Janette and I became friends with a number of women in the town. We informally interviewed them, interpreted the meaning of the collected narratives, and supported each other through difficult times.

The Story of Maama Mally, Alcohol Seller

When Janette and I first met Maama Mally, she told us her story about the suffering of women, marriage, and the fear of HIV infection.

Maama Mally was 17 years old when she married a man much older than herself—a man she describes as "way over 30." She became the primary caretaker of the children from his previous marriages. As well, she had three children of her own with this man. In polygynous family structures, women do not necessarily wield power as wives, but rather as siblings and mothers. After the birth of her third child, Maama Mally felt "forced" to leave her marriage. As she recounted:

> I left because of my in-laws. There were three of his sisters, all divorced and living there. He was the only male in the family. He had built his house in his parents' compound. He liked his mother so much, he never wanted her to cook a meal, so I cooked for everyone. We all ate together—mothers, sisters, and all of their children. They would not help me with any work. As soon as they finished eating, they would go and walk and then eat again. If the meal was not ready, they would quarrel. They would put their clothes out for me to wash. I was married to their brother, so I had to do every bit of their work. Also, they would accuse me of things. I could not stand it so I decided to leave and go to my parents' place. I had asked him to get his own plot and build a house for us so that we could be free of these people, but he refused.

Continuing, Maama Mally explained that some women, when they fail in marriage and return to their parents' homes to live, will mistreat the wives of their married brothers.

Maama Mally packed up her things, weaned the last born, and went back to her father's village:

> In my father's village, I lived in a big house, but separate from my parents. Three of my sisters were there. Divorced, we all had our own rooms and each was free to bring a man. In those days, was there anything to fear? We just used to en-

joy ourselves. If you got tired of a man, you would just leave
him, change, and get another.

Over a number of years, Maama Mally had consecutive liaisons
with three different men. Each of these men was married with
a wife in his own compound. She bore each man a child; each
child died. Desperate to explain their deaths, she and others
concurred that her husband had sent a curse. Eventually, she
returned to his village and again stayed with him.

While Maama Mally was away, her husband found another
wife. Even though the compound was extremely small, the two
women lived in separate houses. According to Maama Mally:

> I used to quarrel with her every day. She had cultivated all
> of the land and when I got there she did not want me to take
> any of the land to grow food for my own children. Every day
> we would get up, work in the garden, meet, and quarrel for
> the rest of the day. There was so much jealousy that when-
> ever he would sleep in my house, she would walk around,
> around, and around it in the night.

Maama Mally said that whenever the husband bought her cloth
or something for her house or even just sauce for *matoke*, there
would be an explosion from the co-wife; and on many occasions, she and the co-wife would physically fight.

Eventually, Maama Mally said that it was painfully obvious
that her co-wife was visiting a traditional practitioner (witch
doctor): "She would go out very early in the morning and come
back with something wrapped in leaves. I do not know what
she was doing with them but my husband used to find it and
always quarrel with her."

This went on for a month before Maama Mally decided to
leave. She decided to join her brother, a cattle trader, in town.
He helped to set her up as an alcohol seller, loaning her money
to buy *waragi*, a very raw form of gin, which she sold both out
of her single room in town and in the mobile markets.

> It is because of problems that I do this. Alcohol selling is not
> a good job. If that's the only way I can feed myself, there is

nothing that I can do. It is a job for people who did not go to school. It is so bad, some women who sell alcohol have ended up being beaten. A man may come to a woman's room, get drunk, and when she asks for her money, he may refuse. If the woman insists, he just slaps her.

Sex often becomes part of the trade. Women acquiesce, as there is always the threat that the man will take away his friends and go drink somewhere else. Expectations for sex increase if the man actually buys *waragi* for her to drink.

Some alcohol sellers drink with their customers. The men are drinking and the sellers also drink. When the sellers get drunk, they act in a way that attracts these men. Some of them get drunk before the men do. They do not even know what they are doing.

I do not play. I do not drink alcohol. I am good to the men because they are my customers, but there is no way a man will joke with me. Sometimes when they are drunk, there is no getting them out of the house. But for me, no man would want to sleep with me anyway. Which man cannot see that I

Single room, mud-and-wattle row houses

am sick? But very many men have been disturbing me. When they do suggest sex, I tell them there and then that I do not want it. Of course, they insist, but so do I. Sometimes a man will come with sugar and bread. He will give them to you, but it is very dangerous to eat these things if you are not going to accept the man.

Maama Mally acknowledges that being an alcohol seller is a dreadful occupation. Most alcohol sellers operate their businesses out of a single room located in the mud-and-wattle row houses where they also eat, sleep, and raise their children. Women often have to plead for payment or pray that their customers will come back and pay for alcohol consumed on credit. Alcohol selling is a burdensome job, but it is viewed as an opportunity for women to find men who will supplement their incomes and property. A friend of Maama Mally sees alcohol selling as a way "to get expensive men":

If I was selling alcohol, some of my customers would be my men. If I was selling alcohol, I would not be suffering financially like this. Yet, I could not allow this because my house is so dirty. There is no bed, no good things. I cannot allow them to see my poverty. But, I have been told that it is no problem. These men put in all of those things in less than a week. Of course, I would have to have sex with them. There's nothing for nothing. I cannot manage such a life. I would rather suffer. I know what women who sell alcohol go through. They do the selling, and in the end, they sleep with them.

As her statement suggests, there are women in the town who realize the risks involved in alcohol selling and "would rather suffer" than engage in it.

Maama Mally's story is tragic. Her story is shared and recounted by other women in this town: many women find themselves similarly burdened, alone, and struggling to live on tenuous incomes. Women who sell alcohol develop fragile relationships with men who provide varying levels of emotional and economic support and, in most instances, demand sex in return.

Cattle loaders and traders are a common sight in the town.

A Trading Centre and Stop-Over Town in Uganda

The town where Maama Mally lives is recognized as a "hot spot" for HIV-1 transmission in Uganda. Located on a major trucking route, the town developed as a truck stop, servicing the needs of truckers who travelled with their lorries from the Kenya port city of Mombasa through Uganda to the land-locked countries in East and Central Africa. It is also a trading centre, attracting agriculturalists, market vendors, and cattle traders. The lure of the cash economy prompts many men and women to migrate here in search of employment. In this setting, distanced from the moral requisites of rural community life, a more relaxed, relatively free sociality occurs. For many women, "sex for food" is the only avenue for feeding their young children. These factors, combined with the fact that it is rare for women to be able to negotiate condom use, have contributed to increases in HIV transmission.

The number of people who live in lorry stops/trading centres and who are presently HIV-positive (HIV+) is astounding. Recent epidemiological surveys in the Rakai district indicate that generally for trading centres HIV+ seroprevalence is as high as 35 percent for the adult population (13-49 years of age) (Wawer, 1991).

The town is a numbing place. Residents call it "Sodom and Gomorrah," referring to the Biblical city where burning sulphur rained on the people as God's punishment for their abominations. Between 1990 and early 1994, there had been a rapid decline in prosperity due to the closure of the Rwandan border and the concomitant decrease in lorry traffic. At the same time, population numbers have declined because of the large number of deaths caused by *silimu* (AIDS).

Beginning with an Ethnographic Approach: Our Original Objectives

The impetus to study this Ugandan town ethnographically derived from the fact that there is little published information on HIV/AIDS in the context of culture. HIV+ seroprevalence rates among bar girls (who at one time "moved up and down the streets like schools of fish") were as high as 76 percent in certain regions in Uganda (Carswell, 1989). Bar girls, their clients, long-distance truckers, and persons who frequently contract sexually transmitted diseases (STDs) are considered to be at particular risk for HIV infection and thus became the initial "targets" for the ethnographic research.

Funded by the International Development Research Centre (IDRC), we undertook to qualitatively assess the nature and distribution of sexual behaviours among these high-risk groups in this Ugandan town. In addition, we wished to identify social-cultural factors that motivate, shape, and influence unsafe aspects of sexual behaviour. We also wanted to ascertain how the AIDS pandemic has affected the sexual health of adolescents and young adults. Lastly, we planned to develop a counselling program targeted at bar girls and patients with STDs who sought treatment at the town's health centre.

We believed firmly in the necessity of developing a "culturally appropriate intervention." The term "intervention," while popular in the medical literature, unfortunately has connotations of control, manipulation, and "doing something to someone." We decided to adopt the notion of "enabling resources" in lieu of intervention. The reason for this became obvious during the initial phase of the ethnographic study. Persons in this town are at risk for more than simply HIV/AIDS infection; they are at "social risk" for economic hardship, illness, dysfunctional and maladaptive relationships, family problems associated with migration, and so on.

The resources required to ameliorate these more broad-based concerns require strategies that have the potential of meeting comprehensive needs and concerns. Culturally appropriate interventions (e.g., primary prevention education) are one dimension of a broader domain of resources that need to be marshalled in response to these community-based needs. Building on the language of "health as a resource for living" (Ottawa Charter, 1986), the research team coined the term "enabling resources."

The ethnographic research would provide the foundation for the development and implementation of a "culturally appropriate intervention." In order for the intervention to be "successful," we felt that a partnership with community members was essential. In the early stages of the research, we had discussed using a participatory action-research (PAR) approach. Soon after the team entered the field, however, it became clear that people in the community felt numb, almost irrevocably fatalistic. Therefore, we decided to marshal a variety of evidences (epidemiological and ethnographic) intended to uncover and illuminate layers of risk before thinking through the steps of community participation and involvement. The Principal Investigator on the research team, Nelson Sewankambo, has commented:

> It is very clear to me that programs already in place are not making an impact on the prevalence of HIV/AIDS. I am not saying that there is no change in the community resulting from these existing programs, but I would like to see much

more behaviour change, especially with respect to HIV transmission. Focussing on clinical studies alone is inadequate. We need to look at other approaches. These alternative approaches need to address the existing problems in a personal way. That is why I got interested in qualitative approaches to the problem, since clinical and KAP (Knowledge, Attitude, and Practice) studies are apparently not enough. Looking at interventions, we need the participation of the community, so that at the end of the day, we have in place complementary approaches: anthropological studies first, followed by participatory approaches.

Getting Started

We started by using classic ethnographic techniques such as in-depth interviews (unstructured and semi-structured), focus groups, and participant observation in order to understand the socio-cultural context of high-risk sexual behaviour in the town. Nelson hired four Ugandan university graduates with degrees in the social sciences (Janette, Barbara, Godfrey, and Addison). Barbara, Godfrey, and Addison are Baganda from Central Uganda; Janette is a Mugesu from Mbale Province. Barbara left the project after eight months to pursue graduate studies in England. The project had been running for seven months when I joined the team in August of 1993. We lived and worked together in a rented house located on the outskirts of the town.

Each of us interviewed community members as opportunity afforded. At this stage, participation simply meant a willingness of individuals to share personal stories, including the sexual aspects of their lives. In some instances, stigma made participation very difficult or painful, as we came to be known as *basawo basilimu* (AIDS doctors). Sometimes, community members thought that the people we visited had the disease even if they were not ill or known to be HIV-positive. In fact, for some women with whom we compiled case studies, this was a constant concern.

The Story of Two Neighbours: Juliette and Josie

A friend introduced us to Juliette, a cooked-food seller in the evening markets. She lives in a place commonly known as the AIDS compound. By this time, we suspected that there were other women besides bar girls and waitresses who were living in precarious economic circumstances and exposed to mobile market men (men with money), creating a significant risk for HIV/AIDS. At first, Juliette was really kind to us, chatting freely. But after the second and third visits, our presence in the compound was obviously difficult for her. She would go to the market to buy tomatoes for her *matoke* sauce and not come back or, as we found out later, she would instruct her child not to talk to us. Janette and I struggled with this, concerned that we had offended her.

Josie, a young woman who later became a close friend, was embarrassed by her neighbour's behaviour towards us and explained the reasons for Juliette's "badheartedness."

> Juliette talks to women around here and says that she does not want anyone to associate her with you. Juliette had *ekisipi* (herpes zoster) on her back and told people it was syphilis. A year ago she had a baby. It took a few breaths and died. So every time you came to find her, she did not want to meet you. This is why she locked her door and went away.

We did not know what the rest of the women in her compound knew—Juliette was very ill—and our visits served as added confirmation that her illness was AIDS. We stigmatized her.

In time, Juliette wanted to talk. She told us how worried she was about her sick mother back in the village. Two of her sisters had travelled long distances to be near their mother so that they could care for her properly. But now, as Juliette said:

> My sister in town has died and the one in the village looks sick. It seems she got "our disease." Our mother is really old now. Who is going to keep her? I wish God could make it so that the old people die first. These days it is mostly the young ones who die first and the old ones die with no help.

Juliette eventually went to the village to bury an elder sister. When she returned to town, her own fears were realized—AIDS was destroying her.

Josie was reluctant to let me hold her six-month-old child, Farouk. Criticized for having a sickly child, Josie constantly was told by women in the AIDS compound to keep him inside. They said things like, "How can you bring out such a child? That one has *silimu*. Leave him inside and not do bother us with him. Take your baby inside, he makes us vomit."

Malnourished and with dripping lesions, Farouk moved only to scratch his rash. He was a pathetic sight, covered with a greenish brown herbal medicine which was caked into the creases of his skin. Neighbours explained his sickness as stemming from an improperly performed "twin" ceremony.

Twins are considered to be an unnatural birth occurrence. For this reason, prescriptive rituals are undertaken to appease the ancestors. Through these carefully constructed ritual events, assurances are guaranteed for the health and well-being of the two children.

Other women in her compound supported Josie by helping to supply her with charcoal and food. She did not have money to pay for her child's treatments. Farouk's father had stopped coming around and no longer provided support, having told Josie: "If you do not allow me to have sex, I will not help you. The time will come when you will start starving. Then you will allow me. People cannot go without food." Josie felt that he did not want to be associated with such a sick baby. She explained:

> Many used to ask him, "Why are you wasting money buying milk for this baby and giving him treatments? After all, he is going to die." He stopped giving me assistance. The child from his other wife, who was at home, was also sick in the same way, which made him believe even more that it was *silimu*.

Later, Josie confided that she was worried her baby was indeed sick with "the thing." She wanted to be tested for HIV.

We arranged to get Josie tested. She told a few friends in the AIDS compound about her choice but she was not prepared to disclose her positive result. People harassed her. Every time we visited, others in the compound took note; women listened through the rat holes behind her mud and waddle walls. Despite their denigrating comments, Josie remained staunchly committed to our friendship. We felt very fortunate.

As the ethnographic study proceeded, we began to understand better the many aspects of people's lives that put them at risk for HIV. The major contributing factor is the life situation of people. As Nelson observed:

> One could argue that ignorance plays a part. If people do not know how a disease is spread, how it is transmitted, they may live certain kinds of behaviour, not knowing that those behaviours contribute to the transmission of the disease. However, over 80 percent of the people in this country know but are unable to change their behaviour because of the situation they find themselves in.

> For example, some women find themselves unable to look after their children, and of course, they want them to survive. They have to find a way to feed them. Women get into and remain in relationships that ultimately put them at risk. They fear that they have no alternatives. They have to continue with their relationships simply because this is where they get economic support for their own survival and the survival of their children. It has to do with economic hardship.

Personal and Methodological Dilemmas

Many community members still believe that we are "AIDS doctors" (*basawo basilimu*) or members of the Ugandan AIDS Support Organization (TASO), and they quickly questioned the peculiarity of our ethnographic research. Previous AIDS researchers working in the community used questionnaires and other survey instruments, and drew blood, activities that led to certain preconceptions about HIV/AIDS research. Interviewing members of the community, "walking about," and writing down life stories and illness experiences were techniques unfamiliar to the community.

Those who are already infected with HIV have been pressing us for more, asking us for treatments, answers, and cures. We have listened to their stories, shared their suffering, and mourned their losses. Embarrassed, we know that we must give them something more tangible than our time, our support, and our friendship.

The government doctor in the community once asked me about our participation at burials and customary overnight gatherings for men to mourn a death: "There are people here who tell us that those boys [Godfrey and Addison] even go and stay with the bodies. They talk about how good they are. Do they have to do that? Is this part of your work?" I was unsure how to respond. But I felt proud, much like the day when I watched Godfrey and Addison returning from a burial, doubling community members on the backs of their bicycles.

Our ethnographic process of data extraction, when framed by an increasing knowledge of human suffering—the tears, burials, and fatalism—created methodological conflicts and personal dilemmas. "Could we continue like this?" we asked ourselves. We felt not. Persons have shared with us their vulnerabilities, the depth of their fears, and their hurt. We could not forgive ourselves if we packed up our fieldnotes and left the community without giving something more.

Our methodological dilemma was deeply personal. We were emotionally attached to these friends. No longer strangers, we had to do something. Our intent had always been participatory, but so far our process had not been. We had reasoned that the question of how to "intervene" would be answered through an ethnographic understanding of the culture of risk for HIV/AIDS. In addition, we needed to understand the basis of influence in the town and gain the support of the formal and informal leaders. In this first stage of the study, we were accountable to the community, but accountable only in the sense that we would check whether we got the stories right. Another level of accountability was urgently required. We needed to respond to community needs in a more immediate, interactive manner.

Adjusting the Ethnographic Research Design

We rented office space on the main street in town. People felt shy about visiting our home on the outskirts of town and we did not wish to encourage this for security reasons. Our intention was to provide a place where members of the community would feel comfortable gathering—a place to discuss experiences and the implications of HIV/AIDS on people's lives.

People now drop by to chat, to discuss, or to read their newspapers. We show them what we do with the ethnographic information, even demonstrate the process of interpreting their expressions in order to understand the complexities of meaning or the discrepancies between beliefs and behaviours. Some see our office sign, "Talking About AIDS: The Lorry Town Study Group," and come looking for treatment or testing. We do our best to connect them with the HIV counsellors of a local non-governmental organization, the Rakai AIDS Information Network (RAIN). More recently, however, we have run more formalized focus groups in the office to corroborate our data and to assess how such a forum might help people in need of support.

Unfortunately, the space has become "gendered"—a place for men to meet with men and women to meet with women. Men and women are often levelled with abuse by acquaintances and neighbours who see them sitting in the office. While women have more to lose when accused of being "infected" or even "prostitutes," some do come to the office and we arrange times to talk, usually in the privacy of their own home. When we ran a focus group with alcohol sellers and needed to arrange a meeting place, the office was not considered an option. We are currently looking for a more "natural" and "safe" place to hold meetings with women—perhaps the resting place used by women returning from their gardens.

Janette, Addison, Godfrey, and Patricia (l-r) outside the Talking About AIDS: The Lorry Town Study Group Office

People want more from us, and we are responding, cautiously at first (through the office in town), but we are committed to supporting community-initiated activities and incorporating flexibility in our approach.

There are, however, serious barriers to developing an environment that promotes sexual health and behavioural changes. The town's history as a lorry stop, responding to the demands of drivers, generated an economic environment characterized by transient commercialism. In the past, people migrated to the town to make quick money as market traders, prostitutes, and water vendors. A culture of individualism characterizes the town. Coupled with poverty, gender inequities, and ethnic strife, it is difficult to build community solidarities and sometimes hard to believe that a community exists in this troubling place. We were naive to assume that HIV/AIDS interventions would be easily accepted, especially given an ethos of fatalism and individualism. Lorry drivers passing through town would not likely respond to the usual types of programs, such as HIV counselling programs, even if available,

Shops and restaurants lining one of the main roads linking the town and villages.

nor would they readily use condoms when exchanging money for sex.

Leaving Town

When I left the town in September 1993, it was hard to say goodbye. Maama Mally was one of the most difficult persons to leave: my heart was in my throat. Her lament that day was about "sickness," and her physical condition was clearly worsening. She had sent her young son, Mally, to her parents' village to be cared for and her eldest daughter had arrived to wash, cook, and go to the market while Maama Mally was "down." Maama Mally could not move as dripping lesions covered most of the lower half of her body. She said it was *omusiipi*, "a belt of burning pain, like the burn of hot water, that goes all of the way into the bones," and was smearing the wounds with Colgate toothpaste to cool and ease the pain. She said to me, "By the time you come back, I will be dead."

After living in the town for 14 months, I went back to

Canada for a short period of time to begin writing my dissertation and returned to Uganda in August of 1994 to continue with the project. Other team members remained in the town. No longer strangers in the community, we continue to talk with, support, and document the experience of residents living with HIV/AIDS.

Ethnographic Realities Informing Participatory Action

There is no question that "something needs to be done," but any activity must be accomplished in a manner that mobilizes the interests and abilities of community members. Our intention is to work with community leaders and, most importantly, with representative spokepersons of the groups most vulnerable to HIV infection and transmission. These include alcohol sellers, mobile market traders, STD patients, long-distance truckers, adolescents, and water vendors.

In this next phase, we believe that a variety of community-based forums will facilitate the generation of appropriate "enabling resources." What will be required is a comprehensive program designed to address a variety of concerns: counselling for HIV/AIDS, economic problems, and gender issues related to the improvement of the sexual health of individuals. But a critical response will only occur if persons like Maama Mally are listened to, and their voices and stories fully acknowledged.

Epilogue: Turning Points—Naivete, Guilt, and Uncertainty

Dennis: When we began thinking about this project we had the epidemiological evidence—the numbers of people thought to be infected with HIV. The numbers were dry, and did not bring to life the reality of people's lives. The narratives we collected from Maama Mally, Josie, and others demonstrated the depth of the suffering that is occurring. We started hooking up with the stories rather than the numbers. After a while, even that became too familiar for us.

Janette: When we came to the town, I did not have any idea about what the community or the people were like. We began by creating relationships with people, by learning or by knowing the place. I did not expect to create friendships like we have of late.

On the one hand, the friendships have enabled us to collect more information and to connect with people and organizations we might not have otherwise. But it has been difficult because I see the people who have become my friends go through difficult times; I have seen them lose their relatives, go through their sicknesses, even starve.

We try as much as we can to help out, but often we cannot do enough. For example, when we first met Josie, she was starving. We tried to help here and there, inviting her for a meal or giving her some things, but we could not really pull her out of that. Godfrey and Addison have been active at burials, comforting, staying overnight, and sometimes actually putting the body in the hole. When Farouk was sick, Patti and I spent a lot of time just sitting with Josie. These things are really appreciated. There have been times we have gone and found people in very poor moods, but the time we spent helped to cheer them up. They would laugh, get out of the bed, and maybe eat something. The last time we visited Maama Mally before she died, she was very sick. She had just bought a new mattress, and we were just playing around—Patti was jumping on her bed and we were laughing. She was sick but she could still laugh with us.

Sometimes, however, I feel that the people do not see what we have given because it is not material. The things that we have given are the normal things that any person would do in a family or a community. It is a part of participating in somebody's life.

I feel like there is something missing. I feel guilty—like

there is something more I should do for them. If the project was to close now, how could we leave the community without feeling very guilty? It would seem like we have exploited them just to collect information, even though this was never our intent.

This is a devastated community. People are poor; people are sick; people are dying. People are coming into the office and demanding, "When are you going to give us the information that you've collected"? People want information but they also want more. They want us to dispense medicines, condoms, and advice. Recently, an influential businessman in town criticized, "We are tired of you people. You just come and sit in the office and read your notes. This office should be kept open until 2 a.m. This is when people are the most active and they want condoms."

I get to a point where I am embarrassed. I see the people "getting finished" and dying. I feel guilty. I remember a boy who came to the office (he has since died) and asked what we were going to do for the community. I said we have not started to do anything, but maybe in the future we will do something. He said, "You think the future is going to wait for us? We are dying. We want to benefit from what there is right now."

Dennis: What could we do? We were stuck wanting to do something in a place hit harder than we had realized. It was only half-way through the project that we actually came to see how bad it was, and the guilt crept in.

Should we have started differently? Was community participation possible in the early stages when, as we came to see, there were enormous social and cultural resistances to working towards something that would stop the deaths? Or is this merely a pathetic rationalization on our part?

We all began to feel burned out. I asked Janette, Godfrey, Addison, and Patti to construct illness genograms demonstrating who was ill and who had died. (A genogram is an anthropological tool that uses symbols to diagram family relationships.)

When the team got together at the retreat in Mombasa mid-way through the project, we put these huge manilla sheets with the illness genograms up on the walls. We were surrounded by them on all sides. All of a sudden we realized how bad it was and everyone went quiet. That was a turning point for the team. It was a moment of transformation—a moment where the reality of these people's lives became very intimate for us.

In the beginning, with only a vague notion of how grave the situation was, we thought that an ethnographic assessment, a community diagnosis of how persons viewed and experienced HIV/AIDS, was required. Once we elicited indigenous notions or popular understandings of how the virus was transmitted, we would know what we were up against. We envisioned starting with a qualitative ethnographic study that would help to identify persons in the community who were most vulnerable to HIV. Eventually, in collaboration with these people, we could work against the resistances.

We came to see that our initial target groups—bar girls, long-distance truckers, STD patients—were indeed at risk, but there were other groups of individuals, such as alcohol sellers, mobile market traders, and adolescent girls, that are even more vulnerable to HIV. We learned that it is possible for bar girls to negotiate condom use with "dailies" but not necessarily with permanent partners. Yet, we now understand that for alcohol sellers, who are living in situations where sex = money = food = support for dependent children, safe sex is not a choice. There is no choice when you are hungry; there are no options. It is a situation of "choiceless choice." (We are grateful to Byron Good of Harvard University for labelling the situation in such a compelling and powerful way.)

Were we wrong in thinking that we should understand the social and cultural resistances prior to deliberate and careful steps forwards? We are not sure. Knowing what we now know of the constraints—the indigenous notions of risk, sexuality, relationships, worry, fear, illness, and death—we think we were right. People who feel so strongly that there is no future, no hope, and no possibility for a life without this disease need a supportive environment to build hope. This was, and still is, our assumption of what we needed to do.

We realized we were in the middle of a living hell here. The retreat helped us to understand why we were so burned out. We underscored our ethical commitment to do more. We realized that complex problems require complex solutions and to just intervene with primary prevention as we had initially proposed was naive. The epidemiological evidence was naive. We needed to understand the reality or context of people's lives.

Nelson: Dennis and I agreed that we must use anthropological techniques to help us understand better the life situation in the town. From the beginning, we wanted people in the town, particularly the bar girls, to be involved in the project not only as study subjects but also as part of the research team. There were very delicate issues to grapple with regarding the design and implementation of the study, which became even clearer as the study evolved. We needed interventions to complement the descriptive anthropological studies. We needed to involve the community members, but the ethical issues raised by their potential participation in data collection were very difficult.

People were used to projects with a top-down approach and questioned the authenticity of our research when we appeared to be just living together with community members. They were used to projects that gave out tangible material goods and did not motivate them to help themselves. They were not used to projects that give back results to the communities so that community members would develop interventions in partnership with outside/external researchers.

The experience has been greatly rewarding, eye-opening, and challenging. In a situation of extreme human suffering caused by ill health, poverty, and drought, one may lose direction. I have witnessed the various dimensions of this suffering. It makes me despair and, like the communities, I lose hope. I ask myself whether what we are doing is useful—whether it is making a dent. Can we really have an impact on the future of these communities? This uncertainty is compounded by the apparent exhaustion and, at times, despair of the research assistants.

An entire population is at risk: adolescents, adults, and even the unborn children. A killer disease, transmitted by an activity fundamental to the continuation of human existence, has developed into a nightmare. And yet, life has to continue.

We have learned an enormous amount. We are in a much better situation now to work with people and hopefully make a difference. We are a little unsure of the best way to proceed. We are willing and ready to learn along the way. The financial resources required to get us started are not easy to get, which leaves us handicapped. Yet, I feel we have a moral obligation to continue to work with the people and help them out of their dilemma.

Patti: As we enter into the second phase of the project, we need to return what we have taken in terms of data and do something with it. The question we keep asking ourselves is, "Can we go back to this community with the data, without bringing anything else? Is that possible when people expect drugs, soaps, creams, and advice?"

Participatory action-research is about creating something sustainable for the future. Many people in this community think only in terms of the present because the future is not predictable. The people who have helped us to understand this disease as a social entity are the ones who will not benefit. Maama Mally is dead. Farouk is dead. People have shared their stories with us because they think we are going to help them. Josie, for example, suffered a lot of stigma by talking to us but I believe she felt our friendship was worth it.

PAR has worked in communities where there is a sense of future and sufficient time for empowerment and mobilization. But everyone in this community believes, "We are dying and getting finished." This has tremendous implications for what we do in the next phase. We want to return the data that we collected, so that the people will own it and they can make decisions about what they feel their needs are.

Dennis talks about helping to provide "enabling resources." This seems to be a more pragmatic way of approaching "interventions." For example, the situation of women in the town is deplorable. We, of course, are not able to remove the constraints of patriarchy in one small project, but what we *can* do is tell people the dangers of an STD. This might enable women in a constructive way rather than the team attempting to mobilize all women to tell all men to go to hell.

It might be easy for some to say, "You should have gone in with the medicines and rice." But this would we have generated a completely different relationship with the people. We might have created dependence, with no real chance for community-based development and sustainable actions. Again, is this just rationalization on our part? We think not. We believe that now we can give back some of the stories: truths that cause them to remain situated in despair. An understanding of the context of their lives gives us a platform for talking through and walking through the trouble in constructive and supportive ways.

Janette: Maama Mally used to ask, "Why do you not give us the rice now if it is rice you will give out. Why won't you give me my share now before I die? By the time you start doing something for the community, I will already be dead."

We keep telling people to wait. Some of them do not have patience any more.

References

Canadian Public Health Association. 1986. Ottawa Charter for Health Promotion. *Canadian Journal of Public Health* 77: 425-473.

Carswell, J.W., Lloyd, G., and Howells, J. 1989. Short communication: Prevalence of HIV in East African lorry drivers. *AIDS* 3(11): 759-761.

Sewankambo, N. and Willms, D.G. 1994. An HIV/AIDS Participatory Action Research (PAR) Agenda Promoting Sexual Health in Lorry Town, Uganda: Developing and Implementing "Enabling Resources" within a "Critical Accountability Loop": A Phase 2 Proposal. Grant submitted to the International Development Research Centre, Ottawa, Ontario, Canada.

Wawer, M.J., Serwadda, D., Musgrave, S., Konde-Lule, J., Musagara, M., and Sewankambo, N.K. 1991. Dynamics of spread of HIV-1 infection in a rural district of Uganda. *British Medical Journal* 303(6813): 1303-1306.

Acknowledgement

We gratefully acknowledge the research funding generously provided by the International Development Research Centre (IDRC Dossier 3-P-90-0204, Health Sciences Division, "Understanding High Risk Sexual Behaviour" [Uganda]). We also thank the Rockefeller Foundation, Health Sciences Division, for supporting an interpretive and planning workshop involving the entire Uganda-based research team. Patricia would like to acknowledge the financial support provided by the Young Canadian Scholars' Award (IDRC).

5

GROUNDING A LONG-TERM IDEAL: WORKING WITH THE AYMARA FOR COMMUNITY DEVELOPMENT

Maria-Ines Arratia with Isabel de la Maza

CR EDITORS' NOTE: This chapter, written by two women both born and raised in Chile, hints at a recurring theme: the value of telling stories. Documenting this participatory action-research experience in the mountains of Chile from an outsider's perspective, Maria-Ines tells her story of returning to Chile after many years in Canada, meeting Isabel, and coming to know the Aymara people who, like the stark beauty of the surrounding highlands, have a harsh but rich reality. Maria-Ines and Isabel write of Isabel's story, allowing us to glimpse Isabel's history and the lessons she has gained from her ongoing involvement with the Aymara. And they speak of Vivi who intuitively discovered the importance of sharing stories with the mountain women, thereby creating an empowering dialogue that centred on the realities of everyday life.

In this chapter, Maria-Ines and Isabel use a "reporting" voice to a significant extent and thereby provide necessary facts and observations. But they also allude to certain images: llamas grazing peacefully in the open plains; Isabel and Maria-Ines "deepening their views" through conversation while driving on rough roads into the remote highlands; and mountain women who, as sisters, experience the fundamental rhythms of daily life and who, as extraordinary survivors, are dealing with disturbing, alienating threats that are eroding language and culture.

How can writers of participatory action-research initiatives pro-

vide the basic elements of who, what, where, and why, but also in-
tensify impressions, helping readers to paint sensitive pictures in their
inner eyes? To feel the energy of the women seated in a circle talking vigorously in the midst of making significant personal and social
changes. To recognize at a deeper level the women's struggle to understand the dominant lowland society in order to protect themselves—"prove their birth, their age, ownership of land"—and to construct their own organizations and purposeful activities.

Whether oral or written, people's stories generally arouse a
greater sense of texture, meaning, and movement. Good use of nar-
rative, capturing people's realities and vibrations, is a meaningful way
of knowing: it gives vitality to our human experiences.

Often (academic) critics will casually dismiss participatory action-
research as "just community development," that is, not legitimate research. The methodology chapter of this book, however, uses quotes
from the six different case studies to support a framework for participatory action-research. Incorporated are numerous ideas from
Isabel's and Maria-Ines' chapter which recognize how knowledge and
social changes are produced in many different ways, and demonstrate
the dialectical relationship between participatory development and
participatory action-research. What appears at first as "just development" is, in many respects, frequently generating needed, critical
knowledge.

Maria-Ines and Isabel both approach PAR as a way of life. They
are committed to "a certain way of being in the world"—a way that
values just, democratic participation and a "love of other human beings" that is "in tune with the 'other'" and trustfully "gives back."
They strive to ground their ideals on a daily basis. ∞

Two to three decades ago, a discussion began among Latin
American social scientists about the uses of knowledge. Out of
these debates, participatory methodologies in research emerged
as a means of integrating different types of knowledge with
critical social action. These aimed at reducing (and perhaps
eliminating) social asymmetries. The goal was to create a new
civil society, a democratic social fabric that recognized the validity of alternative systems of knowledge *for* the people (Fals-
Borda, 1979).

During the long years of the Chilean military dictatorship

(1973-1989), a network of non-governmental organizations (NGOs) was formed. People involved in this network wanted to democratize from the grassroots while organizing to survive in harsh neo-liberal economic conditions. This is the story of one NGO's efforts to undertake social change activities. It is also a story of personal growth.

The Value of Education

My parents always told my siblings and me that our only inheritance would be our education. They invested inordinate amounts of money in making sure that their children had "the best education to be found" in our small resort city in the central zone of Chile. I grew up during the post World War II era, when optimism abounded and learning languages and being a "citizen of the world" were of utmost importance for our future.

After immigrating to Canada in 1971, I pursued a university education, eagerly learning about Paulo Freire's work in Chile where he had been exiled from Brazil in the late 1960s (Freire, 1973; 1983). As an educator with a social conscience, Freire's understanding of the situation of disadvantaged people rang a chord with my own sense of service and mission.

In 1989, I prepared for my doctoral field project in Chile, hoping to work with the Aymara (a minority native group living in the remote northern highlands). I had read that several NGOs were using participatory methodologies for community development and I was curious about how they were doing this. A national plebiscite held in 1988 supported free elections during Pinochet's reign—it was only a matter of time before Chile would be rid of the dictator (or so people thought). These were exciting times in the re-democratization of the country. I felt that a road was opening up ahead of me.

Landing in Iquique

From the very beginning, Iquique seemed quite different from other cities in Chile. It reminded me of a mining camp, with its low housing and flat roofs. The hills were barren, typical of a desert area, but the air had the humid, salty quality that I had known as a child. I was again on the shores of the Pacific Ocean.

On my first morning in Iquique, I visited the offices of CREAR, a non-governmental organization that I had heard was working with the Aymara. After exchanging greetings and short introductions, the director told me that they no longer worked in the highlands. Instead, there were now three NGOs in the region: the Centre for Research in the North (CREAR) based in Iquique, Taller de Estudios Aymara (TEA) in Arica, and Taller de Estudios Regionales (TER) also in Iquique. The NGOs had divided the region geographically among them so as not to duplicate their activities. Disappointed with this information, I considered my options.

As it turned out, I spent the weeks that followed making

Maria-Ines' first images of the highlands: open spaces and llamas

repeated, unsuccessful efforts in Iquique to affiliate with TER. Not knowing the internal politics of the situation, my now somewhat foreign, mild-mannered, and cautious approaches got me absolutely nowhere. I therefore remained affiliated with CREAR for the duration of my fieldwork, but carried out my research about adult education programs with the Aymara independently.

A Brief Aymara History

The Aymara of Chile have lived in the northernmost frontier for centuries, following their migration from the Bolivian highlands in search of new pastures for their camelid (llama and alpaca) herds.

The history of this region has been greatly influenced by the expansion of Chile's political and economic structures following its declared independence from Spain in 1810. First came the Spanish colonial administrators; later on the nitrate barons and, with them, the Chilean state. The discovery of nitrate produced an economic boom that attracted foreign and national capital. This created a veritable bonanza that lasted until the 1930s, dying out completely by the 1950s, and leaving behind a desert littered with ghost camps and towns (Alfaro, 1936).

The Aymara were deeply affected by these invasions of their territory. Their traditional livelihood as llama and alpaca herders was disrupted and the internal constitution of the communities was altered. Attracted by the opportunities in mining, some of the Aymara left their highland villages; many of them never returned, migrating to the growing urban centres. Others resumed their herding activities after a stint of mining, continuing on the path laid down by their ancestors. Some hired out for occasional work on the Bolivian side of the border, while Bolivian Aymara also migrated into the mining camps in search of monetary wages and then remained in Chile (Gonzalez, 1991).

In more recent decades, the region has become a "coloni-
zation" or heavily militarized zone. The Aymara, together with
all northerners, were to be "Chileanized" through various policies, including formal schooling and a compulsory military
draft for 18-year-old males.

The Aymara Today

The Aymara population in 1989 was estimated at 40,000
people (Gonzalez and Gundermann, 1989). Of this total, two-
thirds are settled in the northern cities of Arica, Iquique, and
Calama, with varied occupations. The remainder live in the
low-lying valleys where they practise agriculture and some hus-
bandry, or in the highlands where the main activity is herding.
Migration from rural to urban areas has resulted from the
externally influenced economic conditions and the negative
influences of the imposed schooling system. The young Aymara
with primary education have been forced to migrate to semi-
rural locations to continue their schooling and subsequently
have become detached from their communities. The educational system has not recognized regional or local needs, nor
the existence of an Aymara language and culture, thus implic-
itly devaluing all markers of Aymara identity together with
valuable ancestral knowledge. The communal labour force of
highland communities has been eroded, severely diminishing
their chances of sustaining subsistence agricultural practices.

The Beginning of My Affiliation with TEA

During my year of fieldwork, I gradually became acquainted with the Aymara of the region of Cariquima (see Figure 2: Map of Region of Tarapaca) and spent enough time in
Iquique to figure out what was happening among the NGOs,
particularly within CREAR. I became very critical of CREAR's
approach to development activities in the rural areas. CREAR's

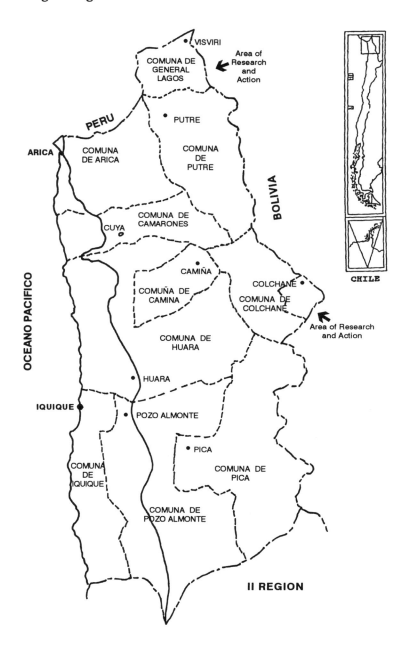

Figure 2:
Map of Region of Tarapaca

work with urban dwellers was instrumental in grassroots organizing in the city, but its work with the rural Aymara was ineffectual. For example, CREAR distributed printed flyers to rural Aymara, but this effort seemed purposeless since the flyers described things that the Aymara already knew. I found the papers blowing around or left in corners of different households. This "consciousness-raising" attempt was nonsensical to the program "beneficiaries"—something was quite wrong. The man responsible for the program at the village level explained to me that he had held meetings to distribute these materials, answer questions, and encourage people's participation with the NGO. He had not been trained in participatory processes within communities. As far as I could see, there had been no real participation and nothing in the villages had changed.

I was under the impression that TEA's orientation was closer to my own notions of community development. TEA's booklets stated that its primary role was to support an economic base for the survival of the communities. Migration to the cities had disrupted previously viable patterns of social organization, leading to changes in subsistence activities and lack of food for the population. TEA's initial thrust was to ensure that people had access to food. When the Aymara requested support, TEA responded by offering technical assistance programs and examining ways to acquire the needed supplies that were no longer produced by the Aymara. Without this base, the communities could not survive.

At an international conference about the Aymara held in Iquique, I learned more about what the TEA staff were doing. In subsequent conversations, two of TEA's anthropologists said they would keep my interest in mind. Months later, an encouraging letter arrived explaining that TEA was starting a set of "schools" for leadership in June of 1990. I was welcomed to join the training team. By this time, however, my year of fieldwork was nearly over; I was to return to Canada at the beginning of July. Travelling to Arica to visit its offices in March and find out more about TEA's plans, I met Isabel.

Three women were planning their next trip into the highlands when I arrived at TEA's doorstep. We chatted informally, referring also to their work and my interests. Isabel was very enthusiastic about the future schools. I later learned that, as one of the instigators of this methodology, her personal and professional investment in the program was high.

Educated as a teacher of history and geography, Isabel has always been inclined to work in social development. Deeply moved by Latin American indigenous cultures and by a desire to find her own roots within them, Isabel chose to live and work with the Aymara. She wanted to contribute but, more importantly, she wanted to respect and value their culture and to learn.

Between 1983 and 1985, Isabel had taken part in several workshops in Santiago on participatory development, which were organized by a North American organization. She learned that participation was not an "anarchic, chaotic, and disruptive" force as the authoritarian government would have Chileans believe.

Vivi, an anthropologist and one of the founders of TEA, had begun to work with village women in 1982. She invited Isabel to work on a project with Aymara women and took her into the highlands where she would gradually gain their trust. Isabel survived the harshness of the highlands, eventually growing to appreciate their stark beauty. She joined TEA when she moved to Arica in 1985.

Isabel's contribution to TEA was a mixture of her university studies in education and the newly learned participatory techniques. At school, she had concentrated on the study of pre-Columbian history and taken courses in cultural anthropology. Isabel discovered that theory and actual practice are not the same thing—Vivi's guidance was crucial. Working with the women's project in the highlands meant spending time in several Aymara villages with the women, organizing the marketing of their alpaca wool. Isabel developed learning modules to provide the village women with basic math for bookkeeping. This program had a high rate of success and eventually resulted in the organization of a woman's cooperative.

Using Participatory Methods for Development in the Highlands

TEA's use of participatory methods began through the field-work that Vivi did with the women in the highlands. Along with her husband, Vivi lived in the Colchane district for over two years. At the time, the local municipality was organizing workshops for women called "Mothers' Centres." While this was yet another way for the military dictatorship to exert con-trol over the population, the urban women responsible for these workshops did not have the time nor the inclination to remain in the highlands. In the right place and at the right time, Vivi was hired to direct the workshops: the authorities did not know that Vivi's political orientation was opposed to that of the state regime. Indeed, she subverted the official purpose of the Mothers' Centres by promoting awareness among the Aymara women and by encouraging them to question their cir-cumstances. This was the start of an empowering process.

The regional staff of the Mothers' Centres marketed most of the llama and alpaca wool items produced by the partici-pants. The Aymara women had no knowledge of how to do this themselves, nor were they aware of the profits being made by the national organization. They were supposedly being trained. Their actual income from this activity was low, although it did make a difference on a household level by providing them with cash. To become autonomous, the women needed to gain the necessary skills to independently sell their wool products in the regional and national markets.

Vivi intuitively discovered that the best way to work with the women was to integrate into the group and share her own experiences. This encouraged the women to tell their stories. The dialogue supported the women's efforts to hold their households together when their husbands departed for the city. Out of this work came several life histories and a compendium of herbal medicines used by the women to heal family ailments. The women began to see themselves in a different light—ca-pable of assuming their new roles as heads of households. More

Weaving—a woman's art—being marketed in Villablanca, 1989

importantly, the women and TEA staff realized that social action needed to be oriented to the local conditions and to the development of skills and information needed for the survival of the communities.

When TEA was officially established in 1986, it continued to sell wool and weavings on behalf of the women for a few years while teaching them about controlling the quality of the spun wool, fast natural dyeing, and developing a line of items to market. Its goal was to organize women in four highland villages—Enquelga, Central Citani, Ancovinto, and Chulluncane—so that they could market their own woollen goods. This included a reappraisal of women's activities and skills to produce and sell marketable crafts.

Women Working with Women

Isabel and several other team members went into the highlands for 15 days at a time and stayed a few days in each village. They met with the women, discussed their situations within the villages, and reviewed how individuals were sharing responsibilities. Those meetings were also occasions to follow up on the women involved in the math program.

Vivi had noticed that at times the women seemed distracted during meetings; some even fell asleep while she was attempting to explain something. The level of discourse used by TEA was much too abstract and conceptual. Communication became Isabel's first area of concern.

As educators, Isabel and Karin (another member of the team) concentrated on methods of conveying appropriate information. Isabel thought about using training materials developed elsewhere, but had no idea whether they would work with native people who did not speak "proper Spanish." Moreover, neither Isabel nor the other team members could speak Aymara. It was obvious that the women's immediate environment and their needs circumscribed their knowledge base. Their knowledge was practical and oriented towards subsistence and the improvement of the level of income for their individual households.

Dramatizations, photographs, drawings, histories, and slides were helpful in communicating information. Although the staff observed a gradual improvement, some women still did not participate because they could not speak Spanish. A bilingual participant acted as a translator, and Isabel was forced to accept that she would always be limited by her ignorance of the Aymara language.

The Aymara language has been gradually losing ground in favour of Spanish; it is only in the highlands that a few people still use and value Aymara. The Aymara in the low-lying canyons and valleys are discriminated against, often speaking Spanish in order to identify with the non-Aymara peasants. Generally, men are better at Spanish since they have been in longer-term contact with the cities, the colonial language, and with Chilean culture. These were all important considerations for TEA: language skills, power structures, gender, and regional cultural variations impact on any dialogue.

Getting to know the Aymara meant first thinking of each

locality and its way of life. Distinctions had to be made between highland, piedmont, and valley settlements. The cultural dynamics were different in each setting so that the same techniques and materials were not effective everywhere. The use of Spanish varied. As well, the different local customs, economic activities, social identity, and relative distance from the city made a difference. Participatory methods had to be adjusted to the local situation and needed to begin with the people's own knowledge base.

The work that TEA staff did with Aymara women was their first test of participatory methodologies. Staff considered their results to be good, but the organization as a whole did not fully recognize the importance of participatory approaches. This learning ground for Isabel and her colleagues began their own processes of growth. Above all, a dialogue with transformative potential was started.

Leadership Training Schools

In 1990, the Special Training (Capacitation) Unit was formed within TEA, with Isabel at the helm. Leadership training was prompted by the Aymara's increasing participation in the regional and national markets, and their requests to find out more about what was"legal," meaning what was acceptable by the dominant administrative system.

Village assemblies provided the mechanism for village consultation and organization of community activities. As was usual in the initial phases of TEA's programs, the assemblies explored the utility, feasibility, and appropriateness of the idea of leadership training schools. The participating communities decided to select two members each to attend the schools while TEA absorbed all costs of the schools, including the participants' transportation.

Some villages with one clearly identified leader also chose a younger, more inexperienced member of the community—perhaps a hopeful successor—to attend. In other villages where

traditional authority had become divided by virtue of migration or had disappeared altogether, the village assemblies voted
to determine who would attend the schools. The choice usually was based upon the personal skills of the candidates, their
literacy, level of education, and ability to relate with the "external world."

The Aymara generally had little awareness of Chilean politics. In planning the schools, TEA hoped to raise people's consciousness about the politics of economic matters. As the
Aymara increased their market activities, they needed to understand the political structures governing these activities.

The first leadership schools were held in a rural setting
close to Arica in the valley of Azapa. This ideal location removed people from their daily chores, allowing them to concentrate on the tasks at hand. Village leaders shared concerns
and interacted among themselves in a different setting, fostering perhaps closer relationships and organization between villages in the district.

One of the most difficult things for staff to accept was that
TEA's view of a democratic Chile did not fit with the more authoritarian Aymara way of structuring social interactions. Yet,
the Aymara themselves wanted to learn more about the dominant external political system that had imposed formal schooling and military draft on their children. Participants disagreed
with our Western democratic values, but most could see that
their survival depended on understanding and working within
the larger system.

The participants had repeated problems in transporting
their goods to market. The police, they told us, would take advantage of their ignorance of the rules and regulations. Frequently, police would confiscate their products, saying that they
were not "legal."

So much of Aymara life was affected by their lack of "legal"
documents of all sorts—documents proving their birth, their
age, ownership of their land, and that they met certain criteria
for government benefits and services (including maternal and
old-age subsidies and health care). This one word, "legal," was

The first leadership school, Arica, June 1992

clearly what Freire (1973) would call a "generative term"—a term generating discussions about the political powers that control various kinds of everyday situations. This process of uncovering the workings of political control is necessary for people's empowerment. Participants specifically asked TEA to assist them in understanding these rules and regulations and how to access funding for community development projects.

In total, four schools were held for the men and four for the women. Out of this first set of schools came the legal birth in 1993 of a women's cooperative—Ccanthati, meaning "dawn." Based in Arica, it took over the marketing of the wool products, with a young Aymara woman trained as director. Ccanthati is now largely independent, relying on TEA for quality control and some management advice only. They have an executive, meet regularly for business discussions, and are placing most of their production in the Santiago market at a fair price. Financial control is in Ccanthati's hands.

One participant, a community leader previously associated with TEA in village projects, became affiliated with a political party and was elected mayor of his administrative district. Another younger participant, a member of a different highland community, was elected municipal councillor. Many leaders have made their own contacts and used them to improve the conditions in their villages. In some cases, however, participants have either not shared their experiences within the communities or they have left their villages altogether. This issue has affected the planning and execution of additional schools.

Lessons Learned

Reflecting on TEA's successes and failures with the first set of schools, Isabel learned that all training must begin from people's own experiential knowledge base and be geared towards finding a response to their more urgent needs. She discovered that, if we are promoting social organization to achieve participatory development, it is not enough to only train the leaders. We also must follow up the leaders' trajectory in the communities and work with the leaders in a sustained fashion to keep the flow of information going. This follow-up is part of the transformative process; it needs to be supported so that dependency on TEA eventually is eliminated.

It is also fundamental that we sustain our social action. When we become distant from the field proper, we tend to forget the importance of the everyday dimensions of people's lives. This leads to further mistakes in our work, as distance interrupts the ongoing dialogue—an integral part of transforming social interactions.

Further, we need to provide appropriate support to the community leaders on a regular basis. When the leaders are at home, their conduct is adjusted to the expectations of the community; their attitudes can appear different to that observed during dialogue sessions in the schools. In the communities, they are in an Aymara context under the scrutiny of their kin and there is a culturally accepted demeanour to be kept in asserting their position. We must know and respect the relevance of context while providing leaders with helpful support.

It is necessary to speak Aymara when working in the highlands. This is an issue to be addressed more seriously within TEA. In the meantime, we must use an Aymara interpreter at all times to ensure that all community members, especially the women and the elderly, who have not previously been exposed to participatory methods, can fully grasp our intent.

Working in small groups enables people to become more expressive and to share their own views and concerns. Practical and focussed learning develops the skills needed to meet the concrete demands of specific activities. As people begin to see the results of their actions, an empowering process begins to unfold.

The residential training schools allowed people to concentrate and not be distracted by their everyday responsibilities. Isabel also found that informal social occasions in the community gave the villagers an opportunity to reciprocate for the hospitality extended to them during the schools. These occasions were another important, yet somewhat neglected, element in TEA's programs.

When staff give personalized attention to individuals, this allows adaptation of materials and techniques to suit a variety of learning speeds and styles. The diversity of previous levels of education and literacy among the participants meant that we must emphasize oral learning while encouraging further literacy training. All educational materials used in the sharing of information must be short, concise, and easily understood. Experiments with literacy alone have not been successful since people's economic needs take precedence over any purely "educational" effort. People's requests for further training are always oriented towards their subsistence.

Motivation techniques frequently employed in popular education settings should be used cautiously; sometimes people dislike the idea of playing games as a learning technique. In general, dramatizations of real situations worked well with Aymara participants.

Beyond the Leadership Schools

New developments affected the continuity of the schools. The democratic government instituted a new system for community development project funding: both TER and TEA were to carry out the initial phases of consultation and negotiation with various communities. CEPI, a special commission for native peoples sponsored by the Aylwin government, also received targeted funding for community projects. Some communities looked for project support from CEPI while others worked with TER in Iquique. Travelling to Arica was no longer deemed necessary by some leaders if they could find support in Iquique or through other contacts. Those closest to Arica continued to work with TEA.

Municipal government elections took place in June 1992, the first since the national democratic elections of 1989. Leaders of all communities involved with TEA were invited to attend workshops about the electoral process. After the elections, TEA members travelled from village to village, explaining to people how an elected municipalitity works as the seat of local political power and how specific community services are administered. At the same time, TEA encouraged the village assemblies to present their priority needs to the appropriate development offices (locally and/or regionally). When this happened, TEA could offer continuing support in the negotiation of claims or the formulation of projects.

In the meantime, TEA carried out promotional work for CEPI, the new government development agency. This work involved a series of workshop meetings with villagers to identify small projects in communities where TEA had not worked before. At the end of this short-term project, workshop participants asked TEA to support political and economic activities in the piedmont settlements and the low-lying agricultural areas closer to Arica.

Recently, TEA reorganized internally and formed a Social Education Area (SEA). Its goal is to foster increased community autonomy through a strengthening of village dynamics that have been weakened by migrations and economic and political pressures. The schools now fall under the responsibility of the SEA. Supporting a more equitable system of opportunities, TEA's vital ability is to share information and analysis with those people who have reduced access.

TEA's long-term experience can open new spaces for constructive change within district and regional government institutions. For this to happen, TEA must work with government staff, technical and professional consulting staff, and social services staff to demonstrate that participation is the key to development and social action. TEA can support government personnel to become more culturally sensitive in their interactions with the Aymara.

Changing the hierarchical orientations of institutions to allow for greater team work is essential. Although Chile has had four transitional years (1990-1994) of democratic government, the regional government administration is still closed to the possibilities of change. This part of the transformative agenda will take time, and TEA's role is to build bridges between the establishment and the Aymara, recognizing that "development" is what people themselves are able to attain through their own empowerment.

The Dialogue Continues

Isabel's life continues to revolve around her activities in participatory development. My own case is different as I have returned to Canada. While she is learning on an everyday basis, my distance from the Aymara communities begins to alter my own perspective.

Our dialogue, however, continues. Both Isabel and I believe that community development initiatives are possible. This is where individuals can fully participate, where involvement can make sense in terms of everyday life, and where consciousness-raising processes can take place in tangible terms.

I have contributed theoretical background that Isabel

Always in dialogue: Isabel with a local leader, Camarones, 1992

needed to support her practice. We have devised field methods to improve the dissemination of information within the villages. We have deepened our views while driving into the remote highlands and preparing specific events. All of these have
been shared learning experiences. Often our efforts seemed to
be imperceptible either because social change was so slow or
because the tidal wave of modernization, consumption, and increasing migration from the rural areas into the cities was overwhelming.

What we initially aimed for, we achieved: rural Aymara are
now working in small, localized projects. But we need to look
at development from a broader, regional perspective. Supporting co-ops that extend beyond the local village is one way of
working towards a common district development strategy. Together with local leaders, TEA is now trying to achieve such a
strategy. The challenge is to find new sources of work as Arica
cannot be the only place where gainful employment is found.
Creating employment in the rural areas will allow Aymara who
wish to remain rural to make a living there, reconstructing a
sense of community.

A new cooperative is legalized: Camelid Meat Producers of General Lagos, Highland District, 1993.

One of the most important lessons I have learned is that a commitment to transformation means long-term involvement. I have found a space where my earlier experiences as a Chilean woman can merge with my intellectual discoveries in Canada. Since I can only support activities in Chile from Canada, my involvement with TEA has become a vital outlet for my own sense of commitment. I also have learned that community development is unavoidably interlinked with global processes that are governed by world market interests quite different from those of local communities. Maintaining a long-term view, we must never lose sight of this ominous reality as we continue to ground our ideals by contributing to the process of Aymara community development.

Epilogue: Building Trust, Seeking Connections

For me, participatory action-research is a philosophy of life. Very hard to put into words, it is a way of being in the world.

It is perhaps easier to talk about the kind of person that is attracted to PAR. One must have a sense of social justice. In my own case, these roots go very deep. One of my first childhood memories was not being allowed to play with poor children. We lived in municipal housing in a new neighbourhood. Just around the corner was a poor family. Walking to school dressed in a pretty red blazer and gloves, I went past their house every morning. Those children had no shoes. I asked myself, "Why is it that I have more than they have? Why doesn't my mother want me to play with them? Why am I not allowed to go into their house?" That was my first conscious experience of poverty—the contrast between our two families bothered me. I grew up feeling that something was very wrong, but I never knew that I could do anything about it until I began studying social sciences.

As a social scientist, I define my role as participating in social action that promotes a better kind of society. Other social scientists, particularly those in Chile, do not see this as an appropriate role for themselves. They prefer to be removed from action—to be the professor, the leader, the policymaker, or the bureaucrat. The separation between the "objective" and engaged stances is an ongoing debate. We should be able to do both.

Engagement in a PAR process demands a liking of people. This does not mean that I necessarily like every person I work with, or even every group with which I am involved. I have met social scientists who, by virtue of their training or life experience, have developed rigid patterns of action or work. Because of the dominant cultural patterns (which are class-structured), they fall into set patterns. In talking to them, I have observed, "I understand why you're following that path, but don't you see that path leads you away from the basic sense of love for other human beings?" This realization has led me to a holistic life—one with more control over what I chose to do or not do.

Dialogue is central to a truly participatory process. What are the dynamics of dialoguing with people from different backgrounds? This returns to the question of the kind of person attracted to PAR. A love of other human beings implies patience and respect. How do I put respect into action? Does it mean saying from a distance, "I respect people." Or does it mean living side by side with people and letting them teach me? PAR requires that I become almost like a child in the other culture, figuring out where people are coming from. Who are they? What do they want out of life? What is their vision? What are their plans? I have to listen first and then relate to people with the knowledge that I bring as an outsider.

Sometimes outsiders are not patient enough. Their sense of time is different from that of the villagers who are perceived as "slow." This, together with the sense of class difference, may lead to an unrecognized tone of superiority, in which outsiders say to themselves, "People should listen to me and appreciate what I am doing. These people are not educated. They are curious and different and I want to know more about them, but they are lesser than I am because they don't have the same background, are not urbanites, do not have a TV in the house, and so on." The process of being a learner does not have to be lengthy. I learn more, much more quickly, by doing things with people than by just sitting watching and listening.

The PAR process is not necessarily about being critically minded—at least in the initial moments. I am just one human being with another human being, trying to establish some kind of connection. Connecting initially with the Aymara women, I later started working with the men. There were times that I needed to be almost like a daughter—to just let people show me the way. Being a woman with two children myself was a fundamental basis for connecting with the Aymara women. Sisterhood does exist. One of the first things that I did was walk around with the kids. They were eager to find out more about me and they taught me about nature and how to fetch water from the well. I would say to the women, "If you have to go do whatever, I'll watch the kids." Or, "if you have to go to the river and do something, I'll do the laundry for you." Friendships developed.

*My friends
from Villablanca*

I always had a sense of "otherness" about me. I was not
from there. I had no kin there, as did everyone else. This feeling of otherness is never entirely lost. With the men, the sense
of distance was greater; it was harder for them to figure out
who I was. Right up until the end they would ask, "But why
did you come here?" No matter how I explained it to them,
there was always a question of "Who are you?" Knowing I was
a mother, the men wondered why I wasn't home with my children. The women perhaps thought the same thing but they did
not act upon it. The men mistrusted me somewhat because I
did not fit their image of a woman with children. Although at
times the men chose not to give me information, they nonetheless respected my "difference"—that wasn't a problem.

People wanted me to do something for them before they were willing to open up to me. They needed to trust me somehow. I did things for people so that they could see I was okay. For example, I wanted to take photos of people. Previously, a film maker had worked in the highlands; the villagers had never seen the film or heard from her again. There I was with a camera. They were reluctant to let me take photographs. I negotiated, "I'll ask permission before taking any pictures. If you allow me to take them, I will send copies to you." Reprints were expensive, but I gave people copies of all my photos. This simple and tangible action—something I did for others—built trust.

One day in talking with an older man in a village, I decided to go a little further. The man was telling me stories about his family, the village, and so on. I suggested to him that I could write a booklet of his story that included some of the photos, and perhaps he could ask the school teacher to show it to the kids and teach them how to read it. He was very enthusiastic about the idea and, upon completion of the booklet, I gave a copy to him as well as the president of the village committee. I then did the same for each of the seven villages in the area. Through this sort of give-and-take, people began to realize that I was okay, that I wasn't there to just take from them or do things that would somehow have negative repercussions.

While all of these characteristics—giving back, building trust, having respect and love for other human beings, and having a sense of social justice—are key factors in doing PAR, there are no rule books. Using prescriptions or set patterns means that sooner or later the temptation arises to impose what is learned from one group onto another. Participatory action-research is much more than an instrument. In Isabel's words:

> If you think about PAR merely as an instrument you lose the basic sense of it. You begin to manipulate the activities to suit your purposes. You are then doing something which is not a participatory process philosophically. If you think you can instrumentalize participatory methods to transfer information, then you are focusing on the information, not on

> people's needs. You cannot do it! It does not work! It is sim-
> ply a waste of time and money.
>
> PAR is about people and their needs. You have to begin from
> where people are at and move along with them. You cannot
> impose a particular process on them and expect them to stay
> with it.

The dynamics of each group are what keeps a PAR process alive; that is where the seed of transformation really lies. As Isabel put it, "Each situation has its own dynamic. In adjusting to each situation, I begin to live that way, always in tune with the 'other'."

Participatory action-research is not a panacea. When urgent actions are needed there are places for other approaches. For example, I grew up in a country where there are frequent earthquakes. When one strikes, other countries offer immediate assistance. Generous people elsewhere are willing to come in and provide charity. But, if we are talking about constructing a different kind of world—a world where people are less polarized because of their surname, birthplace, or economic status—we need to look at different options. Assistance and charity are not going to create this reconstruction. These approaches allow some individuals to benefit but the community is not really helped. In contrast, participatory action-research is about strengthening communities, fostering local organizations, and in the process, transforming realities.

References

Alfaro, C. 1936. *Resena General de la Provincia de Tarapaca.* Iquique: Miguel Bustos Gonzalez.

Fals-Borda, O. 1979. Investigating reality in order to transform it. The Colombian experience. *Dialectical Anthropology* 1: 33-55.

Freire, P. 1973. *Education for a Critical Consciousness*. New York: Continuum.

_____. 1983. *Pedagogy for the Oppressed*. New York: Continuum.

Gonzalez, H. and Gundermann, H. 1989. *Campesinos y Aymaras en et Norte de Chile*. Documento de Trabajo No.1. Arica: TEA.

Gonzalez, S. 1991. *Hombres y Mujeres de la Pampa: Tarapaca en el Ciclo del Salitre*. Iquique: TER.

Acknowledgement

Maria-Ines Arratia's initial research was made possible by a Young Canadian Scholars' award from the International Development Research Centre, Ottawa, and by a doctoral fellowship from the Social Sciences and Humanities Research Council of Canada (SSHRCC). Post-doctoral research was also funded by SSHRCC. This vital support is gratefully acknowledged.

Ms. Arratia would like to commend the long and tedious work on the part of the editorial team to produce an accessible and useful volume for all those interested in generating knowledge with/for people through participatory methods.

6

PASANTÍAS AND SOCIAL PARTICIPATION: PARTICIPATORY ACTION-RESEARCH AS A WAY OF LIFE

Arturo Ornelas

ଔ EDITORS' NOTE: The construction of this chapter is a story in itself. During the production of this book, the Honduran experience continued to unfold. It was retained in people's memories and reflected in their actions; at the time documented largely in Arturo's informal letters to the National Vice-Director of Health of Honduras.

In early 1992 while still in Honduras, Arturo sent us a tape cassette, an initial "talking chapter" accompanied by four diagrams, in which he described the *pasantía* work from his perspective up to that point. Later that year at small conferences in Alberta, Canada, we audiotaped two of Arturo's slide presentations about Honduras. Susan also interviewed Arturo three times: on audiotape in 1992 while observing a follow-up *pasantía* in Honduras, and on videotape and audiotape in 1994 in Calgary, probing his motivations and personal philosophy.

Once transcribed, these tapes created a mountain of notes. With Nancy's help, Susan did an extensive cut-and-paste and edit, sorting out the practical hands-on story and its details, the more abstract comments on participatory action-research, and Arturo's recounting of significant personal life events. Arturo then reviewed the chapter line by line with us, adding or clarifying specific statements.

When asked for permission to include the Honduran experience in the book, Honduran members of the facilitating "Promoter Team" seemed somewhat surprised at the request. They had no objection and commented on the strange (North American) notion of intellectual property, believing that knowledge is for everyone.

Arturo's voice, insightful and provocative, is the one heard in this chapter. We hope that someday the perspectives of participants and co-facilitators will be added to the case study, thereby enriching the account further. ☙

One sunny morning in February, 1992, I ate lunch with the National Vice-Director of Health of Honduras. She is smart and active with a strong commitment to the many poor people of that country. We talked about the most difficult aspects of their national health care system. She observed, "We are too bureaucratic in the Ministry. This problem is compounded by the limitations of the health care system itself." She continued, "Our hospitals are the worst because they are the empires of our doctors." Doctors in Latin America too often mechanize and dehumanize people, especially the poor. They only see parts of the body, not the person, the human being. In that sense, she wanted to challenge their system to transform one clinical hospital into a communitarian hospital.

I asked her, "Why do you want to change just the health workers? Why not change society?" This question launched the "Napkin Plan." We scratched some ideas on a paper napkin. (Napkins are terrific for planning, poetry, and addresses; they are beautiful tools for administration and can even be faxed!)

In 1992, Honduras had built five new regional hospitals, but these hospitals did not have good connections with their surrounding communities. People were reluctant to enter the hospitals because of a belief that they were places to go to when dying, and also because of the arrogance of certain hospital personnel. We decided better links were needed between the hospitals and the people in their surrounding communities. "Do you commit yourself to helping?" she asked me.

When she approached the Pan American Health Organization (PAHO) for funding, PAHO asked, "What is your plan?" Showing the napkin to them she said, "Please understand this open approach. We want to build the program *with* the community members. We need the cheque tomorrow." They were unable to grasp that we needed to start with the needs of the poor people rather than with the logic and rationality of the professionals and institutions. The predominate attitude is that it is "the people" who need to change their behaviours, never the professionals.

In July, she phoned me in Mexico to start work in August. The initial funding from PAHO was only for two months, which I knew was not going to be enough time. This limitation happens when programs are seen as actions to get "products," instead of processes in order to have transformation.

I arrived in the country with no plan of action, only with an open mind and heart to see and learn first, and to live in a little town called La Esperanza, "The Hope." While in the capital city, the Vice-Director said, "Well, Arturo, you're going to stay for six months. I have suggested to different people that they join you, but I am not sure who will actually be on the team." The people invited were nervous as they would need to work with an unknown approach to research and social change. Two nurses agreed to come from the Unit of Social Participation in the Ministry of Health. At the regional level, an educator with 20 years of experience in the Ministry of Health joined us.

> In doing participatory action-research (PAR), you enter into the process as an ignorant. You start by recognizing your ignorance and working with it. Only when you do this, can you truly "know" your own ignorance. Part of PAR is knowing that you will have doubts and uncertainties, periods of "fog" when it is not clear what to do next. They are part of the process. This does not mean that you are a mess of doubts. You do not doubt that you will have doubts! But if you begin, already thinking that you have the truth and the tools to go with that truth, then it is not possible to find reality.

Understanding Historical Context
and Current Realities

The four of us arrived in La Esperanza and decided to spend ten days walking, visiting, and talking with people of the area. La Esperanza is surrounded by 52 communities of about 75 to 150 families each. A small hospital had opened in La Esperanza in February 1992. We saw problems related to high rates of infant mortality, maternal mortality, and malnutrition. For example, of nine children born in one small community at the beginning of August 1992, five were dead by the end of the month. Many women experience complications during childbirth. The birth rate is very high. During our first month in the area, we saw 23 men close to death from malnutrition. (In the Maya tradition, the men eat last in the family.)

Because the people live high in the mountains, there is no extensive agriculture. Their homes and villages are far apart with no public transportation to reach them. Women and children gather wood for fires and water for cooking. Most of the men have alcohol problems.

Why this need to escape through alcohol? These people lost their identity twice, first when conquered by the Mayans and then by the Spanish. They were pushed from the lush valleys into the mountains where their traditional food— bananas, corn, pumpkins, beans, and root vegetables—did not always grow well. They also lost their language. Now only Spanish is spoken. People are their language. With language, people explain their understanding of themselves and of their world. If people lose their language they lose their identity.

To escape their oppressors, the people moved to the mountains, spreading out for protection. A walk of five to seven hours separates the little groups of houses. Their society became closed with its own religion, beliefs, economy, and type of communication. They now cultivate land on the immense ravines. I do not know how they are able to stand up on the steep mountain sides and sometimes I think that the people have wings and are able to fly in order to work the land.

In the valleys, large vegetable gardens are now cultivated by multinational corporations. The corporations use pesticides on the vegetables and then fly the food from United States' military bases in Honduras to the United States in order to sell it in giant food stores. In the end, the American people eat the pesticide poison that was absorbed in the cultivated produce.

The people in the La Esperanza area today live in poverty.

One organization, La Vara Alta de Moises (The Staff of Moises), unifies the population spiritually. This organization exists in every town. People believe that long ago Moses came and spoke to the people, gave them his staff, and said, "This is your identity." Moses told them that they were going to suffer until they regained their liberty, and to regain their liberty they must be united and work together. This belief is what maintained their identity following the loss of their language.

Every village has three families who are Guardians of the Staff. The Guardians beg for food and are unable to change their clothes or wash for an entire year. They sacrifice themselves in order to maintain the traditional beliefs.

The Catholic Church did not like La Vara Alta de Moises and attempted to eradicate the organization by removing images of their saints from church doors and buildings. The Church tried to destroy the human role played by the organization in its communities, to focus on the church itself rather than on the people.

> The Church uses social control, influencing people to think that if they do not believe in the Church, they cannot believe in themselves. "The Church is you and you are the Church" is the message. In Latin America, a person can be with the Church or against the Church but it is impossible to be out of the Church. The same is true of politics in Latin America.

This population believes that a child dies because God wanted the child; if someone dies young that is his destiny. The more a person suffers here on earth, the better it will be in heaven. In that sense, the people do not take advantage of the few good technologies that exist. Health care is not a high priority among the *campesinos*; they are more concerned about jobs, water, roads, cars, and stereos.

> How could health have a higher priority? This is difficult when life has little value. When someone is working all day from 4 a.m. to 11 p.m. and still does not have enough to eat, when he knows that all his ancestors were poor and his children and all his descendants will remain poor, death can be considered a release from suffering.

As *campesinos*, the people are conservative, guarding their small amounts of money, their little pieces of land, their few hens. They must be very careful. There is no confidence and little trust of outsiders. They did not accept us in the beginning.

> How to build trust? This is one of the major questions of PAR. As an outsider, you will always be marginalized until the group trusts you. That trust will be built by working with the group, living with them, doing what they do. They need to discover that you are a human being. When you gain the moral value of being trusted, at that moment you become a part of the group or community, part of the landscape. PAR can then start. Sometimes, authors of PAR literature pay insufficient attention to this element of trust. This is because many take an academic view, focussing on the methodology, philosophy, or theory, rather than experiencing the daily life of PAR.

The people live in a dependent security. We understood that these people work from 4 a.m. to 11 p.m. for years on end and have little decision-making power. The way of life of the oppressor becomes the model of life for the oppressed. The importance of community spirit is to create beliefs in common unity, common goals, and common achievement. When the oppressive system is very strong—strong enough to break communities—these vital beliefs about community are lost.

> When human beings transform nature, a culture appears. By transforming nature, people are transformed themselves.

The result of these changes is culture—for example, how houses are made or how rationalities develop, or the appearance of popular science and technologies necessary for the cultivation of small plots and survival. A culture without change, without evolution, becomes tradition. People become increasingly conservative; their spirit dies.

The team realized the necessity to re-establish self-esteem among the people and also to establish the capability to transform current reality. We needed to work with the people and their current culture with a clear understanding of their historical context.

The Initial Facilitation Team

As a second step, we created a facilitation team of people from three levels of government. At the central level, there were two nurses and one social worker from the Ministry of Health. At the regional level, one educator, one grassroots health promoter, and one supervisor of health promoters participated. At the local level, we expected to develop a team. The only criteria for being on the facilitation team was a desire and openness to learn.

We asked ourselves, "What do we need to be a team?" We decided to allow ourselves the time to get to know each other. We went for walks and to dances. Spending this time together doing different things, we became a team. Everyone began to learn from actual practice.

The essential element of PAR is love. PAR necessitates that the individuals involved in the group care for each other on many levels. If you cannot work on transformation with the love necessary, you become mechanical. If the action is not being humanized, the world is not being humanized. You are acting as a robot, doing mechanical things. PAR cannot happen. From my experience, when team members start criticizing in destructive ways, when people stop loving each other, the team is destroyed and so is any action. Without love we do not create movement. How necessary is the foundation of love.

Thinking about the *Pasantía*

The team did not have any detailed plan, only our experiences and a small library. Planning, projecting, calculating—all these types of activities usually are carried out before starting anything. After working in different large institutions in Africa, Geneva, and Washington, I have found that most of this pre-planning is not useful. The time, money, and energy is not justified. A person cannot plan to "teach" another person, but they can live a process together.

We wanted to create an opportunity where people could come and pass through an experience. We asked ourselves, "What kind of experience should take place?" Everyone rejected the usual workshops, courses, and seminars. Instead, we proposed a series of *pasantías* which, roughly translated, means "passing through" a social experience with a critical eye and a sense of personal fulfillment.

Each participant would bring their own reality, their own experiences of living within a certain context. Working together, participants could imagine and then create the experience themselves. They would begin to "see" their reality, investigate that reality—not only study "texts" but study "context"—and propose actions to transform that reality. They then would start working towards their new vision, all the while learning from their own experiences.

> Social participation means people are directly involved in decisions that affect their lives. If social participation is linked with reality, then people start creating a body of knowledge—a body of knowledge that is actually introduced by a body of doubts. Knowledge is not transmitted, it is constructed. In Latin America, we are working permanently to construct new knowledge. This starts by a recognition of our own ignorance.

> For me the right question is found in the answer. The right
> questions are not asked if all the threads of the answer are
> not present. Sometimes another person is needed to help il-
> luminate those threads that form the answer and then the
> question. So that is why I say that we started building a body
> of knowledge about La Esperanza, its people, and social par-
> ticipation.

Wanting to build the program on the interests of the participants, we did not know what the program would actually
look like beforehand. We wanted to ask the participants what
they wanted to learn, to experiment with, and to reflect on
together. We intuitively thought that a three-week program
could allow sufficient time. For all of us, this was to be our first
experience at leading this type of process.

The *Pasantía* Begins

No one knew how many people were going to come to the
first *pasantía*. The only condition to attend was that the person be interested in social participation. Twenty-five people
were invited to the first *pasantía* and 47 showed up. The individuals were from different backgrounds: professionals, health-
related workers, and *campesinos*. Some had more formal education while others had the richness of life experiences.

The team supplied 300 books and articles, a photocopier,
and a meeting place. We asked the participants what they
wanted to do. They replied that they had come to learn and
inquired, "What is your program?" We described the situation
of the hospital and the need to create "links" or closer relationships with all the communities. We turned the question back
to them, "What do you really think? What are your needs?
Your feelings? Your ideas? Link it to social participation, and
then tell us what you want to know." The participants were
surprised because they were expecting prepared courses and
it was nothing like that.

The participants started discussing the questions in small

groups. A few participants became angry. (Three doctors from the Central level quit the program very early, saying that we were only joking, playing with people. They could not allow themselves the chance to be creative.) We left the participants alone to search out what they wanted to learn.

Initially, they protested this approach. The next day, however, everyone returned with specific ideas for the program. A trend became clear: participants wished to learn from each other, as well as from texts. Individuals might approach learning differently, but we were unified by the same reality.

Living and Learning the Process

Each small group made a presentation about their ideas. Surprisingly, most people wanted to know similar things. Five main items arose: participatory action-research, communication and popular education, community-based health development, evaluation, and spirituality. The next question was, "How do you want to learn these?" People suggested different ways, drawing from various styles of education.

We always started with an active exercise—doing something practical that would get people moving. People should not sit passively while someone lectures for one or two hours, followed by a few individuals asking three or four questions. That formal approach was not what was needed.

> How do you learn to walk? Walking. How do you learn to swim? Swimming. Usually theory is taught first and then the skills for actual practice. Many times the learner never gets to the practice. The exercises promoted everyone's critical thinking and they allowed a sharing of knowledge, continuously building upon reflection and action.

For the next ten days, we worked in the training centre and outside in the communities, examining the experiences of the participants in the five focus areas. Emphasis was placed on analysis and writing, putting in order what people were thinking and feeling. Some people, mostly the professionals, thought they knew everything; this made it hard for them to learn. Occasionally, it was necessary to say to the professional, "Be quiet and let the others talk. Learn from them."

The group analyzed what they wanted to do with the hospital and proposed to do a diagnosis of the overall situation. Different communities extended invitations to the participants. We broke into small groups and went outside of the meeting room to work and learn. Participants started by talking with the people about anything and everything. They performed theatre, sang songs, played music; the children made drawings. Everyone worked on something, for example, popular education or exploring an analysis of participatory action-research. No one implemented a participatory action-research project, of course, because they could not just start that process but instead, participants explored what "research," "participation," and "action" meant for the community people. They tried to catch the popular meanings of these concepts. Everyone also worked in the community, helping to construct a road, building a health centre, or presenting information on different sicknesses.

Simultaneously, participants were sharing, working, and living with the community people, understanding the reality of their daily lives. Through talking and working, the people of the *barrios* began to understand how much they really knew about home health remedies and the history of their area. People became more knowledgeable about health and their own needs.

Theory of the Mattress

We carry our cultures with us wherever we go. When participants went into the mountains for field trips, they scrambled to rent, buy, or borrow mattresses. They carried these mattresses on their backs, not realizing at first that the walk was long hours up and down the mountains. Lice, ticks, and chiggers love mattresses. After the first night, the mattresses were full of insects. The second night was hell, and the third was to sleep with the devil! People then slept on straw mats as the mountain people sleep but, in the end, had to carry the mattresses out of the mountains.

Those mattresses proved to be a wonderful tool for learning. We understood that our beliefs and behaviour affect the reality that we experience. The most important lesson was to realize the need to understand our own weaknesses and hostilities and to have compassion with ourselves.

> I think hostility begins in two ways. First of all, an inner hostility starts when I, as an urban outsider, "lose my mattress." Without running water, electricity, or the comfort of my house, I develop an inner violence when eating only beans, chili, and coffee for days, weeks, and months. There is not the theatre, movies, video, radio, newspaper, 7-Elevens, McDonalds, and pizzerias of our cities. I had not yet discovered the excitement within myself.

> Hostility also is created when I arrogantly insist on going to "teach" somewhere. If I try to teach people in my own language and through my own city culture and behaviour, people's eyes laugh at me. This gives me uncomfortable feelings of resentment. Real and imaginary differences between people create that tension of hostility.

> It is a tug-of-war with myself. Humbly I need to open and start learning. I need to look inside myself. Hostility will always occur. The question is: "Will I pass around it, or will I work through it until the solution becomes evident?"

Extracting the "Juice"

Participants returned to the centre for three more days. We synthesized the experience, asking, "How did your thinking and feelings change while out in the communities? What was your sensorial diagnosis of the communities? What is the 'juice' of the whole experience?"

We use the word "validation" to bring a value to our actions,
in order to show our appreciation of our active efforts. We
bring a value to everything. Doing a critical analysis and
revision is a different question and action. Perhaps that is a
difference between the Anglo-Saxon and the Latin American
concepts of evaluation.

Participants lived with the *campesinos*. We saw how people
were carried to the hospital and why they died. We slept with
the lice and flies and ate beans and tortillas, tortillas and beans.
Being in the community was amazing. The people provided
us with water, food, support, songs, and dances—they gave us
their hearts. Many of the professionals discovered their country. They experienced in a small but very significant way the
life of the poor—and also its richness. The professionals lost
their fear, as did the *campesinos*.

Interconnections form when people work together, learn together, share the same story. Linkages form when fear is lost.

Consciousness is the human capacity to perceive, understand,
and transform. Understanding is a deep comprehension of
situations. When I can see the real size and shape of my perceptions, then I understand in a deeper way than before. I
begin to make internal interconnections between the different factors affecting a situation. Consciousness internalizes
the outside world. It brings the outside world into myself.
It forms points of integration and leaves me available for
transformation. With consciousness, we can comprehend
ethical values like social justice, human rights, love, and solidarity.

Language is a powerful tool used to internalize the world.
Through language the external world is invited into our
minds. We also can explain ourselves through language.
Language and consciousness work together.

Conscientization occurs when a person can understand and
identify the elements of oppression, injustice, and control. If
people share the same conscious capability, they can create
movement for social justice. At that moment, we can speak

of conscientization and actually mean action, the concrete action of consciousness. Concrete actions manifest or reveal consciousness.

Developing Summary Schemas

Participants completed a sensorial diagnosis of the area by telling stories, sharing experiences, and making drawings. Through discussion we understood that, as with many organizations, the Ministry of Health did not have effective communication between the capital, regional, and local levels of health care. Linkages had never existed. The region needed to be linked with the local hospital, which in turn needed connections with the small health centres. The community people had never requested a stronger relationship with the hospital because they also were not unified. Through social participation in the *pasantías*, everyone began to have an increased conscientiousness about their community, including the hospital.

The notion of a communitarian hospital was developed by the *pasantía* groups. Working together, hospital and community people drew the schemas that follow, capturing their ideas for a process that would transform an isolated, clinical hospital into a hospital rooted in its community.

Participants knew that health programs most often are designed by government people working from behind their desks, thinking about reality but not really knowing the community's reality. They recognized it was important to avoid systematic barriers as well as to bring out fears about a communitarian hospital. A communitarian hospital needed to have flexible actions, schedules, and resolutions. In fact, all the hospital personnel needed to participate in the change process.

One day, working with the *pasantía* group, I asked, "If you want to have someone come to your house, what would you do?" Their answer came quickly, "I go to them and invite them to come to my house." My next question was, "If we want the community to come to the hospital, what can we do?" Immediately, they answered, "We go to the community and we in-

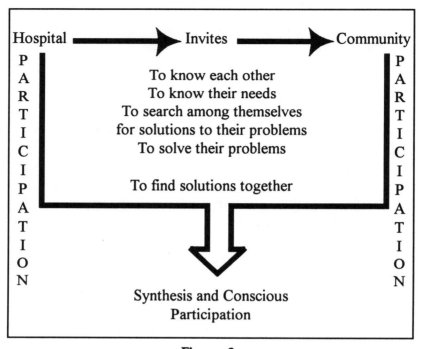

Figure 3:
Schema #1—Communitarian Hospital

vite them to come to the hospital." Coming closer together
would allow everyone to know the needs of the community as
well as those of the hospital. A search for alternatives could
begin, with common actions taken to solve problems. A certain type of participation would appear during this process (see
Figure 3).

Participation can be like a prescription or recipe or it can go
beyond this. To arrive at a cohesive and conscious participation requires a deep commitment.

Making interconnections is the process of searching for and
connecting different ideas, actions, and/or people. Integration of ideas and actions goes one step further. It puts together or merges the elements being discovered. Integration
gives size, form, and colour to the essential connections being made. At that moment, when all is put together at the

right time and place, something tangible occurs. What was abstract becomes concrete. Theory becomes reality; ideas become flesh and blood. It is a moment of truth.

The second schema (Figure 4 on page 154) depicted the need for forming a "promoting team" that would undertake an institutional diagnosis in order to analyze problems and priorities, take action, validate those actions, and conduct any follow-up. In actual fact, different actions started while this process was in its early stages. But participants thought that actions taken later in the process would be undertaken with greater commitment and understanding.

In the third schema (Figure 5), four types of councils were proposed. The first was the *cesar* community advisory group comprised of village people, the nursing assistant, and community health personnel associated with each small health centre high in the mountains. The *cesamo* community advising group was the communitarian council of the area: village people, doctors and nurses, community health personnel, and the city mayor. This area covered the hospital and the 14 health care centres. People were elected by free elections, thereby creating a popular power in health. The two other councils related to a larger scope of territory and incorporated people from higher levels of government.

Reaction of La Esperanza Hospital

For the first *pasantía*, four people from the hospital came as participants: one kitchen worker, one statistician, one young psychologist, and one auxiliary nurse. The facilitation team was angry, "Where are the doctors here? Where are the professional nurses? The hospital administrators? The regional and municipal personnel?"

The hospital director replied, "A hospital is for curation. Doctors work in hospitals, not in the communities. They are too busy." We understood at that point that the director did not support this project.

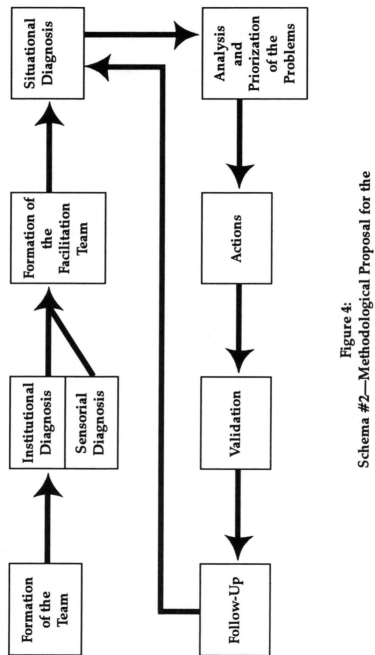

Figure 4:
Schema #2—Methodological Proposal for the
Establishment of a Communitarian Hospital

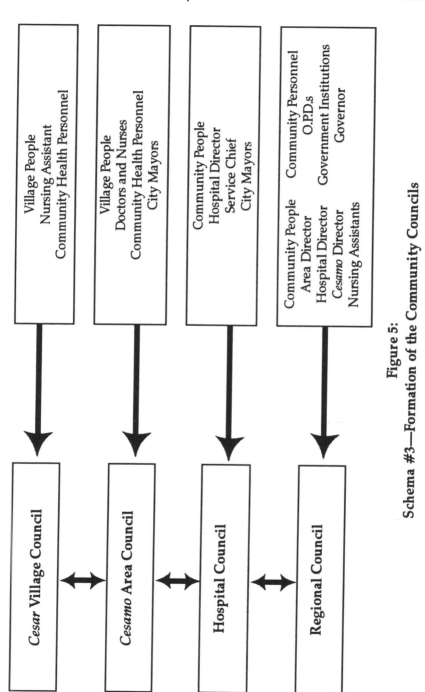

Figure 5:

Schema #3—Formation of the Community Councils

At times, it is important to analyze how one person who is not clear on the objectives and who does not share the same commitment—a person who is committed to his socioeconomic class and not to the people—can harm a process.

All people have consciousness, but not all people can see social injustice. Those that cannot have an alienated consciousness which is a type of sickness. Someone is alienated when they cannot see their own reality clearly. It is more comfortable to believe in the fantasy that society presents. For example, in my society, the Church says that suffering on earth will lead to heavenly glory. In North America, the dominant society tells you to work hard, save money, and go to Hawaii for holidays. Or save money throughout your life so that you can live comfortably in your golden years. Many stereotypes also exist. Poor people are poor because they are lazy, drunk, or ignorant.

This thinking is a social sickness. Believing in these fantasies, as well as the stereotypes, turns reality into a fantasy, and the fantasy becomes reality. That is alienation. How can a person emerge from alienation? Through conscientization. How can a person gain conscientization? Through a PAR process, you will discover your own situation and vocation.

During the first *pasantía*, we went to the hospital to do a survey. It was immediately apparant that some things were very wrong in the hospital. One of the main problems was that, as a hierarchical institution, orders came from the top to the bottom. Nothing went from the bottom to the top. Participants wanted to create a "go-and-come" type of information flow.

The survey findings were given to all the hospital personnel, who agreed with the information. A permanent instrument of reflection within the hospital was vital for sustainable change to happen. This insight later led to the formation of reflection-action circles.

Long ago, love and hate were unified, as were work and idleness. Society today has separated these ideas into "positive" and "negative" components. But the negative elements—hate or idleness, for example—are actually part of the positive elements. They are not separated. Sometimes moments of joy occur on the same day as moments of sadness. The interconnections between the negative and positive components are very important. It is only through these connections that we develop a sense of inner and social unity, of being reconnected with the different vibrations and dimensions of the universe.

Another essential element is the realization of the need for tensions. Everything occurs in a dialectical relationship. Each element is in relationship with its opposite. Tensions form. There are times when a critical eye and questioning is vital along with trust that a group can find its own answers. Patience is found with impatience. The specific needs of the various individuals are in tension with the collective interests. These are examples of inevitable tensions that will arise.

Action-Reflection Circles

As the *pasantías* progressed, everyone realized that a bureaucratic approach could not continue in the hospital. In order to decrease hostility and create firmer linkages, a new structure for communication and problem-solving was needed within the institution. Four action-reflection circles were created: administration, clinical matters, community, and coordination. With everyone involved seated in a circle, problems would be analyzed; the group then would make decisions based on their analysis, which would lead to action and follow-up. Three elements made this process work: people affected by a problem were allowed to stop work immediately when a problem surfaced, a one-hour time limit was set while the group analyzed the situation and made plans to take action, and follow-up was done on the results of the action decisions.

Following a circle of reflection, a sheet was posted in a designated, visible place. It outlined who met, the problem, the discussion, and the actions. Everybody had to know what was happening, including the patients.

Our modern times continue to work with dualities—black or white, good or bad, success or failure. We must have "success"; failure is a catastrophe. We spend our lives searching for things for which success is guaranteed. When the element of interconnectedness between circumstances, people, and ideas is realized, a person stops working for just "success" and does not fear fear itself. A new conception is formed whereby people will recognize vulnerabilities, realize limitations, and develop the discriminating judgment to re-orient actions. Success or failure, as such, becomes part of the experience.

A Referral System Begins

The national facilitation team recognized that there was no effective medical referral system in the La Esperanza area. One assistant nurse served 12 to 15 communities. She made referrals to a professional nurse who in turn worked with a doctor or a dentist. When the facilitation team began working, there were no roads into the mountains. Up to 28 men took turns carrying a sick person out of the mountains to the nearest road. Once there, the long wait would begin for a passing vehicle with a driver willing to take the sick person to town. The hospital was considered a house of death because after several days of travelling, the patient usually died there.

During one of the *pasantías*, participants focussed on developing a referral system that could work in these high mountains. The nurses working in the mountains were not familiar with referral systems or hospitals; on visits to the unfamiliar La Esperanza hospital, fear was visible in their eyes. We had two days of discussion about what "referral" meant and all worked to design a referral process (Figure 6).

Suddenly, just through talking with different people, three ambulances were found. The first one was discovered in the house of the deputy minister; it had been given by the government to the local volunteer fire brigade. Since no such group existed, the ambulance had been stored. The second ambulance came from a German non-governmental organization. The third ambulance was discovered in a garage at the Minis-

Figure 6:
Sistema de referencia

try of Health; it was old but reconditioned. A short time later, 16 Citizen Band (CB) radios were donated. Everything was in place for the referral system.

One night the CB rang: a woman was dying in childbirth in a mountain village. She was carried onto the back of a passing truck loaded with wood. An ambulance was dispatched immediately from the hospital with a doctor and blood. They met the truck midway. Both the woman and the child were saved. This *extraordinario* result was synergistic.

> When I do something that takes me beyond what I have been able to do before, and I discover that I am capable of doing that action, I realize joy. I am, in fact, growing. It is a feeling of movement and satisfaction for both the individual and the group.
>
> Development is an energizing force that grows synergistically. Without linkages between people, that energy is not created. Synergy pushes us to walk on, to go further, to work more. The moments of joy have so much to do with people being together and caring deeply about each other. This, in turn, affects and reflects the actual work being accomplished.

Community people must be able to recognize the symptoms of different sicknesses and know when to send people to the hospital immediately. People from both the villages and the institution renewed their motivation to learn. Plans were made whereby one professional nurse and one health promoter would conduct workshops in the mountain health centres. Meetings in the hospital outlined a plan where hospital nurses would return with the mountain nurses to the villages in order to follow up patients, bringing the referral system full cycle.

At that moment, the hospital administration became supportive because the people became organized. The community began to heal themselves and talk about what was needed.

Rotacion del personal de salud

The mountain nurses, often isolated for many years, wanted to be brought up to date. *Pasantía* participants designed a rotation program between health centre nurses and hospital nurses. Taking turns, the nurses would exchange places, each gaining knowledge and skills while visiting and working for short time periods in the new setting. At first, the program had difficulties. For example, Aida, a nurse that came out from one of the villages, complained that the hospital nurses did not like her and did not help her. Nobody talked to her and she wanted to leave. The hospital nurses responded that they should not have to teach a "peasant" nurse. The Hospital Administrator called all the head nurses together for a meeting. Another lengthy, detailed discussion was held with all the staff nurses.

We examined all positions. This analysis uncovered what it meant to be a "nurse," whether working in the mountains or in the hospital. The hospital nurses discovered that they were making a terrible mistake, and Aida found that she was acting as a "child nurse," accepting a passive role. Aida became a symbol of solidarity.

The program grew. Other rural nurses later had better experiences in the hospital. Nurses from the hospital returned from the mountains changed; they became more open to differences and possibilities and began doing health work in the community. Hospital staff now often visit those in the mountains. By experiencing each other's realities, their understanding and subsequent links became stronger.

How can people learn to appreciate the reality of others? This is done by breaking isolation, going beyond the status quo, and creating knowledge. I am not talking about adaptation but about how to establish commitment.

At different points, doubts or fears about the unknown will occur. Many times these appear as vulnerabilities. At that step, if a vulnerability becomes a weakness, then we will think that we have failed. But vulnerability can become a strength when we recognize that we have limitations, that we are not yet prepared sufficiently to go beyond the immediate situation. Vulnerability, lived with a critical eye and the strength of commitment, can become a beautiful path to walk, allowing us to grow as persons and facilitating the transformation of reality.

El hospital en el comunidad/La comunidad en el hospital

How could the hospital come to the communities and the communities to the hospital? When you are committed to something and become part of it, creativity flows. Eighteen people decided to do something different. They travelled from village to village, living with the families and working in the fields during the day. At night they sang, danced, and invited people to come to a "health fiesta."

They invited seven doctors to take part in the fiesta and planned a 5 a.m. departure in order to arrive on time. Two doctors showed up, the hospital director, and the director's boss. Waiting for the others until 7 a.m., the two lone doctors said that they would not go. I replied that I was going anyway, got in my truck, and drove off. Looking in the rearview mirror, I was glad to see them driving behind me.

Six hundred people were waiting for us to arrive. Of the 18 *pasantía* participants, seven were nurses and went to assist the two doctors who were doing medical consultations. These incredible nurses were really committed to the people and treated the doctors like spoiled children, saying "Yes, yes doctor," and then doing exactly what they, the nurses, wanted to do. Nurses are the "hinges" joining two solitudes, the one of the communities and the one of the doctors.

Meanwhile, the other nine people created a fiesta. Soon the people were drinking and dancing, doing theatre, talking politics, playing football, and playing guitar. By 4 p.m., there were still at least 200 people waiting for medical consultation. I asked one doctor if I could help out. Although not a medical doctor,

EL HOSPITAL EN LA COMUNIDAD

LA COMUNIDAD EN EL
HOSPITAL

Figure 7:
El hospital en la comunidad/La comunidad en el hospital

I have practiced traditional medicine in Mexico and thought group consultations might prove useful. "What happened?" I asked the first patient of the 35 waiting in the group. He replied, "I am sore in my belly and have diarrhea." The diagnosis was parasites. The second patient had the same symptoms and got the same response, as did the third patient. When the tenth patient was asked, "What do you have?" the patient joyfully replied, "Parasites!" People learned to recognize their symptoms in this group learning situation, many of their illnesses being the same and poverty-related. (Of course, problems requiring privacy were handled differently.)

Within four months there were several fiestas. Today most of the doctors attend; they have been pushed into it by the nurses and the people.

> Sickness is poverty in Latin America. The causes are social injustice. Sometimes you have to open a doctor's head and add "social justice" to make the doctor understand. Our educational systems can do significant harm to an individual's abilities to see and understand. Entering university at 20 years of age, I was so smart and beautiful. I came out at 27 years so ugly and dispirited. I know now that the greatest sickness is that of the spirit and it is possible to not even notice that you are weak in spirit.

A Flow of People between the Hospital and the Community

Many women were dying in childbirth because of being transported to the hospital at the last moment when problems developed. People questioned why there was not some type of hostel where women could stay before giving birth. Eighty-two *campesinos* decided to build a maternity home for the mothers beside the hospital. Gathering at the site to discuss the idea, the *campesinos* remarked, "Why not build it right away?" They began digging the foundation that day and continued building every Friday. The hospital provided food, the Ministry of

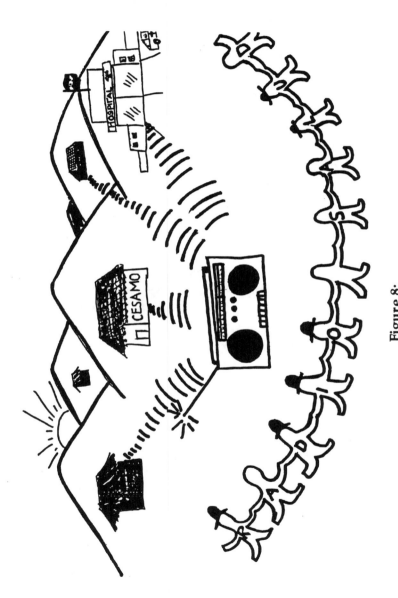

Figure 8:
Radio salud/Health on Radio

Health donated a truck for transportation, commercial enterprises donated roof tiles, and the churches gave beds.

Today, the maternity home has a capacity for 65 persons to be self-supporting. Each woman is accompanied by one other person; they help grow their own food in the huge vegetable garden. The Ministry of Agriculture donated nine cows, some pigs, and chickens. The Pan American Health Organization funded the initial project while the government pays the staff salaries.

A constant flow of people between the hospital and the communities occurs. There is now a teaching room inside the hospital where seminars can be held each year. A program for midwives has started. Another innovation was a ten-day workshop for 82 traditional healers and 25 doctors. The doctors were surprised by the knowledge of the healers. The radio station has donated broadcast time to the hospital, conducting interviews with health personnel and recording 42 different songs related to health (two examples being songs about diarrhea and the grippe or common cold). The radio links those communities with no other means of communication.

Pasantía participants planned to undertake certain actions in their local communities on returning home. Everyone worked on implementing their plans. Three or four months later we invited them to come back, share their experiences, and receive a diploma.

Back in their communities and alone, they are fighting with their bosses, struggling with themselves, trying to explore their own minds in order to acquire a new knowledge. Those moments are the real tests. It is in that sense that we validate the knowledge of loneliness, solitude, and the confrontation with the self. For those will surely happen.

Wisdom emerges when people choose to undertake certain challenges. They compile their resources in order to take action. When a common objective forms, social participation appears and social energy is generated. This in turn leads to a synthesis of ideas, actions, and feelings and results in knowledge construction—the wisdom of the people.

Figure 9:

The Total Reality of the People Is the Point of Departure

Aspirin or Transformation?

So, that is it. That is the *pasantía*. At the beginning in August 1992, four people began the process with a focus on the hospital. Over six months we held four *pasantías*, three weeks each, and two follow-up workshops. Two hundred and sixty-seven people attended in total—people from the different communities, hospital workers, social workers, doctors, nurses, as well as people from the Ministry of Health and non-governmental organizations.

In January 1993, the name of the hospital facilitation team changed to the "Promoter Team of the Process," and the number of team members increased from eight to 22. It now is a committee of the people that works with a much broader view of health, communities, and hospitals.

Eight of the 25 hospitals in the country had started the *pasantía* process by May 1993. Of course, there were also problems. Some people will never understand this type of process or the nature of social participation. The program needed to be sustainable. Issues of permanency and ownership pose difficult questions that are still being resolved.

Our approach began by getting to know the people and their perceptions of reality. The participants came with their experiences. They wanted to learn and listen to others about different topics: popular education, participatory action-research, and community development. Once equal relationships (subject-to-subject) were established, we explored our experiences together, not doing a conceptualization first, but going to people's reality, and then doing a conceptualization. We started with an actual experience—something concrete that can be seen and felt as real—knowing that the war of ideas is a false war. From one idea another idea is created and that creates yet another idea. That infinite wheel is not science or knowledge but science fiction. At the level of practice the limits of a true idea are evident.

We worked consistently on three levels: celebrating the techniques, identifying the process, and then constructing concepts. Participants organized their personal experiences. Practical action was emphasized. This methodology rests on flexibility with action and research as one process. Knowledge from research is applied immediately to the actual reality in order to transform that reality. By the end, they were confident of the knowledge produced through the sharing of experiences. Using creativity to arrive at new knowledge, the people played, wrote poetry, and sang. Everyone explored their own values. Each person had a deeper understanding of their meaning of commitment, responsibility, solidarity, love.

> Ideas are a synthesis of human understanding of a particular phenomenon. This knowledge is not like a photo of a landscape, stilled and static, but rather is alive and moving. Everything is a process.

> The biggest problem in community development is that the poor fight with the poor and not against oppression. Convinced of their own ignorance, people think that their poverty is their fault; the rich are better people. When people understand that this is not true, they can move mountains.

> How can we accept the lies of systems that say the poor are drunks or lazy? How can we accept the thesis that social change can happen without conflict when violence is a permanent condition in the daily lives of poor people all over the world? If we accept this thesis, there is conflict. If we do not accept it, there is conflict. Violence seeps throughout the human condition, increasing from tension, to the building up of anger, and finally hate. The need to heal becomes an absolute necessity.

> If we think in mechanical, non-essential ways, mechanical behaviour results. When we deal with society in technical or mechanical ways, we fail. Everything can be reduced to mechanics when you are a robot. Everything has a sense of meaning when you are a human being. It is up to each of us to choose.

> When a person undertaking PAR is not enmeshed inside the life of the group, when s/he just occasionally participates in

discussion or just interprets what others do, that person remains an outsider. That research becomes a collection of data only, and the researcher is an organizer and transcriber of data. PAR is being seen as a technique or tool. As a person experiences PAR, s/he moves beyond PAR as a technique and begins to understand that doing PAR also means re-searching inside the self. The research "outside" incorporates a search "inside"—to develop in the community also requires an inner development.

Vulnerability, risk-taking, trust, openness, patience, and impatience—all these have to do with PAR as a way of life. When we accept these characteristics as part of the process, we also begin to integrate those qualities more deeply into ourselves. We develop trust in ourselves as well as in others, allowing mutual caring and a sense of place and personhood. These are the spiritual dimensions of PAR. They are as necessary to the process as the dimensions of investigation, action, reflection, and dialogue.

In maintaining a relationship with a community, all actions will be political. We cannot be naive about this. In the last analysis, there are only two "sides" in development: be functional and give charitable assistance, or be transformational. You are either with the people or against the people. There is no middle fence to sit on. With a charitable approach, nothing essential will happen. What is our choice? Aspirin or transformation?

Epilogue: Alienation to Liberation— Personal Reflections

At 20 years of age, I was studying in Geneva and earning money by washing trains in the wintertime. The other washers were political refugees from Greece, Turkey, Spain, and Portugal. Having been labelled communists or socialists in their home countries, they were in political exile. Continually frustrated with their situation, they needed food to feed their families, medicines for illnesses, and schooling for their children. But most of all, my co-workers wanted democracy. Their common bond was a strong desire to be part of the decision-making in their communities and to live in peace and harmony.

I was studying in Geneva in order to be rich and famous. I thought I would then be able to work for peace for my people. Hearing the life stories of the other washers I realized that my perspective was wrong. What I could do as a student, and later as a professional, was to put my theoretical knowledge at the service of my people. I gained consciousness at that moment.

To be in solidarity with people fighting for their liberation, I decided to do fieldwork in Africa. Through many practical experiences, I became transformed myself by engaging in work that transformed people's realities—an important lesson learned over a period of seven years of studying and working.

After Africa, I began working for the United Nations in Latin America. My perspective became bureaucratized. I was visiting different countries, speaking with various officials and professionals, spending money to support their projects, all the while thinking that changes would appear. In several cases, changes did occur but my actions were to push papers, take planes, attend conferences, and write theoretical documents about the different realities of Latin America. Engulfed in my job, my relationships with people became closed; life centered around papers, budgets, and air tickets rather than around people. This is the madness of international or academic bureaucracy. One day, while living in Washington, D.C., I planned to attend a meeting in Ecuador with national directors of education from different countries. Arriving in Daytona on the first leg of the flight, I impulsively returned home and re-entered my house at 3 a.m. Some hours later, I presented my resignation to the United Nations. I was tired and empty, but full of false privilege.

It took me two years to decide to work with *campesinos*. My new job as a school principal in Mexico was repeating a sense of alienation; I was once more receiving an excellent salary, living in a fancy house, and working with too many people that I did not respect. I was again becoming false. At last able to recognize this pattern, I decided to drastically change my life.

This decision meant that I sold the big house, quit my job as school principal, and started living in rustic conditions, carrying water, cooking food over wood fires, and using candles for light. It was a drastic but purifying step. At that time, I started to be Mexican, to be myself. It was a moment of integration and consolidation, although I did not recognize it as such at the time. The elements leading up to that point—the end of my marriage, the unfulfilling work, and lost identity—all contributed equally to provoking a crisis. The critical point for change came, however, when I saw the pattern of alienation.

What is the relationship between my personal crisis of alienation and my understanding of participatory action-research as a way of life? I think that a personal crisis is provoked because of a deep personal alienation. I wanted to come out of my isolation, but was not sure how to go about accomplishing this. A fear of the unknown gave a stronger dimension to this crisis. The crisis itself did not take me out of alienation, but it did push me to acknowledge my situation and do something about it. My consciousness increased because of the crisis.

A personal crisis can lead to personal liberation. But if a person enters into participatory action-research or community work in reaction to a personal crisis, it is possible to transfer the feelings of hurt or anger to everything that is done. That is a danger. But it also is possible to develop a deeper understanding of social injustice because of an intimate knowledge of what it is to be wounded, in pain, or empty.

Living and working over a seven-year period with Mexican *campesinos* and later having additional experiences in other areas, I have regained richness, recognizing the value of studying in Geneva, living internationally, and concentrating my efforts on the survival of my own people. I understand that it is far more important to hold a strong commitment—life then becomes a poem, not written, but lived. In the uncertainty of life with its permanent fog of doubts and moments of joy, the only certitude is that I chose to work with the poor to defeat social injustice.

7

DEEPENING PARTICIPATORY ACTION-RESEARCH

Susan E. Smith

ᚻ EDITORS' NOTE: PAR is an evolving approach to research and the production of knowledge, one that will mature with challenges over time. The author of this chapter, Susan Smith, drew from different sources to write about the philosophical foundations of participatory action-research and develop a PAR methodology framework: the six case studies from Mexico, Canada, Honduras, Uganda, India, and Chile; existing literature; her own experience in PAR; and ongoing conversations and debates with friends and critics.

PAR, as a critical and spiritual form of research, is about personal and social transformation for liberation, that is, the eventual achievement of equitable communities and societies, which are characterized by justice, freedom, and ecological balance. In PAR, a group of people collectively enters into a living process, examining their reality by asking penetrating questions, mulling over assumptions related to their everyday problems and circumstances, deliberating alternatives for change, and taking meaningful actions. The group has ownership over what questions are pursued, and how. Research questions take many forms and are not predetermined, that is, no one person or subgroup enters the process with the major question(s) already specified. The group's process of action-reflection (praxis) strips away the veneer of life circumstances, revealing the foundations of why things are the way they are, and develops increased critical consciousness among group members. The focus is the creation of opportunities for empowering moments of truth and action.

173

A holistic framework for PAR methodology (praxiology) must capture dynamic, lived experience, or *vivencia*, acknowledging people as complex beings with different motivations, perceptions, capabilities, feelings, and relationships, but with shared problems and desires for community and common effort. It must make room for the necessary dialectical tensions and conflicts.

A PAR process consists of spiralling moments within an individual and for the group—knowing self, seeking connections, grounding in context and focussing on fundamental needs, beginning praxis, experiencing conscientization, and awakening. The moments build on each other and constitute intellectual, emotional, and practical movement. What becomes clear is that the intention to do PAR, while perhaps establishing important groundwork and individual or team transformation, does not constitute PAR itself. In situations of disturbing struggle for social participation and changes, people come face-to-face with themselves: these are probably the most difficult moments of all.

When people struggle together to meet challenges and resolve problems, they add to their complexity as individuals, their abilities to care and be cared for, their sense of rooted connectedness, and their capacity to create social justice. Giving birth to the knowledge of hopeful dreams, people in participatory action-research processes can strengthen their commitment to a meaningful way of life.ॐ

SECTION I: Thirst for Liberation

Many forces in the world today prevent us from establishing common goals and from using common resources. Cities grow too big and people are increasingly mobile, driven by strong cultural values of competition, consumerism, and individualism. We in the industrialized world, having created unsustainable ways of living, find it difficult to work and live together. Our patterns of social domination—people insisting on power over others, particularly men over women—result in a weak society characterized by isolation, lack of meaningful purpose, and numbing silence. Oppression today manifests as personal and social alienation and results in high levels of human and ecological damage.

We tend to have "small circles of family and friends formed to [our] taste, leaving greater society to look after itself." Alexis de Tocqueville described this rise of individualism in North America. Writing in the 1830s, he called it a "calm and considered feeling which disposes each citizen to isolate himself from the mass of his fellows and withdraw into [such] a circle" (Bellah et al., 1985: 37). As individuals we experience competition on a daily basis and are well versed in its demands. At the same time, we have only "sporadic flashes of togetherness, glimpses of what might be if only people would cooperate and their purposes reinforce, rather than undercut, one another" (*ibid.*: 198).

What is "community"—this sense of togetherness that periodically flashes into our lives? A community is a group of socially interdependent people "who participate together in discussion and decision making, and who share certain practices that both define the community and are nurtured by it" (*ibid.*: 333). Community (common-unity) is achieved when people work on common objectives, and have common successes. This form of collective society broke down when economic and practical interdependency was no longer necessary in the industrialized world (Macpherson-Smith, 1994: 96). A strong cultural focus on the individual ensured greater personal autonomy, but when extended to the point of individualism, resulted in the sacrifice of community, alienation of self from others, and rampant consumerism.

Participatory action-research (PAR) emerged to satisfy a tremendous need for liberation and recovery of community. PAR, as an approach to the creation of knowledge and the improvement of life, arose from the work of marginalized people in Tanzania, Brazil, India, and elsewhere in the early to mid-seventies. These people, often surfacing from long histories of colonialism, were dissatisfied with the usual Western academic research methods as a means for addressing problems and wanted to formulate alternatives. PAR is an "intellectual and practical creation of the peoples of the Third World when traditional academic research approaches and findings did not stimulate needed social and economic changes" (Fals-Borda, 1988: 2). Efforts converged to counter domination in societies: feminist research and literature, Black and indigenous movements, transformative adult education, historical materialism, and community development have all influenced the development of PAR as a philosophy and methodology for social knowledge and change.

The Power of Knowing

Knowledge is an ever-deepening understanding of the many complexities of reality. To have knowledge is to have a certain truth about reality; to do "research" is to produce (new or recovered) knowledge for specific human purposes. Knowledge is produced through many means; no one method has exclusive rights over what is to be considered legitimate knowledge. No research is neutral, devoid of a value base or assumptions about the order of life: all research has an ideological basis. A research ideology—the body of ideas and ways of thinking held by its practitioners—is reflected in the type of research questions examined, the methodologies used, how findings are disseminated, and the sources and amounts of funding.

Research in its pursuit of truths is not the sole domain of highly trained university-based scientists. Today people undertaking participatory action-research acknowledge that "knowledge is power" and confront those who want to monopolize the definition and production of knowledge. Vigorous and valid research can be conducted by people in everyday circumstances; PAR is a credible, needed source of knowing our world. People's science can help us find out where we have come from, who we are now, where we want to go, and how to get there.

This chapter has three distinct parts. The first section outlines three different forms of inquiry and explains ideas that form the foundation for participatory action-research. The second section focusses on the methodology (praxiology) of PAR and presents a PAR framework, while the third contains discussion and lessons based on experience for people wanting to engage in PAR.

What Is Participatory Action-Research?

PAR is about personal and social transformation for the liberation of oppressed people. People create knowledge within a PAR process which "is simultaneously a tool for the education and development of consciousness as well as mobilization for action" (Gaventa, 1991: 121-122).

A group of people collectively enters into a living process, examining their reality by asking penetrating questions, mulling over assumptions related to their everyday struggles, deliberating alternatives, and taking meaningful actions. They strip away the veneer of life circumstances, revealing the foundations of why things are the way they are. This back-and-forth, action-reflection process develops increased critical consciousness among group members. People in PAR are overtly political, working to change the status quo where unjust social, economic, and decision-making structures exist, to break free of constraints, and to open up possibilities on both inner and outer levels. PAR is "openly ideological research" (Lather, 1986: 63), an approach that makes its values and purpose transparent.

The Values of PAR: Capacity, Equity, and Commitment

PAR is based on three important values: (1) all people have the capacity to think and work together for a better life; (2) current and future knowledge, skills, and resources are to be shared in equitable ways that deliberately support fair distributions and structures; and (3) "authentic commitment" is required from external and internal participants (Fals-Borda,

1991: 4). Authentic commitment means to persist at every level and over the long term towards the shared goal of social transformation. Given the tensions inherently present in any process of change, these values will be tested at different times.

People are not "objects" to be studied (as in conventional empirical or interpretive methods) but are full "subjects" in the research process. They are actively involved in decision making and in taking actions, with ownership of the resulting consequences and knowledge. This is different from being "objects," that is, acted upon by others and living out their decisions. This definition, popularized by Paulo Freire and others promoting liberatory approaches to education and research, has a potential point of confusion with conventional research. Most research treats people as objects while labelling them as subjects.

To have "subject-subject" relationships in a PAR process is to have egalitarian, authentic participation among those involved. To participate essentially means to have meaningful influence (control) on how decisions are made, how resources are used, and how information is produced and distributed. Or, as Fals-Borda explains, to participate means to break up asymmetrical relationships of domination and submission with dependence (*ibid.*: 5).

Recognizing almost all action as political, those doing PAR assume that all work has implications for the distribution of power in society (Maguire, 1987: 37), and that control of knowledge production is central to maintaining power (Tandon, 1981: 23). Forming more democratic ways of living necessitates active attention to the distribution of power, to the relationships between individuals and groups, and to knowledge production.

Forms of Research

Different authors have classified research in various ways. Drawing from Habermas (1971) and Kemmis (1991: 99) placed research into three forms: positivist (empirical-analytic), interpretive (historical-hermeneutic), and critical. Maguire (1987: 15-20) discussed research forms in terms of dominant (empirical-analytic) and alternative views. Guba and Lincoln (1994: 109-112) identified four forms: positivism, postpositivism, critical theory, and constructivism.

How does PAR compare to other types of research? The table on page 180 captures our understanding and experience with the different forms. Each of the three major forms of research (empirical-analytic, interpretive, liberatory) is based on a distinct paradigm. A paradigm or mindset is a specific world view about the nature of society and how knowledge is produced and to be used. Each has underlying, taken-for-granted assumptions. These assumptions derive from an ideology and constitute "different lenses or windows from which to observe and make sense of social reality" (Maguire, 1987: 14). By placing the three forms of research side-by-side in a table, it is possible to compare their methodologies and (epistemological and ontological) assumptions (see next page).

EMPIRICAL-ANALYTIC INQUIRY

Currently empirical-analytic inquiry remains the dominant form of social science research. This type of research generally is grounded in positivism: the detached scientist asks a question or proposes a hypothesis, formulates a research design, and observes people from a distance, taking note of observable phenomena and verifiable, distinct facts. The underlying assumption is that "truth" is represented by these observations and facts. The intent is to produce replicable, technical information that causally explains and predicts human behaviour.

INTERPRETIVE INQUIRY

Researchers undertaking interpretive inquiry seek to capture meaning. They hold that different people have different, subjective perceptions of reality, and that there are therefore multiple realities and multiple truths. Researchers using an interpretative methodology choose a certain "phenomenon" to explore and usually interact with the selected subjects during

Table 1: Forms of Research

	EMPIRICAL-ANALYTIC INQUIRY	INTERPRETIVE INQUIRY	LIBERATORY INQUIRY (E.G., PARTICIPATORY ACTION-RESEARCH)
Purpose	Experimental science in search of causal explanations and laws in order to make predictions.	Interpretive science in search of subjective meanings and understanding in the world of lived experience.	Liberating (humanizing) science to create movement for personal and social transformation in order to redress injustices, support peace, and form democratic spaces.
Nature of Reality	A unique, real, social world exists to be studied by independent observers. Recognition is given to distinct, positive facts and observable phenomena.	Pluralistic and relativist (multiple realities dependent on individual's perceptions). People make purposeful acts based on their perceptions of feelings and events and so shape their realities by their behaviour.	"The social world is humanly and collectively constructed with a historical context" (Maguire, 1987: 22). People are active subjects in the world and are constantly in relationships of power: with the self, with others, with nature.
Nature of Knowledge	Objective truth exists. Objectivity (detached neutrality) and a value-free science is possible and desirable. Logical, deductive, rational findings. Knowledge is an end in itself.	Knowledge is a social, subjective construction. Language contextualizes the meaning of data. The method used justifies the knowledge produced.	People can change their levels of consciousness through learning. Objectivity does not exist. Fundamental human needs drive the process of inquiry. Holistic dimensions of knowing.
Methods	Experimental. Begins with a hypothesis. Validity and reliability are important. Defined time frame. People are "objects" of study. Quantitative data produced. Frequently dependent on complex statistics. Theory and practice are not directly related.	Interactive, sometimes close, processes between researcher and subjects are needed to obtain meaningful data and insights into human behaviour. Qualitative data produced, e.g., of methods: interviews, participant-observation, case study, grounded theory.	Dialectic of praxis (action-reflection process) within the historical and social context. Participants are active with ownership over questions, objectives, process. Many different, often creative, methods, e.g., interviews, stories, drama, songs, surveys.
Knowledge Produced	Technical; instrumental.	Interpretive; interactive.	Critical; spiritual.
Values Reflected	Deterministic application: people are prepared for a given form of social life (Kemmis, 1991: 99). Concerned with "maintenance or evolutionary change of status quo" (Maguire, 1987: 13). Greater efficiency and control over behaviour and the environment.	Humanistic application: "growth metaphor with self-actualization of individuals within meritocratic forms of social life" (Kemmis, 1991: 99).	Transformative process. Belief in people's capacity to work together for equitable decision-making and fair distribution of resources. Authentic commitment over the long term is needed to achieve individual and group-community empowerment.

a human event, such as a birthing experience or particular type of interaction between specific people. Researchers observe, listen, and talk, producing qualitative, written data. In order to grasp the realities of others and maintain objectivity, interpretative researchers will bracket off or set aside their personal values and perceptions. They may or may not make visible their race, gender, class, and personal interests during their inquiry and its analysis and interpretation.

Generally speaking, researchers want to deepen their understanding of the phenomena—what do people think, feel, and do during this event? What are their individual perceptions and interpretations of reality and how do these relate to and influence their subsequent social actions? The production of this interpretive knowledge is intended to strengthen understanding within and between people in the existing society.

LIBERATORY INQUIRY

The purpose of liberatory or critical research is the creation of movement for personal and social transformation in order to redress injustices, support peace, and form spaces of democracy. As in interpretative inquiry, the social world is seen as "humanly and collectively constructed within a historical context" (Maguire, 1987: 22). Human subjectivity, human consciousness, and power relations are central concepts. "Objectivity," in the usual sense of detached determination of observations and facts, is not possible. Rather, people are active subjects of the world; their needs are the point of departure for knowledge production and justification (not knowledge for its own sake). Participatory action-research is a type of liberatory inquiry.

CONTRASTING VALUES IN RESEARCH

From a liberatory/critical perspective, empirical-analytical and interpretive research, when based in positivism, insist on a "false dichotomy between personal politics and scholarly research" (Maguire, 1987: 9). Positivistic research deliberately divorces personal feelings, values, and motivations of the researcher from the research itself, regarding these as damaging to science.

Rahman argues that:

> Any observation, whether it is detached or involved, is value biased, and this is not where the scientific character of knowledge is determined. The scientific character or objectivity of knowledge rests on its social verifiability and this depends on consensus as to the method of verification. There exist different epistemological schools (paradigms) with different verification systems, and all scientific knowledge in this sense is relative to the paradigm to which it belongs (1991: 14-15).

Consistent with this argument, those undertaking liberatory inquiry (including PAR) contend that all research has an inherent subjectivity: the viewpoints of the individuals involved are always present, although not always visible.

The technical knowledge produced through empirical inquiry is used often used to expand "control over people and the environment" (*ibid.*: 16). When interpretive inquiry is approached solely in a "researcher-other" mode, it is criticized for setting power issues aside and largely supporting individual growth and adaptation *within* existing social life (Kemmis, 1991: 99). The people being studied are still treated as objects of research—as informants whose knowledge is "mined" for understanding by outsiders. Doing something about the contradictions and inequities found in the lives of the majority of the world's people is not seen as central to the inquiry. The three forms of research can be clearly differentiated by examining their underlying purposes.

PAR has not been considered research by those oriented to other paradigms because PAR researchers assume an involved, non-neutral stance that is characterized by a lack of control by the external researcher over the problem, the methods, and the timing, as well as a closeness between the participants and the external researcher. While these criticisms still surface from time to time, the approach slowly is gaining clarity and credibility.

While liberatory researchers reject positivism, they recognize the potential value of technical and interpretive knowledge that can be gained through empirical and interpretive inquiry. PAR can converge with conventional research, producing a more comprehensive, insightful knowledge. Ultimately, all researchers concerned about social justice grapple with the question, "Knowledge for whose benefit?"

Principles of PAR

PAR has multiple dimensions, each giving shape to the overall experience. Each PAR initiative will vary in content, emphasis, and evolution. To different degrees, depending on the group and their situation, people engaged in PAR processes:

- *Intend liberation.* Liberation is the eventual achievement of equitable communities and societies which are characterized by justice, freedom, and ecological balance.

- *Develop a compassionate culture.* They care about each other and strengthen their commitment to a shared struggle. Their stories, experiences, and values converge at certain points. They seek connections with each other and build a sense of community, person, and place. The creation of dialogue for an evolving partnership means addressing vital questions such as: Who are we? Why are we here? What do we believe? What is our purpose? How can we work together? The influence of mutual support and questioning, along with the organization of common work, promotes the awakening nature of doing PAR.

- *Participate in cohesively dynamic processes of action-reflection (praxis).* Such processes are organic, ever-changing, nonlinear, open, and continuous without predetermined time limits or fixed questions, and are interactive and unique to each group. People move between moments of analysis/education, investigation, and action—back and forth from one moment to another, sometimes staying with one moment for a lengthy period before moving on and at other times quickly passing through a moment. How something is done or discussed is as important as what is being done or discussed. "Each project persists in time and proceeds according to its own cultural vision and political expectations until the proposed goals are reached. Or it may end forthwith through impatience and/or repression" (Fals-Borda, 1991: 7).

- *Value what people know and believe by using their present reality as a starting point and building on it.* They recognize the vital importance of historical and current context and so retrieve past history and relate this information to present circumstances and structures. PAR groups honour popular knowledge, believing that people's feelings, beliefs, and personal experiences are vital ways of knowing.

- *Collectively investigate and act.* Groups work together on needs about which they have strong feelings. Through dialogue, they decide on their major questions and actions. Often very practical, their actions promote structural changes rather than personal adaptation to oppressive environments.

- *Consciously produce new knowledge.* The group embarks on a transforming path, making decisions, and taking on activities that are grounded in members' experiences. They seek new, in-depth understanding, using multiple—often creative—means for knowledge generation and documentation. Problem-posing as well as problem-solving techniques are used.

People are the essence of PAR work. Individuals with a common need come together to form a group with a specific purpose. Continual dialogue is critical to a PAR process and supports a climate of mutual trust, openness, and cooperation. The group will ask important questions, ones that it will "own" and investigate in order to understand the forces at play and the consequences of actions. These questions can appear in many different forms and can change over time. So long as an involved group remains intact (despite changes in individual membership), a PAR process can continue.

Self and group awareness grows through ongoing participation. As individuals and as a collective, people learn from experience, discovering many important lessons; emotional, sometimes painful, tensions appear along with moments of joy. They develop increased critical consciousness of who they are and the means for change.

PAR Is Praxis

People often tend to polarize ideas into dualities and present them in an "either/or" fashion, thereby implying a "black or white" choice between the ideas. This linear way of thinking frequently restricts critical analysis and the imagining of alternatives. Another approach is to think about dialectics: elements or forces acting in relation to each other. These can appear to be opposites and interact in tension (a tension dialectic) or can synergistically influence each other (a relational dialectic).

With dialectical thinking, people recognize the ongoing shaping and reshaping that occur between certain forces. For example, individuals make up a group in a PAR process. This constitutes a seemingly simple dialectic between an individual (in the group) and the group itself.

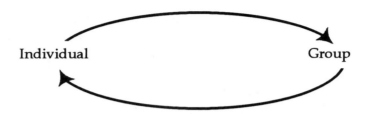

Critics of PAR point to the potential that "consensus tyranny," "tyranny of the group," or "tyranny of the committed" can overshadow consideration of individual welfare. It is essential to attend to the group as a whole and to the individuals as separate beings if any progressive momentum is to develop. This becomes increasingly difficult, however, when varying, often competing, motivations and interests arise.

The Dialectic of Praxis

The PAR approach developed primarily as a praxis, another type of dialectic. Individuals make connections with others, recognize a common need, and know it well. Then a praxis begins—reflecting, taking action, and reflecting on that action.

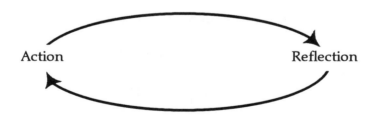

PAR develops a repetitive, transforming rhythm of reflection-action, action-reflection in which spiralling moments of "think, discover/recover, and do," "think, discover/recover, and do" extend into the future. Picture reflection and action as alternating in foreground and background. As one process is emphasized by a group, the other remains temporarily in the background. Later, this reverses. Later still, it reverses again, extending into the future for as long as the PAR group sustains itself.

Using only one process without the other is limiting. Reflection alone leads to informed passivity. Action alone leads to sporadic, sometimes chaotic, results with much potential for authoritarian controls over decision-making. PAR is a marriage of both processes: thoughtful reflection on reality corresponding with informed action. People integrate their cultures and histories, contribute their moral understandings, and find practical and intellectual knowledge. Strengthening their ability to develop sound judgment and make wise decisions, they move towards a new reality.

Theory and Practice

People's needs spark a PAR process. The group moves from a feeling level about needs, to thinking and understanding, to action and transformation. Changes happen, not because people become more informed (although this certainly occurs) but because their needs drive transformation. Once a process has begun as a result of people's needs, learning continues.

PAR groups develop unique learning cycles—what actually happens will be different for different groups. The experiences of individuals within a group also will vary. PAR processes are dynamic: ever-changing and ongoing, having no clear boundaries, and recognizing that transformative processes are never completed. This ambiguity is deliberate, as it allows responsiveness to the particular situation and the people involved.

A PAR process, building on what is known by the group members, begins at practice. The PAR group develops an evolving praxis between practice and theory: from the practice comes the theory; from the theory, the practice.

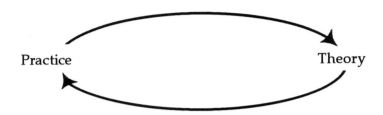

Theory, as a set of organized, related ideas, does not dictate practice. Rather, theory emerges when people hold a particular experience "at arm's length in order to mediate and critically comprehend the type of praxis needed within a specific
setting at a particular time in history" (Giroux, 1985: xxiii).

Praxis essentially refers to movement—intellectual, emotional, and practical movement. People undertaking PAR create movement from what exists now (the reality) to what could
be (a vision of the future) at individual and collective levels.
The focus is not prediction but possibilities.

PAR Is about Power

As young children, we initiate relationships in four overlapping spheres. A person develops within the self as a living,
spiritual being; dynamically with others; in relation to nature
(all elements of the environment); and mysteriously with God
(a greater spirit or Creator). Each sphere is a source of power,
the character of which is determined by history, context, culture, and personality. To understand personal and social identities and the means for change over the long term is to attend
to these different spheres, acknowledging their mutuality and
the influence of significant actions, attitudes, thoughts, and
feelings.

Events that touch the inner self can deepen and enrich the
soul, often in unexpected ways. Conversely, other events can
inflict individual and/or collective damage. This also lays down
a soul memory and affects all four spheres of relations.

POWER-OVER

The terms "power-over," "power-with," and "power-from-within" are from Starhawk (1987) *Truth or Dare: Encounters With Power, Authority and Mystery*, who refers to these three types of power and their relations to each other. The notion of "power" usually refers to "power-over" relationships based on domination and authority whereby a person or group can potentially determine the behaviour of another person or group. Power-over uses physical, economic, or social punishment—or its possibility—as the means for control. Generally, oppressive power relations in industrialized societies are taken for granted; few notice the power-over ideologies that are subtly and constantly communicated via casual conversations, literature, media, and more formal interactions. Power-over relations, consistently reinforced by attitudes of individualism and competition, characterize the majority of our institutional systems, including religious institutions, and use resources like money, food, information, caring, and love as the bases for control (*ibid.*: 19).

Dominating power intensely (and frequently at the subconscious level) affects all four spheres of relations. As a result, personal body, mind, and spirit become fragmented, manifesting in an inner violence that can have multiple symptoms of loneliness, obesity, addictions, depression, insecurity, lack of confidence, low self-esteem, passivity, and a willingness to obey. Current rates of physical, emotional, and sexual abuse of children, spousal battering, street crime, and school yard disturbances testify to fearful social violence, a reflection of authoritarian and controlling relations with others. Widely documented ecological damage points to severe disruption in human relationships with nature.

In a persistent search for clear cause-effect explanations and measurable, objective, and provable facts, researchers have effectively divorced spirituality from science. This type of controlling, intellectual pursuit denies people's need for close communion with a loving Creator and devalues the possibility of age-old wisdom. Many researchers feel embarrassed or fearful when faced with these intangible possibilities and dismiss them as irrelevant.

> We have so allowed the scientific approach to the world to
> take over our perceptions that we are afraid to mention such
> [spiritual] experiences for fear of being laughed at or vilified.
> When we do, we find ourselves stammering, struggling for
> words, never being able to convey in language to our own
> satisfaction exactly what it felt like or looked like or what
> sensations it evoked in us. We struggle against skepticism,
> our own as much as anyone else's, and in time we lapse into
> silence about them and a whole, valuable dimension of hu-
> man experience remains unsung and unvalidated (Butala,
> 1994: 55).

Inner Power

But other types of power exist. "Power-from-within" arises
from connections and bonding with other people and the environment and awakens a person's deepest abilities and potential. This type of power emerges to sustain us as human beings. It is felt in acts of "creation and connection, in planting,
building, writing, cleaning, healing, soothing, playing, singing,
making love" (Starhawk, 1987: 10)—acts that care for the soul,
providing strength and renewed meaning to life on earth.

Shared Power

"Power-with" is a form of social power, meaning people's
relationships with each other. It is power that is shared among
people who value each other as equals (*ibid.*: 8-9). This does
not mean that all individuals are viewed as the same or as
having similar personalities or identical capabilities. It does
mean that people seek to establish equitable (fair) relationships
and opportunities. Power-with relations allow mutual influence; people's perceptions are shaped and reshaped as they exercise respectful caring. Shared power is fluid, moving in response to the interconnected energies within a group. It is fragile and can be slow to develop, continually requiring disciplined listening, patience, and openness. Power-with also refers to a balance with nature: human beings living in harmony
with all forms of life.

THE POWER OF TRUTH: A SPIRITUAL JOURNEY

A moment of truth resonates: a silent but clear tone vibrates; an understanding dissolves, replaced with the glimmering new comprehension; or truth arrives abruptly, hitting like a ton of bricks, a physical sensation. Another echoing layer of the complexity of life is revealed.

Through their actions and reflections, group members determine and hold a shared truth about their reality. People experiencing a certain truth expand; they are "more" than before: more complex, more conscious, more knowledgeable, and perhaps more ready to enter into new learning and relationships accompanied by fresh questions and confusion. Based on their perceptions of "right" direction and considerations of possible alternatives, participants again take action. Individuals and the group can then re-examine their understanding and thus continue their production of knowledge.

The power of truth works in many ways. To have truth is to have knowledge that is based on understanding; a synthesis of feelings, thoughts, and actions. People shape their understandings of truth in order to make sense of their experiences and of the effects of their actions in *all* four spheres of relations. The power of truth can strengthen personal will to share power. Coming face-to-face with a truth can eventually affirm and fortify inner passions and capacities. Or shared power and inner power can merge within an individual or group—sometimes joyfully, often arduously—to unveil a truth. As we learn we deepen our understanding of the multiple interconnections and communications between all life forms, evoking a vital sense of human humility.

But this does not mean that there exists only one truth—*the* truth—to be discovered, a positivistic notion. Nor is it helpful to hold "respectful" belief in "multiple realities," a commonly held tenet of interpretative inquiry. This can mean becoming value-relative and thus immobilized for action. It also implies tacit permission for exploitation of people by more powerful people. Instead, there exists one reality with multiple perceptions and interpretations of that reality.

192 NURTURED BY KNOWLEDGE

There are many examples of wrongful (unjust) actions taken by individuals, groups, and societies who held a conviction of the rightness of their truth. A critical point here is that knowledgeable understanding and "right" action must take into account all four spheres of relations; to act unjustly towards others in gross or subtle ways is to neglect attention to this dynamic interplay of relations.

INSIDERS AND OUTSIDERS

There are two broad types of people involved in PAR: people internal (sometimes called "insiders," meaning those knowing and actually affected by the immediate circumstances and problems) and people external to the setting ("outsiders"). By entering into PAR, all become participants ("actors," "stakeholders," "players") working for a shared purpose of social transformation. By definition, since each comes from different realities, a dialectical tension is created between external and internal participants which "can be resolved only through practical commitment, that is, through a form of praxis" (Fals-Borda, 1991: 4). Each participates in and contributes to the PAR process. The sum of knowledge from both, for example, drawing from experiential and academic spheres of knowledge, can make "it possible to acquire a much more accurate and correct picture of the reality" (*ibid.*).

SHIFTING POWER RELATIONS

People in PAR work to shift power-over relations to power-with and power-from-within. Fueled by the forces of truth and understanding, this desired shift in power types ends controlling domination, dependency, and retaliative actions. This shift requires that participants grasp the nature of the power-over relations, which form most of our social identities, and clearly acknowledge the existence of dominating power and its effects, rather than denying its presence and impact or remaining fearful.

One overall goal of PAR is to achieve states of being, in which people are more aware, connected, heard, capable, and productive. People in a PAR process work to integrate shared, democratic power within the group and into society; to strengthen the personal, inner power of individuals; and to create opportunities for empowering moments of truth.

SECTION II: PAR Praxiology—The Methodological Process

CONSCIENTIZATION

Paulo Freire speaks of *conscientizacao*, or conscientization, as a process of rehumanization. Conscientization occurs when people "achieve a deepening awareness both of the sociocultural reality that shapes their lives and of their capacity to transform that reality" (1985: 93). Individuals learn to see existing social, political, and economic contradictions more clearly and to take action against unjust relations and structures. This strengthens people's conscious existence "in and with the world" (1985: 68).

THREE LEVELS OF CONSCIOUSNESS

Freire found three interrelated levels of consciousness: magical, naive, and critical (1973, 1985). People at the first stage of consciousness, the *magical*, are trapped by a myth of assumed inferiority and live within a culture of silence. More powerful others dominate and effectively control ideology, relationships, infrastructure, knowledge, and technology. These regulating factors merge, forming a living context that silences those without controlling power. Those living out this domination internalize the context—it becomes part of who they are and how they see themselves. They actively contribute to their own oppression. Strong behaviour patterns result, having been formed over a long period of time.

Feeling important and having magical explanations for their life circumstances, people at a magical level of consciousness cannot name their dehumanizing problems and so retain an attitude of passive acceptance: "Rather than resisting or changing the reality in which they find themselves, they conform to it" (W. Smith, 1976: 45; see also Zachariah, 1986, for a summary of Freire's work). People deny or avoid existing problems or define them in terms of physical survival. They do not and cannot question (W. Smith, 1976: 45).

People with a *naive consciousness* have reformist attitudes. They see the system as essentially sound and viable. Certain individuals or groups, however, have corrupted important policies, values, and norms. These people have caused existing problems; the fault lies with them. People with naive consciousness "see how the oppressor's actions are harmful and intentional, but they attribute [the] cause to individual maliciousness" (*ibid.*: 75) and try to defend themselves from the effects of this individual's or group's actions.

Sometimes naive people guiltily blame themselves for the violations of policies and norms, and may engage in "horizontal violence" whereby peers blame each other for problems rather than analyzing and addressing the issues. For the most part, those with naive consciousness want to become more like the dominant group and take actions that focus on self-improvement. Or individuals may appear outwardly different yet remain invested in replacing elements of the same power-over system—"tinkering" with or reforming the existing system—rather than truly promoting a shared power alternative.

Conscientization denotes a process of becoming more fully human and raising *critical consciousness* or self-awareness through collective self-inquiry and reflection. Freire noted two essential phases in the development of a critical consciousness: (1) unveiling the world of oppression and (2) expulsion of the myths created and developed by the old order. Gaining freedom means rejecting damaging images of one's own culture, replacing them with pride and acquiring abilities for self-reliance in order to function autonomously (Freire, 1973; 1990: 40).

In these two phases, people first develop a deepened awareness about their reality while paying particular attention to the existing social forces. With this critical awareness, they then "need to gain confidence in their collective abilities to bring about positive changes in their life situations and to organize themselves for that purpose" (Tilakaratna, 1991: 136). Any process of conscientization is difficult. People's images of themselves as subordinates form an inertia that may prevent their active participation in a research process that involves decision-making and actions (Rahman, 1991: 17). An additional consideration is that outsiders, however well-intentioned (consciously or not) can drive a process with their own ideas of what should happen.

BREAKING THE ECHO

People with critical consciousness recognize the necessity for actual transformation. It is not sufficient to tinker with serious, systematic problems. With probing dialogue and analysis of the immediate reality and the larger, more global context, they reject harmful ideology, take liberating actions, and develop a healthier sense of self-worth. They break their "echo" of the dominant group and "win the right to speak" (Freire, 1985: 73).

As people reflect, engage in dialogue, critically question relationships and circumstances, and gain new perspectives, they expand. Their spheres of awareness increase; they know that they know more. They become increasingly capable of taking thoughtful actions to alter their conditions. They continue to live in their world, expressing themselves through culture, work, and language, and recognize more conscious actions and relations.

Moments of awakening become determining events as a person's comprehension shifts and deepens. New lights of truth enter. Richer understandings are absorbed and integrated into one's being; this is a personal, transforming event, rendering the inner self more complex. A more dynamic self is in the making.

CHANGING CONSCIOUSNESS: *VIVENCIA*

Active participation in PAR is a lived experience that is called "vivencia" by Fals-Borda: "Through the actual experience of something, we intuitively apprehend its essence; we feel, enjoy and understand it as reality, and we thereby place our own being into a wider, more fulfilling context" (1991: 4). Ongoing participation helps people to be curious, take risks, understand complicated realities, and gain enough power to work for improvement. Important incidents occur that shift perceptions, resources, behaviour, and restructure relationships. When participants consciously follow the unfolding of these events from different perspectives, they produce knowledge.

How can *vivencia* be captured in a methodological framework? Those writing about PAR methodology usually cite the uniqueness of each experience, carefully explaining that no one model will capture every example of PAR. (See this chapter's endnote for a historical overview of methodology as written by various authors.) The models, when taken at face value without reference to the authors' philosophical text, generally imply that PAR largely is distinguishable from other forms of research by its action component, and by being carried out on a group basis (rather than by external researchers independently).

Writers sidestep or resist making governing generalizations from a specific case. While the actual, lived experience will emerge directly out of the context, needs, and people involved, it is possible to identify broad patterns and frame a PAR process.

Any framework will, by definition, simplify a given event or process. To be simple for the sake of clarity, however, does not mean being simplistic. A holistic model of PAR must capture *vivencia*, making room for the necessary dialectical tensions and conflicts. It will incorporate people as complex beings with differing motivations, individual capabilities, and feelings; varying moments of joy and anguish; multiple relations to each other; and shared needs for community and common effort.

Praxiology Framework

A PAR process consists of spiralling moments. Each present moment incorporates the past and circles around into the future. At times, people will be very much in the present, examining what currently exists or taking actions. Retrospective moments occur when the group members cast a look back, recovering and absorbing relevant history or analyzing what they did and interpreting the meaning of their actions and subsequent effects. At other times, the participants take on a future orientation as they deliberate alternatives and the potential consequences of their actions.

A PAR framework has cumulative moments of knowing self, seeking connections, grounding in context and focussing on fundamental needs, beginning praxis, experiencing conscientization, and awakening. Often overlapping or simultaneous, the moments occur within an individual or for a group, build on each other, and constitute movement. (See Figure 10.) The term "praxiology," used by O. Fals-Borda and M. Rahman (1991), provides a label for the methodology of participatory action-research.

The authors of the six case studies in Mexico, Canada, Honduras, Uganda, India, and Chile describe personal and social moments and actions. Rather than sweeping their feelings and questions under academic or intellectual carpets, the authors (all starting as external agents and outside voices to the settings) put themselves into the picture and reveal many of their own reactions, doubts, and learning. The writers of the Uganda and India chapters in particular tell of their struggles to deal with raw emotion, inner conflicts, and troublesome questions during their efforts to start PAR processes. They speak of guilt, embarrassing uncertainty, confusion, and frustration. The intention to do PAR, while perhaps establishing important groundwork and individual or team transformation, does not constitute PAR itself. In situations of disturbing struggle, we come face-to-face with ourselves: these are the most difficult moments of all.

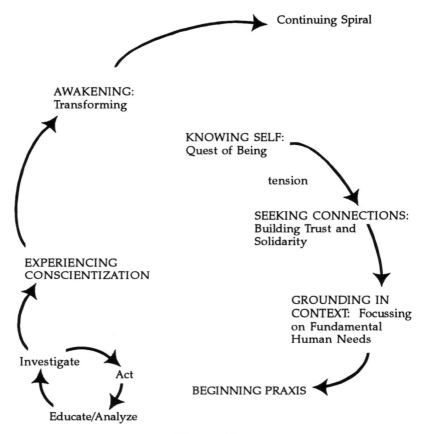

Figure 10:
Framework for Participatory Action-Research Praxiology

Knowing Self: A Quest of Being

A person initially enters into a PAR process in response to an inner tension. This tension could be a vital, clearly identified question or need; a vague, nagging doubt; or a genuine love of people and desire for social justice. The tension forms a personal motivation—a drive—and causes the person to seek out others and to look for something different. The personal sense of self is opening, ready in some way to receive stimulus: how much depends on the individual.

When I began writing my proposal, I had never heard of participatory action-research. I just knew that I wanted to go into a community, learn something, and give back to the people (Seymour).

As an educator with social conscience, Freire's understanding of the situation of disadvantaged people rang a chord with my own sense of service and mission. . . . These were exciting times in the re-democratization of the country. I felt a road was opening up ahead of me (Arratia in Arratia and de la Maza).

Deeply moved by Latin American native cultures and a desire to find her own roots within them, Isabel chose to live and work with the Aymara. She wanted to contribute but, more importantly, she wanted to learn and to respect and value their culture (de la Maza in Arratia and de la Maza).

Increasingly concerned about child rehabilitation services, I noticed that most rehabilitation efforts focussed on changing the child to fit the environment, rather than on changing the environment. . . . My research training was in epidemiology and biostatistics with experience in conducting experimental research studies. I wondered if cross-sectional surveys were able to elicit the needed information. I began to search for a different research methodology . . . (Law).

I became a farmer because my father was a farmer. I followed in his footsteps. I farmed land, grew crops, and milked cows . . . . The tradition of doing the same job over and over again and not completing a cycle of production made me look for something more in life. On the one hand, this tradition gave me a sense of security. On the other hand, it gave me a sense of insecurity—of not having sufficient purpose or meaning in life. The seeds of discontent had been there for a long time (Debbink in Debbink and Ornelas).

I began working for the United Nations in Latin America . . . my actions were to push papers, take planes, attend conferences, and write theoretical documents about the different realities of Latin America. Engulfed in my job, my relationships with people became closed; life centered around papers, budgets, and air tickets rather than around people . . . I was tired

and empty, but full of false privilege. It took me two years
to decide to work with *campesinos*. My new job as a school
principal in Mexico was repeating a sense of alienation. . . .
At last able to see this pattern, I decided to drastically change
my life (Ornelas).

Seeking Connections: Building Trust and Solidarity

Through deliberate or chance encounters, individuals find
each other, share stories and experiences, listen to each other
and start to make people-to-people connections. As a group
and as individuals, they recognize their common interests and
unique positions. They begin to know each other, moving from
isolation to connectedness with supportive linkages that can
strengthen motivations to participate.

> I was quite dependent on [Mr. Pande's] guidance in terms of
> how I should approach the village and recruit women to be
> interviewed. The way to "enter" a village still eluded me
> somewhat. I could physically get myself to the village, but
> whose door would I knock on first? (Seymour).

> I connected initially with the Aymara women and later
> started working with the men. There were times when I
> needed to be almost like a daughter—to just let people show
> me the way. Being a woman with two children myself was
> a fundamental basis for connecting with the Aymara women.
> "Sisterhood" does exist (Arratia in Arratia and de la Maza).

> All participants [of focus group discussions and individual in-
> terviews] stated that it was important to get back together
> in some way to discuss the information. In fact, several em-
> phasized that without getting back together, this research
> process would be similar to other research where they had
> completed questionnaires but had never received the results.
> These experiences had been very frustrating and they did not
> want it repeated during this study (Law).

> When we came to the town, I did not have any idea about
> what the community or the people were like. We began by

creating relationships with people, by learning or knowing the place. I did not expect to create serious friendships like we have of late (Nakuti in Spittal et al).

Feelings of trust, often slow to develop, between the individuals and within the group become vital as people test relationships and actions. Stories, values, and needs converge and create a sense of community and potential energy. Sustaining a sense of community means rejoicing when movement occurs—any type of movement that the group appreciates—enjoying and celebrating the moment.

> As *campesinos*, the people are conservative, guarding their small amounts of money, their little pieces of land, their few hens. They must be very careful. There is no confidence and little trust of outsiders. They did not accept us in the beginning (Ornelas).

> We asked ourselves, "What do we need to be a team?" We decided to allow ourselves the time to get to know each other. We went for walks and to dances. Spending this time together doing different things, we became a team. Everyone began to learn from actual practice (Ornelas).

> People wanted me to do something for them before they were willing to open up to me. They needed to trust me somehow. I did things for people so that they could see I was okay. . . . Through this sort of give and take, people began to realize that I was okay—that I wasn't there to just take from them or do things that would somehow have negative repercussions (Arratia in Arratia and de la Maza).

> We tried to help here and there, inviting [Josie] for a meal or giving her some things, but we could not really pull her out of that [starvation]. Godfrey and Addison have been active at burials, comforting, staying overnight, and sometimes actually putting the body in the hole. When Farouk was sick, Patti and I spent a lot of time just sitting with Josie. These things are really appreciated. There have been times when we have gone and found people in very poor moods but the time we spent helped to cheer them up. They would laugh, get out of bed, and maybe eat something. . . . The things we

have done are the normal things that any person would do in a family or a community. It is a part of participating in somebody's life (Nakuti in Spittal et al).

[T]he cows became an excuse to let our hearts grow as human beings. That is the beauty of the cows. At the beginning, the Canadians came to see their cows and, later, the Canadians spoke only of the people of Mexico (Ornelas in Debbink and Ornelas).

Grounding in Context: Fundamental Human Needs

The group, recognizing a common question or quest, must know their context well by consciously exploring the setting and becoming more aware of the various forces at play. Drawing on personal experiences as well as their thoughts and feelings, people work to understand their circumstances and its immediate and underlying determinants. This critical unveiling of context provides a deepening sense of place.

I arrived in the country with no plan of action, only with an open mind and heart to see and learn first, and to live in a little town called La Esperanza, (The Hope). . . . In doing participatory action-research, you enter into the process as an ignorant. You start by recognizing your ignorance and working with it. Only when you do this, can you truly "know" your own ignorance (Ornelas).

The people live in a dependent security. We understood that these people work from 4 a.m. to 11 p.m. for years on end. They have little decision-making power. The way of life of the oppressor becomes the model of life for the oppressed (Ornelas).

Over 80 percent of the people in this country know [AIDS transmission information] but are unable to change their behaviour because of the situation they find themselves in . . . . Women get into and remain in relationships that ultimately put them at risk. They fear that they have no alternatives (Nelson in Spittal et al).

"People want to show you in their own way that they are well nourished and don't have to finish everything on their plate. After you leave, what you don't see is that they literally lick the bones of the chicken that you ate." Samuel added, "You'll never see that because you are a foreigner" (Debbink in Debbink and Ornelas).

[The *campesinos*] cared very much about the cows, but they cared more about their own families and even their own families did not have salt. So why should they spend money to buy salt for a cow? (Debbink and Ornelas).

Energy points—issues or strengths that generate energy— sharpen in focus through dialogue and provide the first layer of "glue" holding the group together. The group does a preliminary exploration of this energy, clarifying its needs or issues, discovering its strengths, and setting provisional goals. Although each group's energy points and goals will differ, in a direct way they will relate to the nine universal, fundamental human needs: subsistence, protection, affection, understanding, participation, idleness, creation, identity, and freedom (Max-Neef, 1991: 32-33). Max-Neef describes these needs as universal, that is, applicable to all people. A tenth need, transcendence, he notes as also important but not yet universal.

TEA's initial thrust was to ensure that people had access to food. When the Aymara requested support, TEA responded by offering technical assistance programs and examining ways to acquire the needed supplies no longer produced by the Aymara. Without this base, the communities could not survive (Arratia and de la Maza).

Experiments with literacy alone have not been successful since people's economic needs take precedence over any purely "educational" effort. People's requests for further training are always oriented towards their subsistence (Arratia and de la Maza).

The group discussion centered on the "sorts of things" that make it easier or harder for their children to participate in everyday activities in a variety of environmental settings, including the home, neighbourhood, school or nursery, or community (Law).

The starting point for praxis is a focus on fundamental human needs as determined by the people who are impacted by the problem. To be grounded in context is to discover the vital importance of really knowing complex circumstances—an unveiling of reality as a tight web of causation and consequences. Many times, previously held assumptions break down as internal participants ("insiders," those living out the circumstances) and external participants ("outsiders") uncover the relevant operating forces.

> [Prior to arrival in India], I had concluded that health was a priority for villagers. This, however, might not have been the case. My whole project may have been based on a false assumption. I had not actually asked women what were the priorities in their community. . . . While time was a major problem, the real obstacles were my pre-set goals and expectations. I needed to realize that these could be adapted to a situation (Seymour).

> Indeed, it is sometimes hard to believe that a community exists in this troubling place. We were naive to assume that HIV/AIDS "interventions" would be easily accepted, especially given the ethos of fatalism and a culture of individualism (Spittal et al).

> I remember a boy who came to the office (he has since died) and asked what we were going to do for the community. I said we have not started to do anything, but maybe in future we will do something. He said, "You think the future is going to wait for us? We are dying—we want to benefit from what there is right now" (Nakuti in Spittal et al).

Beginning Praxis: An Open-Ended Process

A group in PAR works with a shared purpose for social change. Participants begin an ongoing praxis: a back-and-forth dialectic of reflection and action regarding their differing perceptions of a shared reality. Within a culture of dialogue, the group "problematizes," investigates important questions, and acts on its questions. The emergent phases of analysis/education, investigation, and action focus on naming and defining reality, finding out more about specific areas of interest, and working to create transforming possibilities. Equitable participation as a form of sharing control between members will vary from group to group in its development and dimensions.

> The team did not have any detailed plan, only our experiences and a small library.... We asked ourselves, "What kind of experience should take place?" Everyone rejected the usual workshops, courses, and seminars. Instead, we proposed a series of *pasantías* which, roughly translated, means "passing through" a social experience with a critical eye and a sense of personal fulfillment.... We wanted to ask the participants what they wanted to learn, to experiment with, and to reflect on together (Ornelas).

> [T]here are no rule books. Having set prescriptions or set patterns means that sooner or later the temptation arises to impose what is learned from one group onto another. Participatory action-research is much more than an instrument.... (Arratia and de la Maza).

Everyone needs to be critical, using all senses for discernment, in order to demystify events and clearly understand the actions taken by various parties. Participants often will recover relevant history and relate what has happened in the past to the present situation. Well-developed PAR initiatives give conscious attention to shifts in power, either on individual or group levels.

ANALYZE/EDUCATE: NAME AND DEFINE REALITY

In an analytical/educational phase, people define the nature of their situation. Freire calls this "naming reality" where people problematize their world, grasping a more comprehensive picture of their context and themselves by asking questions such as:

- What is the problem?

- How do we feel about this problem or need?

- What are the circumstances? (context, consequences)

- Why? (causes, history)

- Who says so?

- What could be? (vision of the future, goal)

- What do we need to learn?

We asked the participants what they wanted to do. They replied that they had come to learn, and inquired, "What is
your program?" We described the situation of the hospital
and the need to create "links" or closer relationships with all
the communities. We turned the question back to them,
"What do you really think? What are your needs? Your feelings? Your ideas? Link it to social participation and then tell
us what you want to know. . . ." Initially they protested this
approach. The next day, however, everyone returned with
specific ideas for the program. A trend became clear: participants wished to learn from each other, as well as from texts.
Individuals might approach learning differently, but we were
unified by the same reality (Ornelas).

Village assemblies provided the mechanism for village consultation and organization of community activities. As was
usual in the initial phases of TEA's programs, the assemblies
explored the utility, feasibility, and appropriateness of [an]
idea (Arratia and de la Maza).

Analysis of data took place throughout the study and was
shared continually with the participants and all members of
the research team. . . . Participants then reviewed their written information. They discussed several issues related to attitudes and physical barriers in the community, schools, and
recreational programs. A common concern was that parents
had to search for information and fight the "system" on their
own (Law).

I asked some [community] people what had happened to this tractor and why they did not use it. They said it was not theirs. I asked, "Who owns this tractor?" One person explained that it belonged to the village leader who had used it for only one year and then let it sit idle. Another thought it belonged to all of them. I asked what was meant by "it belongs to all of us." The man explained that five years ago the Ministry of Agriculture donated it to the community just before the elections. It belonged to the community but because the leader of the village was the only person who knew how to drive the tractor at that time, he took it for himself. He then sold the services of the tractor to the people at a rate they could not afford . . . (Debbink in Debbink and Ornelas).

[The Albertan] farmers began to ask other questions such as, "Why is the price of corn so low that the *campesinos* cannot support themselves?" The deeper questions of "why" emerged. They built a link between the low price of grain in Alberta and the low price of corn or beans in Mexico. Our awareness as farmers expanded beyond our own borders (Debbink in Debbink and Ornelas).

INVESTIGATE: FIND OUT MORE

People "wonder at their world" during an investigative cycle and focus on particular problems or needs, asking:

- What else do we need to know? What questions do we have?

- Why?

- Who says so?

- How can we find out more? What methods should be used?

- What are the risks?

- What new skills do we need in order to do this well?

- What does this new information/knowledge mean?

208 NURTURED BY KNOWLEDGE

Participants lived with the *campesinos*. We saw how people were carried to hospital and why they died. We slept with the lice and flies. We ate beans and tortillas, tortillas and beans. Being in the community was amazing. The people provided us with water, food, support, even dance—they gave us their hearts. Many of the professionals discovered their country. They experienced in a small but very significant way the life of the poor—and also its richness. The professionals lost their fear. As did the *campesinos* (Ornelas).

Everyone worked on something [in the community], for example, popular education or exploring an analysis . . . of what "research," "participation," and "action" meant for community people. They tried to catch the popular meanings for these concepts (Ornelas).

So much of Aymara life was affected by their lack of "legal" documents of all sorts — documents proving their birth, their age, ownership of their land, . . . This one word, "legal," was clearly what Freire would call a "generative term." It was a term that generated discussions about political powers that control various kinds of everyday situations. . . . Participants specifically asked TEA to assist them in understanding these rules and regulations and how to access funding for community development projects (Arratia and de la Maza).

After further discussion, parents decided to contact Participating Families–Ontario for more information. On December 9, 1991, a parent from PF–Ontario met with the participants . . . . Participants talked about how they could link up with Participating Families. They decided to form a group and draw up plans for the coming year . . . (Law).

The important thing was that we could increase our organization as a region, thanks to these cows. We could strengthen our understanding of people living in Canada. Most of the cows survived. Many Canadians, more than 100, passed through the houses of the *campesinos*. They experienced the conditions of the *campesinos*. They became more aware and more enlightened about the meaning of poverty, ignorance, social oppression, and social injustice (Ornelas in Debbink and Ornelas).

Five *campesinos* wanted to take the tractor and asked me if I would go with them. They had talked about it among themselves all the while. Three months had passed during which people learned what the tractor was for, why it was there, who gave it, and so lost their fear. They were clear about how this tractor was to benefit the community so that the previous pattern of one family owning it would not happen again. At that moment, the group had all the answers. They knew exactly what they were going to do. This one afternoon they decided to take the tractor—to take power for themselves (Debbink in Debbink and Ornelas).

ACT: WORK FOR CHANGE

The group will organize and work together to take action. They are "planful" within praxis, considering such questions as:

- What can we do (about the problem)?

- How? when? where?

- What are the obstacles/barriers?

- Who will do what?

- Who will benefit?

- What are the risks?

- How will we know if it works?

- What new problems will be created?

- How do we document our work and share our knowledge with others?

We had two days of discussion about what "referral" meant and all worked to design a referral process. Suddenly, just through talking with different people, three ambulances were found. . . . A short time later, 16 Citizen Band (CB) radios were donated. Everything was in place for the referral system. One night the CB rang: a woman was dying in childbirth in a mountain village. She was carried onto the back of a passing truck loaded with wood. An ambulance was dispatched immediately from the hospital with a doctor and blood. They met the truck midway. Both the woman and the child were saved. This *extraordinario* result was synergistic (Ornelas).

People questioned why there was not some type of hostel where women could stay before giving birth. Eighty-two *campesinos* decided to build a maternity home for the mothers beside the hospital. . . . They began digging the foundation that day and continued building every Friday. The hospital provided food, the Ministry of Health donated a truck for transportation, commercial enterprises donated roof tiles, and the churches gave beds (Ornelas).

Out of this first set of [leadership] schools came the legal birth in 1993 of a women's cooperative—Ccanthati, meaning "dawn." Based in Arica, it took over the marketing of the wool products, with a young Aymara woman trained as director (Arratia and de la Maza).

On January 20, 1992, participants formed a parent support and advocacy group, Participating Families–Cambridge. The goals for the group included advocacy, information gathering and sharing, and parent training . . . (Law).

Several days before the cows were to arrive, the [water truck] motor was still apart—all apart. I worried. . . . Everyone was about to help unload the cows and herd them to the nearby field. As the [cattle] truck backed up, I questioned a friend, "Where's the water truck?" He replied, "I don't know. They left at 11 o'clock this morning." It was then 11 p.m. and they weren't back yet. . . . As we were lifting up the door of the truck, up drives the water truck. The men got out. They walked up to us and said, "Huh! We're early. The cows aren't even off the truck yet!" (Debbink in Debbink and Ornelas).

After an action is completed or while it is in progress, the participants talk together, establishing a sense of distance with the event(s), and look retrospectively to examine what has happened, why, and their personal reactions. Many aspects of their questions and situations will become more obvious. Often individuals will gain insights and pose new questions and problems to the group.

RESEARCH QUESTIONS WITHIN PRAXIS

The participants' questions belong to them—they develop ownership over what is pursued and how. In PAR, research questions take many forms; they can be written down or remain oral, be formally or informally worded, and be simple or complex. They are not predetermined; no one person or subgroup enters the process with the major question(s) already specified on behalf of the group. The group's questions can change with experience over time as new, more relevant queries are discovered. Experience will be the significant teacher; as the group members gain experience, their work together will mature.

METHODS/TECHNIQUES WITHIN PRAXIS

Different people likely will have different responsibilities and roles at different times. It is not likely or usually necessary that every person be involved in *every* action taken (to do so probably would bog down the group's momentum). What is important is that the participants agree on how the major decisions are to be made and that they actively contribute to decisions regarding what actions and steps are to taken and how.

Some people, often an outsider initially, may take on facilitation roles or guide the use of different methods and techniques. These include oral histories, interviews, group discussions and dialogue, study circles, community surveys, community mapping and drawings, video productions, popular theatre, dramas, community radio, role-playing, dancing, brainstorming, feasibility studies, public meetings, open-ended surveys, fact-finding tours, exchange visits, songs, and story narratives. All of these generate data in differing forms.

The group analyzed what they wanted to do with the hospital. The proposition was to do a diagnosis of the overall situation. Different communities extended invitations to the

participants. . . . Participants started by talking with the
people about anything and everything. They performed
theatre, sang songs, played music . . . (Ornelas).

"Intentional nudging" was the principal method used to encourage participants to take control of the research process.
[The external research team] believed it aptly described a process by which we would bring participants together to listen
to each other, learn from each other, and decide for themselves what action they wanted to take (Law).

The "right" technique or method to be implemented can be
planned by the group beforehand or it can be of the moment,
arising from the group's context, questions, and interactions.
Sometimes the objective is to deliberately and carefully obtain
systematic information but, at other times, people want more
spontaneous, inventive ways to express what is happening in
their heads and hearts. Dancing, songs, popular theatre, and
poems, for instance, call upon the self in very different ways
than do community surveys or interviews. All constitute alternative types of knowledge—people (re)discover their abilities
to use and integrate different ways of knowing.

SYSTEMATIZING EXPERIENCES WITHIN PRAXIS:
FOG AND TENSIONS

When group members systematize their experiences—
organize the data, see it as sufficient, and do analyses while
identifying gaps and relationships—they build new levels of
understanding. Participants obtain and use information that
they identify as relevant and credible, thereby giving a social
validation to the content. Content that was "subjective," held
as an opinion or belief by an individual, gains "objectivity"
when it moves to being held in common by group members.

During a PAR process, doubts and uncertainties—periods
of fog—will arise when how to proceed is not clear. These periods are awkward but natural, causing individuals to find their
way and, if approached with persistent openness, they may
lead to vital, liberating discoveries.

I feel like there is something missing. I feel guilty—like there is something more I should do for them. If the project was to close now, how could we leave the community without feeling very guilty? It would seem like we have exploited them just to collect information, even though that was never our intent (Nakuti in Spittal et al).

I could not even begin to evaluate the [first group] meeting until several days later. I wandered around in a strange state of revelation and exhaustion. The revelation had come over me slowly, first during the meeting as an undefined sensation which later formed itself into the question, "What did you expect?". . . . I had taken a premature shortcut and was still reeling from the effects (Seymour).

[The cows] joined the flow of the river of *campesino* life. At the same time, these cows disturbed that life—created distractions. The cows caused divisions within the community . . . the cows became a political event. . . . Some *campesinos* wanted to sell the milk to other areas in order to buy feed for the cows. Others said, "No. Why should we sell the milk only to buy feed for the cow. We need to improve our own nutrition." An important tension arose. People began asking themselves vital questions related to the health of their communities (Ornelas in Debbink and Ornelas).

Engagement in PAR reveals individual motivations, fears, and intellectual positions. Tension and conflict also are expected. In the midst of analysis or planning, individuals face crucial moments. Some people will hesitate to continue or will withdraw. With internal or social changes, there will be provocations to emotional security, differences in opinion and beliefs, and risks to personal safety in repressive situations.

Back in their communities, [*pasantía* participants] are alone, fighting with their bosses, fighting with themselves, trying to explore their own minds in order to have a new knowledge. Those moments are the real tests. It is in that sense that we validate the knowledge of loneliness, solitude, and the confrontation with the self (Ornelas).

People want information but they also want more. They

want us to dispense medicines, condoms, and advice. Recently, an influential businessman in town criticized, "We are tired of you people. You just come and sit in the office and read your notes. This office should be kept open until 2 a.m. This is when people are the most active and they want condoms." Maama Mally used to ask, ". . . Why won't you give me my share [of rice] now before I die? By the time you start doing something for the community, I will already be dead." We keep telling people to wait. Some of them do not have patience any more. I get to the point where I am embarrassed. I see the people "getting finished" and dying. I feel guilty (Nakuti in Spittal et al).

Those in a PAR process struggle to build, not just resist or destroy. This creative capability is dependent on the participants' mental and emotional readiness, their willingness to risk and their ability to achieve agreement and mutual support.

The community could have asked several other people [to take responsibility for driving the tractor], but they went to the village leader specifically because they did not want to break solidarity with him. They wanted to demonstrate that they were not taking the tractor away from him, just making it available to everybody. They were, in a sense, not keeping power but rather sharing power. The village leader accepted (Debbink in Debbink and Ornelas).

Experiencing Conscientization

Conscientization is a moment of disintegration and reintegration when a person or group (often suddenly) understands elements of internal and social oppression and injustice.

If people share the same consciousness, they have a shared capacity to perceive, understand, and transform. They can create movement for social justice. At that moment, conscientization means action, a concrete action of consciousness. . . . When ideas, actions, and people are put together at the right time and place, something tangible occurs. Ideas become flesh and blood—it is a moment of truth (Ornelas).

What developed for all of us is that we came to know each other in a way that got rid of some of our myths—myths that families held about each other and myths that I held about families with children with disabilities. We developed a real sense of community looking at the commonalities that we shared. With greater respect, we saw that we could achieve more by working together as partners rather than alone as individuals (Law).

I heard a lot of talk about humanization, democratization, solidarity, retaking power, and so on. I was trying to piece together in my mind what all these words meant. During my first year [in Mexico], I worked on a project in one village. Now, much later, I understand what happened. [This tractor story] illustrates how the structure of society limits our thinking. As a community, as a group of people, we live in fear—the fear of confrontation, the fear of stepping out of where we are. . . . The point is that we all must determine our own reality and not have it predetermined for us (Debbink in Debbink and Ornelas).

After a while even [the stories] became too familiar for us. We were all feeling burnt out. . . . When the team got together at a retreat, . . . we put these huge manilla sheets with the illness genograms up on the walls. We were surrounded by them on all sides. All of a sudden we realized how bad it was and everyone went quiet. That was a turning point for the team. . . . We realized we were in the middle of a living hell here (Willms in Spittal et al).

Changes happen on an inner level. People reach a critical stage of consciousness where they see their relationships to each other and to their world and its structures in a revealing new light. Individual knowledge accumulates to become social knowledge as the group verifies what it knows and understands. Conscientization creates energy within and between group members.

Participants felt very strongly about the research experience. They stated that the research process, with the focus groups and interviews, had allowed them to express feelings so that could then move on to facilitate change on behalf of their chil-

dren. They discovered that others had similar issues and difficulties to face. . . . As a result, they were no longer as isolated (Law).

Even though I do not want to believe that sending the cows
to Mexico was a charitable act originally, I know it was. In
the beginning, deep down, I don't think I knew any different because of my traditional upbringing. . . . What began
as an act of charity by me and other Alberta farmers is becoming an act of solidarity. Solidarity is an act, not of giving,
but of common struggle—a fight for the common goal of
social justice. . . . This requires constantly stepping out of a
situation, looking at it, and reflecting on it (Debbink in
Debbink and Ornelas).

When participants went into the mountains for field trips,
they scrambled to rent, buy, or borrow mattresses. They carried these mattresses on their backs, not realizing at first that
the walk was long hours up and down the mountains. Lice,
ticks, and chiggers love mattresses. After the first night, the
mattresses were full of insects. The second night was hell,
and the third was to sleep with the devil! People then slept
as the mountain people sleep, but in the end, had to carry
the mattresses out of the mountains. Those mattresses
proved to be wonderful tools for learning. We understood
that elements of our beliefs and behaviour affect the reality
we experience. The most important lesson was realizing the
need to understand our own weaknesses and hostilities and
to have compassion with ourselves (Ornelas).

Awakening: Transforming

To awaken is to possess fresh creativity for construction.
Discovering a greater sense of self and other, individuals and
the group gain in inner and shared power. Each person has
enriched the soul, adding to the mystery of life. Each emanates
a greater spirit energy.

At the first group meeting when study results were shared,
some parents realized that all the parents had common experiences and concerns. Others stated that they began to feel

> committed to the parent group and the process of action when the same people kept coming. . . . It was at this point that they realized that together the parent group could "make things happen. . . ." Participants believe that they are making "slow but sure" progress. . . . "It's like we've launched a ship." Participating Families–Cambridge is viewed as their own creation (Law).

But with this act of transcendence, the group is again submerged in a unclear vision. If the group is able to continue a PAR spiral, it enters a new phase.

Vulnerability, risk-taking, trust, cooperation, openness with healthy suspicion, and patience with impatience are the spiritual dimensions of PAR. They are as necessary to the process as the dimensions of investigation, action, reflection, and dialogue. When we accept these qualities as part of the process, we also begin to integrate them more deeply into ourselves. We develop trust in ourselves as well as in others, allowing mutual caring and a fuller sense of place and personhood.

> A PAR process demands that the people involved are human beings. This does not mean that I necessarily like every person I work with, or even every group . . . [But] a love of human beings implies patience and respect. How do I put respect into action? Does it mean saying from a distance, "I respect people." Or does it mean living side by side with people and letting them teach me? (Arratia and de la Maza).

By actively working for change, we are transformed, deepening and rendering more complex our personal state of being.

> The women began to see themselves in a different light — as capable of assuming their new roles as heads of households (Arratia and de la Maza).

> The retreat helped us to understand why we were so burnt out. We underscored our commitment to do more. We realized that complex problems require complex solutions and to just intervene with primary intervention as we had initially proposed was naive (Willms in Spittal et al).

One of the most important lessons I have learned is that a commitment to transformation means long-term involvement. I have found a space where my earlier experiences as a Chilean woman can merge with my intellectual discoveries in Canada . . . my involvement with TEA has become a vital outlet for my own sense of commitment (Arratia in Arratia and de la Maza).

I found the writing process [of this chapter] to be a very painful process. . . . The editors asked me to . . . "put myself into the story." As an academic, I am not encouraged to do that elsewhere, because then I open myself up to questions about my objectivity. The writing process made me realize how ingrained the positivistic, quantitative world view was, in some respects, still in me (Law).

To enter into PAR, the "permanent dance with yourself," is to reconnect the self with others and with the universe. A time of awakening leads to unprecedented possibilities, extending the spiral and intensifying commitment.

We initially believed that we were accountable to the community, but accountable only in the sense that we would check whether we got the stories right. Another form of accountability was urgently required. We needed to respond to community needs in a more immediate, interactive manner (Spittal et al).

When I first returned from India, I could only think about the project in terms of what I had not done. . . . Then slowly and reluctantly, I sorted through the data and wrote a report and this chapter. Over time I was able to reframe my work and accomplishments, legitimizing an incredibly valuable, intense learning experience (Seymour).

What my experience has made me think about is the nature of participation and the need to do more than just give back information. We needed to be partners in looking at what needs to be researched. I have changed what I study and how I do it (Law).

Living and working over a seven-year period with Mexican

campesinos and later having additional experiences in other areas, I have regained richness. . . . I understand that it is far more important to hold a strong commitment—life then becomes a poem, not written, but lived. In the uncertainty of life . . . the only certitude is that I chose to work with the poor to defeat social injustice (Ornelas).

SECTION III: Developing Movement

In the industrialized world, we participate in the domestication of others and of ourselves. We agree to the taming of the human spirit. The draw of false security—the promise of insurance for what is not insurable, life in life—dulls and finally destroys what we as breathing, thinking, creative, and compassionate people are capable of. We submit to penetrating messages from professionals and the ever-present commercial media that tell us how to be, what to do, and how to do it. The challenge of imagining and thereby creating a fulfilling, synergetic life is replaced by a reliance on expert opinion, procedural manuals, legitimated standards, and measurable criteria. We swallow but cannot thrive on this pre-chewed material, the bland pap of professions.

> In mass society, ways of thinking become as standardized as ways of dressing and tastes in food. Men begin thinking and acting according to the prescriptions they receive daily from the communications media rather than in response to their dialectical relationships with the world. In mass societies, where everything is prefabricated and behaviour is almost automatized, men are lost because they don't have to risk themselves (Freire, 1985: 88).

In a strange contradiction, when we demand secure outcomes—false cushions of protection—we actually cocoon ourselves in anxious insecurity. By not entering into the complexities of power and relationships, we wrap ourselves in layers of self-centered uncertainty, deadening our abilities to hear, think, create, and care. Too often we then treat ourselves and others

violently, manifesting our internal state through subtle or bla-
tant humiliation and control. We are easily manipulated by others because of inconsistent belief patterns and an insecure identity (a security of self—I know who and what I am and we are—
which is very different from the false security of things).

Who are the oppressed? Who are the oppressors? These
are threatening questions, but it is possible that we are simultaneously both. When we have many roles (as workers in the
community; as employees in institutions; as parents and
spouses at home), our multiple spheres of interaction overlap,
and are sometimes fragmented and complicated. Our complexity is such that we can be both oppressed and oppressor, liber-
ated and liberator. What is consciously believed and enacted
in one realm may not be consciously believed and enacted in
another. Critical insight derived at home or elsewhere may take
considerable effort to develop at work, or may not appear at
all. These are our contradictions.

Expelling Invisible Oppressors

The invisible oppressors—the internal states of fear, guilt,
loneliness, emptiness, arrogant self-interest, or bored disinter-
est, what Boal called the "cops in the head" (1995: 8)—represent a type of suffering different from the blunt, physical repression found in many settings. But they constitute suffering
nonetheless. Found among both the affluent and poor, these
are the inner demons that "whether exposed to the light of day
or fled into the shadows, are always alive, always active, and
all the more terrible the darker they are, all the more uncon-
trollable for dwelling in darkness" (ibid.: 34).

When we carry invisible oppressors within, we become
alienated from ourselves and from others. We are weakened,
developing an undesirable insecurity that diminishes our human potential. This inner violence, affecting all those around
us, is reflected in anxiety and timidity, in a resistive arms-
crossed silence, in an over-active "fix-it" attitude that refuses

to stop and think, or in condescending remarks that humiliate.

> Every relationship of domination, of exploitation, of oppression, is by definition violent, whether or not the violence is expressed by drastic means. In such a relationship, dominator and dominated alike are reduced to things—the former dehumanized by an excess of power, the latter by the lack of it. And things cannot love (Freire, 1973: 10-11).

We live in an intricate world of multiple roles and interactions that cut across gender, class, work, education, culture, and race. The spheres of possibility cross over: sometimes I limit myself; many times I am controlled by others; at still other times and in other realms, I am free. This is why it is impossible to say "this person has a critical consciousness" or "that person has a naive consciousness" and be done with it. Our blind and weak spots are always present and, although they may shrink or move depending on roles and circumstances, they prevent us from ever seeing fully. Thus, to know clearly is to always retain a shadow of doubt. This is a doubt of wisdom: we can never know all.

But it is fair for individuals in a group to say "in this particular time and setting, we demonstrated a critical consciousness. We questioned a problem, unearthed root causes, understood personal and social forces to a deeper degree, and did something about our situation." While it is not possible to simply classify individuals into categories of consciousness, an experience of conscientization creates a lasting memory in a person; it alters the sense of self and, with the taking of an action, changes reality. The individual grows in awareness. Freire observes: "A deepened consciousness of their situation leads men to apprehend that situation as an historical reality susceptible of transformation. Resignation gives way to the drive for transformation and inquiry, over which men feel themselves to be in control" (1970, 1990: 73).

To live with the invisible enemies is, in part, to suffer at one's own hand; to uncover this oppression is to suffer, and then heal. This healing develops compassion for one's self and for others. To suffer, heal, and feel compassion is to grow more peaceful at heart, to find a freedom of solidarity, to have more unity in one's self, and to be more united with the others.

The important question is not about validity or proof (in fact, the only fact is that no one knows; nothing is absolute), but about protest and freedom. As Freire says, it is how to unveil the world of oppression and expel the domesticating myths and damaging images, or to put it another way, how to create liberating movement within the person and between people. In the words of Krishnamurti, "If I want to live a really peaceful life in which there is deep abundance of love, all the violence must go. Now what do I have to do?" (cited in Boychuck Duchscher, 1994: 20).

Six Ways of Knowing

There are five ways of knowing found in a person's mind, body, and spirit, and there is also the way of dreams—the "oneiric"—in the subconscious dimension. The ways of knowing connect so that messages flow between them to form an overall impression. To understand something in a comprehensive way is to give attention to the knowledge that comes from these different dimensions.

Authors have labelled ways of knowing and learning differently. For example, Griffin (1988: 105-131) discussed six interrelated capabilities that enable learning: emotional, relational, rational, metaphoric, physical, spiritual. De Bono (1985, 1991) used six colours to represent ways of thinking: positive and logical, facts and figures, emotion and intuition, negative logical, creativity, control of thinking. Boal (1995: 21-22) spoke of the affective (emotions, sensations, and thoughts) and the oneiric (dream) dimensions. The ways of knowing discussed in this text draw from both Boal and Griffin.

Most formal schooling focusses on the rational mind, the intellectual ability to gather, organize, and use information— to analyze situations. But the other ways of knowing are equally important. People vary in their attention to, and their use of, the different ways, sometimes relying much more on the ones that are developed and familiar.

The ways of knowing emerge from six sources:

The rational mind. The rational or intellectual way of knowing is the human capacity to think, to analyze, and to use logic (Griffin, 1988: 116), with resulting thoughts and ideas.

The creative mind. The creative way of knowing is the capacity to remember and imagine, to create. (Griffin calls this the metaphoric capacity.) Memory (the storehouse of ideas, sensations, and feelings) and imagination (the "premonition of reality") are complementary parts of the same psychic/creative process (Boal, 1995: 21).

The heart. The heartfelt way of knowing is the capacity to feel. People's emotions affect the quality of their interactions and their work and greatly influence learning. If unattended, negative emotions, such as feeling threatened, frustrated, fearful, or hurt, can hinder learning or result in avoiding, blaming, or attacking behaviours. People will often resist a change if they anticipate having negative feelings as a result of the change. In Menlo's words: "Persons do not resist change; they seek it as part of their inherent nature. What persons resist are expected consequences which will diminish their self or social esteem" (cited in Griffin, 1988: 109).

Accurately naming a person's emotion and accepting it for what it is often is a liberating act and can open up room for change. Positive emotions such as happiness or excitement can help people find meaning and enjoyment and can provide guidance for choosing the right alternative at the right time (*ibid.*: 108-109).

Chisholm spoke of "emotional collisions" in research. Most participants, in particular the external researchers, underestimate the conflicts and confrontations that will appear in a participatory research process, as well as the amount and types of personal emotions aroused when we see "ourselves as human beings" (1990: 253). She suggested that many researchers will take safe refuge through abstract theorizing. Emotions, when recognized and incorporated, are an enrichment and not a weakness of research. They can help people to recognize contradictions and confusions and to gain clarity about power relations.

The body. The physical way of knowing is the capacity to sense and to move, to do. We use our five physical senses of sight, sound, touch, taste and smell as ways of obtaining information about the outside world. Another way of knowing is intuition—our sixth and often ignored sense that helps us to immediately apprehend, to know the intangible without being told. Intuition is often felt as a physical sensation at "gut level," which is then picked up by the mind and heart. In the bodily dimension, people have physical sensations, and use their hands and feet to move in action.

Dreams. Everyone dreams. The dreamful way of knowing are these messages from our subconscious dimension, the layered memories of the soul that rest in another realm of consciousness. But like a newspaper delivered daily to our door, we can choose to read them or not. Our capacity to dream allows us to penetrate beyond physical reality and to collapse present, past, and future into one domain. In a dream all is possible, all is real, and the bizarre is frequently the key to interpretation.

The spirit. Spirit is the life force that is present in all living things. In one aspect, spirit is about a person's energy (or "chi") which circulates in pathways in the body, much like blood circulates in vessels. Energy flows (within a person and between people) and, when flowing well, is cleansing and healing. The intensity of the energy flow, whether drained or rejuvenated, affects and reflects a person's well-being.

Another aspect of spirit relates to willful purpose. To have a healthy spirit is to be purposively on a good path, a path with heartfelt reason. The spirit-led way of knowing is the capacity to *be* and to have energy for purpose in life.

In combination, the different ways can check and balance each other, keeping participants from "going overboard in one direction" (Griffin, 1988: 125). People, attending to and integrating all of six ways of knowing, discover and form their spirituality—the meaning of being human. Spirituality is of wonder and of understanding, of being connected to all living entities.

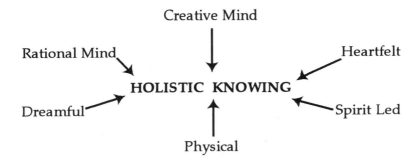

PAR developed as people worked to alter relationships based on domination and repression, the oppressor and the oppressed. Writers about PAR stressed praxis, the importance of using critical analysis and of taking political action to change the control of resources and decisions. Analysis and action, the rational and the physical ways of knowing, were to redress social coercion and suffering. Most case studies or discussions of PAR have this emphasis (see, for example, Park's et al. *Voices of Change*, 1993, or Fals-Borda and Rahman's *Action and Knowledge*, 1991).

A fuller understanding emerges from giving conscious attention to all six dimensions of knowledge. This is especially important for dispelling the invisible oppressors that are lodged in the identification of self. Those engaged in PAR can heal by banishing the internal messages that diminish the human spirit: changing "I can't" to "I can," and "We are not capable" to "Let's do it."

PAR Elements: Participation, Dialogue, Energy, and Strategies

Participation

Active participation in any group process is, by nature, political. To truly participate in a reflexive process is to have authentic influence (a measure of control) and involvement—in making decisions, taking actions, using resources, and obtaining information. These elements define the political character of participation. (The amount of influence or involvement will vary from person to person, group to group, and situation to situation, thereby differentiating levels of participation. There are lesser degrees of involvement, for example, when individuals participate by receiving benefits, giving information, or being consulted. These may be very appropriate in specific situations but must be distinguished from authentic or full participation.)

Individuals who freely resolve to participate are likely to desire meaningful actions and dynamic interactions with others. For whatever reasons, they are willing to invest *of* themselves in the group and are open to challenge and movement, although probably not to equal degrees. This resolution promotes active learning: the transformative processes that develop people's capacities as they discover and use new-found abilities.

Activity overcomes passivity: people initiate exploration of ideas and circumstances, instead of "waiting to be told what things mean and what to do" (Shor, 1992: 18). Because "consciousness is reflexive" with reality, "[w]e can reflect on reality, values, words, interpretations in ways that illuminate meanings we hadn't perceived before. This reflection can transform our thoughts and behaviour, which in turn have the power to alter reality itself if enough people reconstruct their knowledge and take action" (*ibid.*: 22).

Participation helps people to extend beyond what they already understand and do. For those venturing into uncharted waters, authentic participation ultimately is based on trust.

Trust in one's self, in others, and in the group's purpose builds a stronger foundation for participation, one that can help us discover what it means to live with a good heart.

But this is not always the case. People may well have full participation within a group but be intent on harmful or dangerous practices (for example, street drug gangs). The character of participation is only one dimension; the group's motivation and intention are equally important.

DIALOGUE

Individuals talk together. Their "talk"—verbal and non-verbal communication—becomes "dialogue" when they interact reflectively and reflexively, each desiring to be open to the others, to understand the self and the others; each influencing the others. They allow their thoughts, feelings, and questions to surface in order to deepen their insights, interpretations, and consciousness. People in dialogue become more fully aware of underlying assumptions, emotions, and the various dimensions of a situation or idea. They examine their own beliefs and actions as well as those of others, at some point realizing that "the challenge of examining the outside world is never as difficult as the examination of the world within" (Galbraith, 1991: 4).

Those in dialogue develop a "stream of meaning" flowing between them, allowing "the softening up, the opening up of the mind" and heart (Bohm, 1993: 10, 13). As a group, they share meaning and a common consciousness of their outer and inner realities, imagining what is possible in a more holistic, comprehensive way, and thereby achieving greater clarity and acceptance. They move topics under discussion from a practical lived base into the abstract realm of understanding. The reverse also can occur: abstractions can become concretized, practical, and tangible.

> Dialogue requires an intense faith in human beings; their power to make and remake, to create and recreate. . . . Founded on love, humility and faith, dialogue becomes a horizontal relationship of mutual trust . . . [that] cannot exist unless the words of both parties coincide with their actions.

Nor can dialogue exist without hope. Hope is rooted in our human incompleteness, from which we move out in constant search, a search which can be carried out only in communion with other people. . . . Finally, true dialogue cannot exist unless it involves critical thinking which sees reality as a process, in transformation . . . [and] constantly involves itself in the real struggle without fear of the risks involved (Freire, 1970, 1990: 80).

Energy Points

When people have strong feelings about a need or a problem, they are far more likely to take action on it. While working in literacy education in Brazil, Paulo Freire developed a method to stimulate the energy of a group or community in order to break through apathy and create change (Freire, 1970, 1990; Hope, Timmel, and Hodzi, 1984: 40; Wallerstein and Bernstein, 1988: 383). The method is a potentially transformative one if a group directs previously unorganized energy towards a common purpose.

A facilitator, or preferably a team of facilitators, determines the generative themes of a group or community—those themes that generate or elicit energy. This often is done through a listening survey or other methods in which facilitators listen and observe carefully: what do people do, who does what, why is it done that way, what issues arouse emotions, and what words are used to describe the issues (Hope, Timmel, and Hodzi, 1984: 40).

The facilitators critically analyze their findings in order to determine the major generative themes. Each theme is seriously considered from economic, political, and cultural perspectives in order to produce appropriate codes. A code represents a generative theme; it can be a picture, poster, story, song, play—any creative means of conveying a familiar yet vital problem. A series of codes can capture several generative themes or portray one theme from various angles, conveying the interrelated dimensions of most problems. A code is different from an information-giving tool—for example, a social marketing poster tells people to wear bicycle helmets while a code might portray a problematic situation centered on street accidents. Codes raise questions; they do not suggest solutions.

The facilitators present the codes to the participants with the purpose of focussing attention and stimulating discussion within the group. Good codes will pose problems and provoke questions in the minds of participants, prompting them to probe and discover for themselves and to imagine different possibilities. When people suddenly come to life—alive with emotion, whether it be excitement, anger, worry or fear—they have touched upon a generative theme: "There is the energy that could lead to action. Of course, many discussions filled with feeling do not lead to action. They waste away in fruitless grumbling or wind around and around in circles, unless the energy is gathered, channelled, and directed" (*ibid.*: 57).

ENABLING STRATEGIES

People can combine critical inquiry (conscientization) *with* personal growth by engaging in praxis and giving attention to human relationships. Participant ownership of decisions reflects a belief in people's capacity for self-direction and allows for the building of a strategic sequence of activities that is steadily responsive to the evolving needs and the rationale of the group. The creation of enabling space for learning can be achieved through different strategies, activities, and techniques (tools).

A satisfying activity provides an opportunity for the expression of feelings and thoughts related to a particular area of interest. People gain insights and guidance for making decisions by exploring the activity and how it relates to their reality and experiences. Encouraging creativity and risk-taking, an enabling or growth strategy awakens the imagination to new possibilities and allows new roles and abilities to be experienced, helping participants to develop confidence and esteem. "A growth strategy," as described by Srinivasan, "does not confer or bestow power but simply summons it forth, helps it to become manifest, causes it to rise as in a leavening process, helps to germinate and brings to fruition what is already there in a latent or dormant state" (1992: 68).

Well-chosen activities that incorporate a variety of techniques allow people to focus by providing a degree of structure within openendedness, an often-needed reference or starting point. An activity's design will depend on what is being considered; for example, different activities can stimulate an exploration of feelings, an analysis of a situation, or the making of a decision about priorities. Activities can get people up and moving or they can create quiet space, a period of no agenda or of silent reflection. The objective is to introduce non-directive activities that:

> ... [E]voke a wide range of attributes, capacities, and dispositions including creativity, observation, investigation, projection, problem analysis, problem solving, planning and evaluation. To the extent that activities are meticulously designed to serve these purposes, we have found that learners emerge from the experience with increased capacity for self-direction. There is nothing "instant" about this process. It has to be built cumulatively, brick by brick (*ibid*.: 50).

The challenge for the facilitator and the group is to match the moment with the right means.

External Agent "Doing" PAR: Challenges of Participation

PAR is a long process, requiring a sustained commitment; involvement most often will be intense, bound with tensions and risks. Crossing notable cultural and geographic distances causes bewilderment at times—a disorientation—particularly in the initial stages of entering an unknown community.

> The first three weeks in Banaras were probably the most stressful weeks of my life. The environment alone, although fascinating, was overwhelming—a chaotic mosaic of bizarre noise, sights, and smells. My existence had a surreal, dreamlike quality over which I had no control. I fluctuated between

enjoying these strange new experiences and being immobilized by anxiety at the thought of carrying out the project. .
. . I had no idea how or where to start (Seymour).

Working through an interpreter and across cultures and
across socio-economic strata made my task complex and frustrating (Seymour).

Knowing the context and understanding people's perceptions,
circumstances and relations adequately takes patience, energy,
and a certain courageous curiosity.

One step [would be] to understand the area itself. That could
take a year or longer. I would have to start small and get a
grounding of what the area is like and what things could be
possible. Otherwise, I would again find myself throwing
darts, hoping to hit something important (Seymour).

PAR requires that I become almost like a child in the other
culture, figuring out where people are coming from. Who
are they? What do they want out of life? What is their vision? . . . I have to listen first and then relate to people with
the knowledge that I bring as an "outsider" (Arratia in
Arratia and de la Maza).

In PAR, the external agent becomes a participant in an
evolving group process. Academic researchers accustomed to
other forms of research frequently find this to be an unnerv-
ing loss of researcher control over the question(s) to be pursued.
Jumping into the unknown and not having pre-set procedures
or methods can be equally disturbing.

I found it tremendously hard initially to not know where
things would go or what would happen (Law).

I was accustomed to having control over the research process
and study results. . . . The greatest problem in assuming the
role [of facilitator] was to listen, understand the participants'
stories, and accurately use their ideas as the basis for further
discussion. I struggled at times not to allow my thoughts to
bias action decisions. Not knowing where the research pro-

cess would lead was difficult, as was avoiding the temptation
to push things too quickly before the intentions of the participants became clear (Law).

Engagement in PAR challenges the usual notions of participation: it is no longer sufficient to just verify information or
data, interacting with individuals or a group from the periph-
ery—to "check whether we got the stories right" (Spittal et al).
An expectation of participation can cause inner and methodological turmoil in external researchers by raising serious
doubts about their prior assumptions or about decisions to not
take particular types of action. Conflicting feelings of confusion, guilt, or embarrassment within the external researchers
become woven into the stories of the other group members.
External researchers may find themselves pushed to admit (at
least to themselves) that they do not know what to do next
(often a troubling plight for those reporting to or dependent
on agency support and/or funding).

> Our methodological dilemma was deeply personal. We are
> emotionally attached to these friends. No longer strangers,
> we had to do something. Our intent had always been par-
> ticipatory, but so far our process had not been (Spittal et al).

> Embarrassed, we know that we must give them something
> more tangible than our time, our support, and our friendship
> (Spittal et al).

> Despite my feelings of having been misled by CIDA, I also
> felt an enormous burden of responsibility towards the agency.
> I had to do something positive with the grant. I felt guilty
> and doomed for failure. These feelings, waxing and waning
> over the following ten months, became my guiding force. In
> fact, as the project work began in the village, I took on added
> guilt, feeling that the participating women would gain noth-
> ing from the project. I would become yet another researcher
> floating into their lives for a fleeting moment and then float-
> ing out again (Seymour).

Meaningful social change takes time and considerable effort. It is possible to know this on an intellectual level and yet not comprehend what that really means until actually working in a specific situation. Time pressures take over; an anxious urgency for results can predominate, undermining participation.

> My time was running out; I felt that if I did not take this rather unilateral approach [of almost didactic presentation of information], the information would not be disseminated and nothing would be accomplished. The decision left me feeling somewhat dissatisfied, realizing that this approach was far from a participatory one. I felt trapped by time, allowing it to dictate my approach and expectations. . . . The process of discovery and change was really just beginning for the women and myself as I left Akhri (Seymour).

The difficulties are compounded when people live or work within institutional or state restrictions, extreme poverty, or slow cultural disintegration characterized by hopelessness. At a minimum, these settings require an experienced team of external researchers.

> Participatory action-research is about creating something sustainable for the future. Many people in this community think only in terms of the present because the future is not predictable. . . . The people who have helped us understand this disease as a social entity are the ones who will not benefit. Maama Mally is dead. Farouk is dead. PAR is difficult because it takes time. It takes a long time. . . . PAR has worked in communities where there is a sense of future and time for empowerment and mobilization. Everyone in this community believes: "We are dying and getting finished." This has tremendous implications for what we do in the next phase (Spittal et al).

Multiple Roles of Catalytic Agents

Those initiating PAR require a persistence to work against great odds, coupled with an urgent will to learn. They recog-

nize that strong forces work against or negate the possibility
of needed changes, and they question how to take micro-level
momentum to a macro, more global, level. Just because
changes are necessary does not mean they will actually happen.

> Often our efforts seem to be imperceptible either because so-
> cial change is so slow or because the tidal wave of modern-
> ization, consumption, and increasing migration from the ru-
> ral areas into the cities is overwhelming (Arratia and de la
> Maza).

Doing PAR requires a commitment beyond a curiosity about
a phenomena or a shared common interest like a hobby or casual pastime. Interpersonal relations and communication are
at the crux of PAR; only with love for humanity and the Earth
do people create social movement and sustainable ways of living.

> From my experience, when team members start criticizing in
> destructive ways, when people stop loving each other, the
> team is destroyed and so is any action. Without love we do
> not create movement (Ornelas).

> My inner being was changed by living and working with the
> Mexican *campesinos*. I discovered how to give to others be-
> cause I love people and want to share in the struggle, not be-
> cause I feel guilty or want something in return (Debbink in
> Debbink and Ornelas).

Within cultures of oppressive silence or naivete, collective
efforts to meet, analyze, and take actions are not likely to happen spontaneously. People's state of "powerlessness prevents
them from organizing themselves or doing research" (Park,
1993: 9). Among disadvantaged populations, an external individual or team generally initiates a PAR process, usually taking on vital, catalytic roles. Of course, organized and experienced groups have very different internal needs from those of
unorganized individuals who are living in silence or are stuck

in enertia. Their starting points for PAR processes differ considerably.

Catalytic agents, people who actually can be either external or internal participants, take on roles that shift in emphasis over time. Both Fals-Borda and Tilakaratna in *Action and Knowledge* (1991) use the terms "external" and "internal," "catalytic agents," and "stimulating PAR." While not universal terms in PAR literature, they best express important concepts for discussion.

The roles of these agents can include becoming grounded in (knowing) the setting, organizing a group, facilitating meetings and events, analyzing information or data for return to the group, documenting processes and events, advising as resource people, training other facilitators, providing moral support, linking local or regional groups, as well as monitoring personal assumptions and behaviour. Catalytic agents strive to use specific skills and roles appropriate to the needs of the PAR group and the overall circumstances. Their personal characteristics of personality, skills, experiences, and attitudes affect the development of their roles and relationships.

Lessons for Stimulating PAR Processes

Experiencing a PAR process results in often difficult lessons. Important points for stimulating PAR are:

Know your own philosophical basis. Consciously develop a learning attitude. Clarity regarding personal values and beliefs is important because it provides personal grounding and an overall direction. Catalytic agents as participants in a PAR process are not neutral in the conventional research sense in order to maintain a desired distance or objectivity, but they are slow to declare positions or allegiances to particular individuals or positions until they are very familiar with a situation.

Hostility is created when I arrogantly insist on going to

"teach" somewhere. If I try to teach people in my own language and through my own city culture and behaviour, people's eyes laugh at me. This gives me an uncomfortable feeling of resentment (Ornelas).

If a person has a very set view of the world, if he/she really needs control and answers all the way along, that person is going to have tremendous difficulty doing PAR (Law).

Get guidance, especially if inexperienced in participatory processes, group facilitation, or conflict resolution. PAR is not a solo process to be undertaken as an outsider. There is a wide range of skills required for PAR that are different from those of conventional research: "personal skills of self-awareness and self-reflexiveness, facilitative skills in interpersonal and group settings, political skills, intellectual skills, and data management skills" (Reason, 1994: 335). Apprentice with a mentor (someone with notable PAR experience), form a facilitating team, or do both. (This is different than obtaining resource people for specific skills or information needed by the group.) Apprenticing and using teamwork is still "learning by doing," but is likely to be less painful.

PAR is a humbling experience—recognize personal limitations and the value of alternative perceptions. Engage in a PAR process *only* if you have seriously considered the inevitable commitment of purpose, time, and energy. This is not a casual or lighthearted activity (although people in PAR do play!).

Start with the people: know the multiple threads of their setting intimately. Be in tune with their perceptions and rhythms. Do a "sensorial diagnosis" of the setting: consciously relax; open all of your senses, absorbing the smells, sights, sounds, and sensations of the environment and its elements. Discipline yourself to be sensitive to small details. Be curious about your surroundings and aware of what is happening inside you— your feelings, thoughts, and reactions.

Each situation has its own dynamic. In adjusting to each situation, I begin to live that way, always in tune with the "other" (de la Maza in Arratia and de la Maza).

When we become distant from the field proper, we tend to forget the importance of the everyday dimensions of people's lives. This leads to further mistakes in our work, as distance interrupts the ongoing dialogue—an integral part of transforming social interactions (Arratia and de la Maza).

Consider doing a "bridge activity." This is a small, short-term activity that is conducted to help with the process of entering and getting to know the overall group/community and its members. A bridge activity will provide opportunities for members to size up and get to know you. Choose this activity carefully, as it must be appropriate to the setting and its people.

Getting to know the Aymara meant first thinking of each locality and its way of life. . . . The cultural dynamics are different in each setting; the same techniques and materials are not effective everywhere. . . . Participatory methods have to be adjusted to the local situation and must begin with the people's own knowledge base (Arratia and de la Maza).

Make different connections of energy and trust. These take time, effort, and sincere intention. Determine the energy points that will bring people together into a group. Be attentive to establishing and maintaining trust with participants.

The PAR process is not necessarily about being critically minded —at least in the initial moments. I am just one human being with another human being, trying to establish some type of connection (Arratia and de la Maza).

We tried to ensure that participants were relaxed and comfortable. We actively listened to what they said, often asking questions to probe further into their experiences and ideas. We followed their lead in determining the direction of interviews (Law).

As an outsider you will always be marginalized until the group trusts you. That trust will be built by working with

the group, living with them, doing what they do. They need
to discover that you are a human being. When you gain the
moral value of being trusted, at that moment you become a
part of the group or community, part of the landscape. PAR
can then start (Ornelas).

*Facilitate the group's analysis and interpretation of their life situ-
ations and root causes of needs* (Tilakaratna, 1991: 136). "PAR is
about people and their needs," according to Isabel de la Maza.
"You have to begin from where people are at and move along
with them. You cannot impose a particular process on them
and expect them to stay with it" (Arratia and de la Maza).

To facilitate does not mean being mechanical or passive.
Nor does it mean imposing particular methods, techniques, or
views. It does mean actively working with people to investigate the setting clearly, getting new information, and drawing
conclusions. The ability to do this type of balanced facilitation
develops with practice and with attention to cues and feedback.

> You [the catalytic agent] facilitate the reflection, the action,
> the reflection, the action and reflection. You become part of
> them at the moment when they open their hearts and their
> minds to you. . . . At that moment, you can start working with
> them and facilitate different techniques or methods to exam-
> ine reality and transform it. It is a long process—quite, quite
> long. It is not easy. You need to be very critical and help
> them demystify the situation (Ornelas in Debbink and
> Ornelas).

Work with the group to conduct a "situational diagnosis."
This goes beyond a sensorial diagnosis as people dig to a
deeper level, obtaining information from various sources (including their own experiences) to unearth the determinants
(root causes) of a problematic situation. Often this analysis
takes time as the circumstances of a situation are layered and
must be revealed one by one. Many questions will require
further investigation and reflection. Work with participants to
analyze their perceptions and information and interpret their
meanings in order to form a bigger contextual picture of prob-

lems and their causes.

> You begin by recognizing a need and knowing it well. Then
> you start taking action. Reflecting on that action with the oth-
> ers . . . a dialogue starts about the need and about the action.
> The intention of the dialogue is to discover the intimacy of
> the subject. . . . You discover or learn when you eat this soup
> (Ornelas in Debbink and Ornelas).

> We always started with an active exercise—doing something
> practical that would get people moving. . . . Emphasis was
> placed on analysis and writing, putting in order what people
> were thinking and feeling (Ornelas).

Determine if the group will systematically document its
thoughts, feelings, process, activities, and effects of its work. If
so, how will this evidence be created, maintained, and regularly reviewed in order to obtain validity among the group.
What means will the group use to ensure that everyone has
access to necessary information regarding ongoing developments?

Help people to organize themselves for their chosen actions. Consider the creation of their own democratic, non-hierarchical organizations (Tilakaratna, 1991: 136). For a new group's first action, encourage a small but significant action that will likely be
successful. This will build confidence. Work with the group
to anticipate logistical problems or skill deficiencies and identify the means to resolve these.

> After the elections, TEA members travelled from village to vil-
> lage explaining to people how an elected municipality works
> as the seat of local political power and how specific commu-
> nity services are administered. At the same time, TEA encour-
> aged village assemblies to present their priority needs to the
> appropriate development offices (Arratia and de la Maza).

> Personalized attention to individuals by staff allows adapta-
> tion of materials and techniques to suit a variety of learning
> speeds and styles. The diversity of previous levels of educa-

tion and literacy among participant means we must emphasize oral learning, while encouraging further literacy training
(Arratia and de la Maza).

Promote ongoing validation of the group's work: assist in regular cycles of group review of processes, activities, and effects.
Work with participants to diagnose their strengths and problematic areas in order to build from there. Celebrate and learn
from events carried out by the group; these celebrations can
provide vital group cohesion.

> I was naive to think that women from differing castes and
> religions could immediately engage in group discussion or
> even be interested in meeting and talking to each other. In
> my supervisor's project, I had watched a diverse group of
> village women from various hamlets discussing water sani-
> tation. That group session, however, had emerged out of
> many months of work in the village, beginning with small
> groups in individual hamlets (Seymour).

Assist the group to identify internal facilitators (Tilakaratna,
1991: 137). With the group, plan to further develop their abilities. Be conscious of the eventual disengagement of external
participants.

> If we are promoting social organization to achieve participa-
> tory development, it is not enough to only train the leaders.
> We also must follow up the leaders' trajectory in the commu-
> nity and work with the leaders in a sustained fashion to keep
> the flow of information going. This follow-up is part of the
> transformative process (Arratia and de la Maza).

> During the first few months after PF–Cambridge was formed,
> I observed changes in the parents' participation in the group.
> Participants assumed greater control of meetings and deci-
> sions. My role altered to being more of a support person than
> a facilitator (Law).

*Monitor your personal perceptions and positions and their influ-
ence on the group's process.* Recognize the interactions between

people's values/beliefs, attitudes, and perceptions with subsequent behaviours, including your own. Anticipate conflict and tension: learn how and when to name tension appropriately so that the group can deal with it. Approach particpants who are not content with the process and learn more about their perceptions and reasons. Whenever possible and appropriate, be transparent about your personal motivations, intent, and actions. *Any* hint of manipulation of the group will result in mistrust and breakdown of the process.

> It was important to us, as the initial link between participants during interivews, to share participants' suggestions about possible actions, although it was tempting to manipulate the research process by relating participants' suggestions in a way which favoured our ideas. . . . The PAR process would be ineffective if I, as a researcher, unduly pushed or influenced any decision-making . . . (Law).

The Question of Validity

> [T]he question of what constitutes proof was a very subtle and difficult one. Would it not be wiser to turn the principle into its opposite and say, "If in doubt, show it *prominently*"? After all, matters that are beyond doubt are, in a sense, dead; they do not constitute a challenge to the living (Schumacher, 1977: 11).

Researchers have argued that the empirical notion of validity does not hold when examining interpretive inquiry, and they propose different criteria to judge its truth-value or congruency with reality. Many new or reworked terms have been suggested to determine the soundness or "authority" of a study, including self-critical, intensity, systematic, relevance, rigour, trustworthiness, transferability, dependability, confirmability, logical inferences, credibility, thick-and-thin description, verisimilitude, triangulation, findings grounded in data, appropriate category structures, degree of research bias, and constant comparison. These criteria or methods appear in various combinations, depending on the author.

> ... [A] text is valid if it is sufficiently grounded, triangulated,
> based on naturalistic indicators, carefully fitted to a theory
> (and its concepts), comprehensive in scope, credible in terms
> of member checks, logical, and truthful in terms of its reflec-
> tion of the phenomena in question (Lincoln and Denzin, 1994:
> 579).

THE SILENCE IN PAR ABOUT VALIDITY

Reliability, the extent to which findings can be reproduced
in another study using the same method, has been discarded
by researchers as not appropriate in both interpretive and
liberatory/critical forms of inquiry. In contrast to the heated
debate carried out by interpretive researchers and some critical theorists, writers about PAR are noticeably silent on the
question of validity. Patti Lather, however, has suggested that
emancipatory research should address four validation methods
in order to "protect our work from our own passions and limitations" (1991: 69). These methods are:

- *Triangulation.* This is the incorporation of multiple methods and sources of information and various theoretical
  schemes to cross-check information and strengthen the
  trustworthiness of data;

- *Construct validity.* This is reflexivity that builds in systematic ways to critically question actions and practice
  and thereby construct knowledge;

- *Face validity.* This is the return of data to the participants
  for analysis and interpretation to increase credibility of
  data; and

- *Catalytic validity.* This is the use of "a process that re-
  orients, focusses, and energizes participants" to take actions for transformation (*ibid.*: 65-69).

Lather believes that researchers who paid attention to these measures would decrease their "rampant subjectivity" and help to produce rigourous social knowledge for a more equitable world.

Resisting the temptation to just fill in evidence under these four headings, we return to the silence about validity (or any alternative term) in the writing about PAR. What is the silence about? It is a silence of doubt. In *Doing Participatory Research*, Maguire observes: "Even self-identified progressive people, while dedicated and caring, often doubt the value and validity of ordinary people's knowledge when it is created outside of dominant social sciences approaches" (1987: 243).

It is also a silence of protest, resisting the valourization of knowledge: the attempt to stabilize knowledge and to determine its limits. When new knowledge enters an academic realm, it is dissected and used to construct theory that appears in publications; it becomes "codified and incorporated as part of the dominant system of knowledge" (Schapiro, 1995: 40). Peter Reason hinted at this in his discussion of participative inquiry: "In some way to write (and to read) "about" these people's experience in coming to understand their own worlds is to repossess it as an academic subject that can be studied from outside" (1994: 325).

More critically, Schapiro described the co-optation of knowledge and the inescapable shift in ownership:

> [Valourization] inevitably entails a reformulation of the knowledge so that it conforms to the prerequisites and definitions of that larger system. Understandings gained from passionate involvements in the field must be abstracted, codified and rationally systematized in order to be accepted as knowledge at all (1995: 40).

The painted lines on a tennis court define the game's legitimate playing area. The valourization of knowledge paints the same kind of familiar but constricting boundary so that PAR is defined and seen as legitimate. But how do we then understand a holistic, organic process?

Imposition in Order to Judge

Researchers develop theory, an organized body of ideas, from data. The building of theory, conceived in most disciplines as the gateway to the achievement of professional status, sometimes seems over-intellectualized and inaccessible. It has become an arduous exercise that is discussed in difficult language. At other times, theories seem simplistic as little attention is given to context, history, or motivations.

Our current attitudes towards research and theory-building have become fragmented and frozen so that we operate stiffly within finite boundaries. We devalue the potential of people's everyday experiences because they do not live up to standards determined by some external body. The conventional understanding of science has been "valid" but unable to monitor the healthy development of ideas and technology. This non-holistic approach has inflicted much damage by robbing us of liberating confidence, creativity, and a sacred identification with people and nature.

All thoughtful people construct theories about their work, homes, and communities; in essence they analyze their contact with life and develop a critical attitude. Their ideas are constantly being added to, reshuffled, discarded, and thereby reconstructed. People's theories, like themselves, generally mature within the lifecycle. Theory-building in the human sciences requires a concentrated effort but it is an effort that flows with life.

People in PAR, a whole-spirited inquiry, own their process and are concerned about the quality of their work. Working within a PAR approach requires having faith in the ability of people to develop higher levels of discernment. It also builds wisdom as people experience empowering opportunities that help them to become more self-questioning and curious. A group of people undertakes and sustains inquiry because the process is relevant and legitimate for them; if it was not, they would stop. They consciously develop faith in their ability to monitor themselves.

The point is who determines what is relevant and legiti-

mate. If people are faced with the *imposition* of external ration-
ally based criteria about acceptable standards and require-
ments, they lose ownership over their process. This corrupt-
ing influence makes little sense. Determining the measures and
criteria of validity in order to *judge*, "Is this 'good' PAR?" or "Are
the data and findings legitimate?" is the arrogance of the universities. These questions douse the flames of people's experiences and actions. "Within the Western world," John Gaventa
has written, "popular knowledge is constantly being created in
the daily experiences of work and community life. The legitimacy of such knowledge, too, is constantly being devalued and
suppressed by the dominant science" (1991: 128).

THE CENTRALITY OF VALUE IN PEOPLE'S WORK

The actual process of establishing validity in PAR is participatory (Fernandes and Tandon in Park, 1993: 17) and has to do
with the question of "value": what value do participants place
on their work? The participants "see" themselves and their
world and decide how these views can change. They determine how their analysis and interpretation is coherent with
their experiences and actions. They use their emergent conclusions to guide their praxis: "Critical knowledge validates
itself in creating a vehicle of transformation and in overcom-
ing obstacles to emancipation—both internally and with respect
to the external world" (Park, 1993: 16).

Vivencia, research in and of life, is process-oriented and
based on principles of holistic personal and social development.
Validity is shaped by people's expectations, by their praxis, and
by the promise of possibility. At the beginning, they decide on
certain principles, assumptions, and expectations and, throughout their work, they expand on their understanding of these.
This requires flexibility, openness, and permeable boundaries
of interacting and knowing. Participants, as individuals and as
a whole, will struggle with a primary question: How true will
they be to their expectations of each other and to participation
in their process? To what extent will their expectations of trust
flourish? This is the rigour of participatory action-research and

only the group members can answer this question.

Peter Reason referred to two related limitations that can affect participatory inquiry: "unaware projection" and "consensus collusion." People can deceive themselves through unaware projection: "We do this because inquiring carefully and critically into those things we care about is an anxiety-provoking business that stirs up our psychological defenses. We then project our anxieties onto the world" (1994: 327). Consensus collusion occurs when people "band together as a group in defense of their anxieties [so that] areas of their experience that challenge their world view are ignored or not properly explored" (*ibid*.: 327).

By using growth-centered strategies, people can more readily acknowledge their anxieties and reduce the effects of projection or collusion. Learning to be more sensitive to emotions can help participants to reveal and understand the underlying anxieties that prevent a more comprehensive view of reality. Regular cycles of action-reflection and the establishment of safety, trust, and participatory norms can help individuals to thoughtfully challenge assumptions and perceptions. These characteristics heighten the validity of the group's inquiry. They can make it "possible to see more clearly and communicate to others the perspective from which that knowing is derived, and to illuminate the distortions that may have occurred" (*ibid*.: 327).

Participants can establish the space that they need to validate their progress by: "checking-in" on feelings and thoughts; having regular validations; raising, exploring, and clarifying ideas, emotions, and reactions during reflection circles and other activities; tolerating ambiguity—the inevitable "fog"—until enough pieces are in place to provide direction; maintaining a short planning cycle; creating expectations of trust, norms of participation, and a safe climate. People's work has validity because it is real—it happens.

REPRESENTATION OF EXPERIENCE:
A LEGITIMATE TEST OF VALIDITY DOCUMENTATION

It is important to not blur the distinction between an actual lived process and the documentation of an experience. All writing is the art of interpretation, as events pass through the filter of the writer. The task of the writer is documentation: to *represent* an experience as fully and truthfully as possible. Any representation can be challenged on its features and on its presentation—this is a legitimate test of validity documentation. An account of an experience can and should come under close scrutiny: Is the representation a reflection that is true to the experience? Is it truly fixed? "Good interpretation takes us into the center of the experience and into the heart of the matter" (Denzin and Lincoln, 1994: 502).

A good representation, by capturing people engaged in a multifaceted process within a complex context, can provide a perspective that allows readers to consider possible applications in their own situations. "People look for patterns that explain their own experience as well as events in the world around them. 'Full and thorough knowledge of the particular' allows one to see similarities 'in new and foreign contexts'" (Stake, 1978, cited in Merriam, 1988: 174).

Individuals who are charged with the responsibility of written documentation have to deal with many decisions about the text, for example, the points of emphasis, the use of terms, and the style of writing. Depending on the purpose and type of documentation, the group members may guide the making of these major decisions and determine a process for reflexive loops back to the group.

A text becomes more representative when it:

Places the experience in context. The writer's task is to provide a reading on the setting. This orients the reader to the broad and local circumstances that affected the participants in the research process and it should include a discussion of the motivations and assumptions of the various parties.

Details the experience. The writer's challenge is to be comprehensive, to give thick descriptions of the people and their multiple voices, perspectives, and relationships. Descriptions should also include the process, the content, the time involved; the climate, the problems, and the consequences of actions. Documenting dialogue is difficult but it demonstrates a caring "ethic [that] values individual uniqueness and the expression of emotionality in the text, and seeks writers who can create emotional texts that others can enter into" (Denzin and Lincoln, 1994: 510).

Details matter: they allow the reader to get a fuller picture of what happened, how, and why. The writer ponders how to treat obvious and subtle dynamics, decisions, turning points, and shifts in emphasis. As well, the writer chooses how to best present the experience so that it is a sensitive, critical, and accurate account that speaks for itself as much as possible. Carr and Kemmis observe: "To be valid, an interpretive account must first of all be coherent: it must comprehend and coordinate insights and evidence within a consistent framework" (1986: 91).

Creating a thorough text usually means making regular and self-conscious recordings and notes during the inquiry. Readers should be able to grasp the methods which were used for collecting and handling data from the raw field notes through to the final text (Huberman and Miles, 1994: 439).

Reveals and reflects on emergent knowledge. The writer attends to the four forms of knowledge: experiential, practical, propositional, and presentational, as outlined by Heron (1992: 158). All of these (potentially) form in PAR: experiential knowledge obtained in direct experience; practical knowledge that is skill-based (how to do something); propositional knowledge expressed as statements or theories; and presentational knowledge, the process of ordering tacit experiential knowledge into patterns expressed as dreams, stories, and imaginative images. These forms incorporate rational knowledge with other ways of knowing, such as knowledge that is based on experience, on practical skills, and on the tacit level of dreams and intuition.

Writing about the new knowledge is actually interpretation within interpretation. The data must "pass the test of participant confirmation" (Carr and Kemmis, 1986: 91) whereby the participants are able to recognize the data as congruent with their experience. People validate their knowledge, becoming more consciously aware that it emerged from their perspective and their process that was set in a particular time and place. Those who document and therefore again interpret must know, along with the participants, that the knowledge is "open to all the ways in which human beings fool themselves and each other in their perceptions of the world, through faulty epistemology, cultural bias, character defense, political partisanship [and] spiritual impoverishment" (Reason, 1994: 327).

As participants go through cycles of action and reflection, the writer also shows reflexivity in writing by regularly returning data to participants and by critically reflecting on the developments as they occurred, and later during the writing and re-writing. The writer actively searches for points of convergence and points of divergence, for dialectics, and for movement. "A critical text," as expressed by Denzin, "is judged by its ability to reveal reflexively these structures of oppression as they operate in the world of lived experience" (1994: 509).

Reveals personal transformation. PAR is a human and spiritual science in which the head, heart, hand, and spirit reside openly together. Engagement in PAR is an encounter with reality and with possibility: participation can shift people's inner consciousness and their perceptions of powers-within-life. The writer who participates in PAR, like other researchers in the human sciences, "must allow that experience to change her so that the new culture is seen through new eyes, not eyes conditioned by the scientist's own culture" (Harman, 1988: 18). How does the text demonstrate the willingness of the participant/writer to be changed? How is an openness to learning from and with others shown?

Whole-spirited inquiry can lead to changes in personal consciousness and spiritual energy as well as to changes in social structures and relationships. Participants will focus on learning and on the pragmatics of action and will re-form their senses of themselves, some more than others. Writers learn by identifying with the other participants, by being part of the whole, and by being vulnerable in the sense of being open, sensitive, and willing to invest parts of themselves in the research. W. Harman observes, "The scientist who would study in the area we have termed 'spiritual science' has to be willing to go through the deep changes that will make him or her a competent observer" (*ibid.*: 18).

Participants develop increased critical consciousness and openly incorporate a "compassionate consciousness" (*ibid.*: 16). This is the spirit energy of humanness. They will cultivate intellectual prowess through the development of their rational and analytical abilities and, equally important, they will seek spiritual strength through the development of heightened intuition and compassion for others and for themselves. These abilities form the foundation of people-centred, liberatory inquiry. The challenge for the writer is to capture all rational, emotional, spiritual, and practical movement while remaining mindful of the difficulties in doing this.

PAR and Development

People in liberating situations develop capabilities and gain just entitlement and recognition of rights. A web of liberation forms when people are able to:

- Investigate and obtain correct information and know the meaning of that information;

- Learn adequate skills that enable them to do their work well;

- Participate actively in decision-making with the means to change what is undesirable and continue the desirable;

- Critically analyze complex life situations, enabling recognition of the implications of actions and anticipation of what may happen next;

- Obtain sufficient resources to risk action; and

- Develop sufficient inner power and spirit (confidence, self- and group esteem, meaningful influence) to risk action.

These factors tightly interlock; all are vital for gaining fuller, more advanced states of being and interacting. On personal, group, or societal levels, they provide essential support for human development.

There is a dynamic relationship between people-centred development approaches in communities and participatory action-research: each forms and informs the other. People-centred development is a capacity-building process by which people become awakened to achievable individual and collective lifestyles and move forward towards an improved quality of life (Ariyaratne, 1990: 54). By broadening political and economic participation through democratic means, sustainable development strengthens people's capacities to create viable communities characterized by humaneness, justice, and dignity.

The PAR process, complete with inevitable tensions, can move communities to become more human and more developed, thereby changing reality. This changed reality, in turn, helps groups and communities grow in confidence and to enter into new learning cycles with greater challenges.

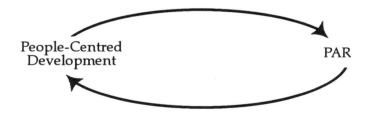

People-Centred
Development
PAR

Engagement in a PAR process can be high-risk work. Particularly in regions controlled by repressive regimes, association with PAR activities can mean personal loss of employment, position, and support systems. Challenging unjust, dominant modes of thinking and organization can also mean threats or death; engagement is not entered into lightly nor naively but many have decided that the benefits of involvement in PAR outweigh its risks. "Perhaps the time has come to tiptoe no longer, but to quietly, firmly, self-confidently insist on the need for a restructuring of science to accommodate all, rather than just part, of human experience" (Harman, 1988: 21).

When people consciously combine the various dimensions of critical analysis, interpersonal skills, practical abilities, and inner growth, they have synergistic potential for the development of capacity. People in praxis strengthen their thinking skills through consistent patterns of critical analysis. In part, this is done by asking questions, by considering various perspectives and interpretations, and by examining alternatives and consequences of actions. Interpersonal skills mature when individuals work together and focus attention on group dynamics, communication, conflict resolution, and cooperation.

Practical abilities grow with opportunities for hands-on practice, using technology appropriate for the setting. Exploring questions such as "Who am I?" and "Who are we?" allows opportunities for clarification of values and principles and supports spiritual quests for a greater purpose in life.

When we struggle together to meet challenges, we add to our complexity as individuals, our abilities to care and be cared for, our sense of rooted connectedness, and our capacity to rehumanize our world. Giving birth to the knowledge of hopeful dreams, we regain commitment to a meaningful way of life, no longer "in fear of stepping out."

Par Is a Tree, a River, and a Mountain Path

*PAR is like a tree, deeply rooted in people's realities,
grounded to the earth and, at the same time,
stretching upwards to the sky.*

*PAR flows like a river; open-ended, finding its way.
Sometimes deep and calm; at other points,
shallow and turbulent.
Complete with cascading waterfalls,
seemingly stagnant swamps, and converging deltas.*

*Those creating knowledge and change through PAR
climb up mountains.
Following a small path of investigation and discovery,
we will circle the mountain many times,
with each turn finding a broader, more enriched view.*

Endnote: PAR Methodology—Overview of Authors

A. W. Fernandes and R. Tandon (1981)

In 1981, Fernandes and Tandon developed a step model of "ideal" PAR (1981: 25). They focussed on the joint inquiry process leading to actions and consolidation of learning and outlined typical steps. Their emphasis was clearly on the collective nature of the research. Their model is represented schematically in the 10 smaller boxes in Figure 11 on the next page.

During her PAR project with battered women in New Mexico, Maguire recognized the importance of building and maintaining trusting relationships with and among participants (1987: 140). She added "Entering, Experiencing, Establishing Relationships with Actors in Situation" (the large box to the left in Figure 11) as the first step in the Fernandes and Tandon model. This combined representation is important in understanding the evolution of PAR methodology over the last two decades.

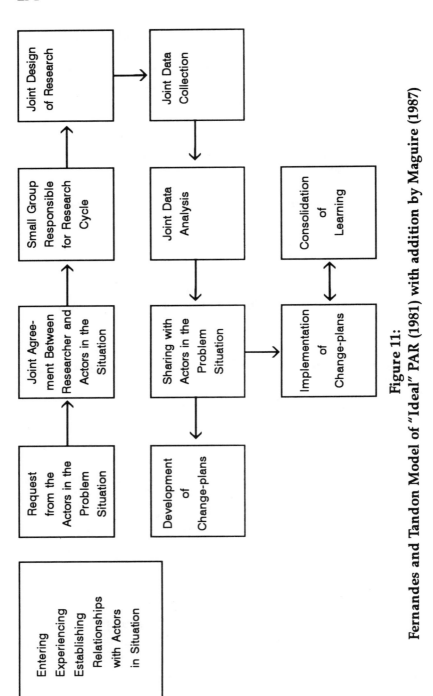

Figure 11:

Fernandes and Tandon Model of "Ideal" PAR (1981) with addition by Maguire (1987)

Vio Grossi et al in P. Maguire (1987)

In 1983, Vio Grossi, Martinic, Tapia, and Pascal had outlined five broad phases for conducting PAR (Maguire, 1987: 49-51). Incorporating guidelines from Hall (1975, 1981), as well as ideas from Fernandes and Tandon, Maguire used these five phases to frame her project:

Phase 1: Organization of the project and knowledge of the working area. The external researcher gathers and analyzes information about the area and the main problems. Either the external researcher invites specific organizations to join in a PAR project, or s/he responds to a request by the internal group.

Phase 2: Definition of the generating problematics. The external researcher uses problem-posing techniques and dialogue to enable the group to identify and understand individual perceptions of the most significant problems.

Phase 3: Objectivization and problemization. Participants link their interpretations of problems to the broader context. They compile questions and themes which will be investigated.

Phase 4: Researching social reality and analyzing collected information. The group designs a process to investigate specific problems. Various methods may be used for information-gathering, classification, analysis and conclusion building. The group develops theories and solutions to problems.

Phase 5: Definition of action projects. The group decides what actions to take. The process and products of research can be of direct and immediate benefit to those involved.

As with Fernandes and Tandon, Vio Grossi's methodology model grounded the initiative in the local context and major problems (phase 1), and incorporated the group development of relevant questions and themes for pursual (phase 2). It also highlighted the joint inquiry process (phases 3, 4) and the action component (phase 5).

P. Park (1993)

Park saw PAR as a process of recovery and discovery that "provides a framework in which people seeking to overcome oppressive situations can come to understand the social forces in operation and gain strength in collective action" (1993: 3). His "composite portrait" of key moments in the process was not intended as a step-by-step, how-to guide—"an unrewarding and futile effort in PAR." Park's framework was:

The beginning (preliminary phase). The "external change agent" enters a community and learns as much as possible. Upon becoming accepted as a researcher, s/he explains the purpose and obtains help from "key individuals." This organizational aspect can require considerable time and effort. "Where there is little shared life, participatory research must first create a community base before it can do collective investigation, not to speak of action and reflection" (*ibid.*: 18-19).

Problem formulation. Community members define their collective problem, which will be investigated. Dialogue generates factual as well as interpersonal and critical knowledge. The group "see[s] the larger picture of structural contradictions which causes their economic miseries and social dislocations" (*ibid.*: 15).

Research design and methods. By drawing upon available and relevant social science methods, participants develop the research design and decide how data are to be gathered and analyzed.

Data gathering and analysis. Collective orientation or training regarding methods takes place. Data are gathered, analyzed, and reported. Participants discover the dimensions of the problem and use these to guide collective actions.

Utilization of results. Systematically organized facts help the group identify meaningful and appropriate actions to be taken. Action can take place concurrently with research and can lead to the formation of collaborative ventures and political alliances. When successful, "[PAR] lives on in the radicalized critical consciousness and the renewed emancipatory practices of each participant" (*ibid.*: 15).

Seeking *Vivencia* in Research

The models of Park and of Vio Grossi, while using slightly different words and phrases, both had five phases with parallel ideas. The earlier model by Fernandes and Tandon with Maguire's addition, although less consolidated, was consistent with the other two. The models suggested that PAR methodology is largely distinguishable from other forms of research by its action component and by being carried out on a group basis (rather than by external researchers independently) with a liberatory intention.

Any framework will, by definition, simplify a given event or process. However, in these models, especially in Park's, there is a disconcerting overlay of procedure from the language of more conventional research methodology, as though PAR was being fitted into a suit of legitimacy—one size too small with little breathing room. In developing the praxiology framework used in this chapter, allowance for the expression of *vivencia* was vital.

References

Ariyaratne, A.T. 1990. Literacy and sustainable development. *Literacy, Popular Education and Democracy: Building on the Movement Proceedings from the Fourth World Assembly on Adult Education, January 8-18*. Bangkok: International Council for Adult Education et al. (pp. 54-55).

Bellah, R., Madsen, R., Sullivan, W., Swidler, A., and Tipton, S. 1985. *Habits of the Heart*. Los Angeles: University of California Press.

Boal, A. 1995. *A Rainbow of Desire*. London: Routledge.

Bohm, D. 1993. For truth try dialogue. *Resurgence* 156: 10-13.

Boychuck Duchscher, J. 1994. Acting on violence against women. *The Canadian Nurse* 90(6): 20-25.

Butala, S. 1994. *The Perfection of the Morning An Apprenticeship in Nature*. Toronto: HarperCollins Publishers.

Carr, W. and Kemmis, S. 1986. *Becoming Critical Education, Knowledge and Action Research*. London: The Falmer Press.

Chambers, R. 1983. *Rural Development: Putting the Last First*. London: Longman Scientific and Technical.

Chisholm, L. 1990. Action research: Some methodological and political considerations. *British Educational Research Journal* 16(3): 249-257.

de Bono, E. 1985. 1991. *Six Thinking Hats*. New York: Penguin Books.

Denzin, N.K. 1994. The art and politics of interpretation. In: N.K. Denzin and Y.S. Lincoln (Eds.) *Handbook of Qualitative Research*. Thousand Oaks, California: Sage Publications (pp. 500-515).

Denzin, N.K. and Lincoln, Y.S. (Eds.). 1994. *Handbook of Qualitative Research*. Thousand Oaks, California: Sage Publications.

Fals-Borda, O. 1988. *Knowledge and People's Power: Lessons with Peasants in Nicaragua, Mexico and Columbia*. New Delhi: Indian Social Institute.

_____. 1991. Some basic ingredients. In: O. Fals-Borda and

M.A. Rahman (Eds.) *Action and Knowledge: Breaking the Monopoly with Participatory Action-Research.* New York: The Apex Press (pp. 3-12).

Fals-Borda, O. and Rahman, M.A. (Eds.). 1991. *Action and Knowledge: Breaking the Monopoly with Participatory Action-Research,* New York: The Apex Press.

Fernandes, W. and Tandon, R. 1981. *Participatory Research and Evaluation.* New Delhi: Indian Social Institute.

Freire, P. 1970, 1990. *Pedagogy of the Oppressed.* New York: Continuum Publishing Co.

_____. 1973. *Education for Critical Consciousness.* New York: Seabury Press.

_____. 1985. *The Politics of Education: Culture, Power and Liberation.* New York: Bergin & Garvey Publishers.

Galbraith, A. 1985. The adult learning transactional process. In: M. Galbraith (Ed.) *Facilitating Adult Learning: A Transactional Process.* Malabar, Florida: Krieger Publishing.

Gaventa, J. 1991. Toward a knowledge democracy: Viewpoints on participatory action-research in North America. In: O. Fals-Borda and M.A. Rahman (Eds.) *Action and Knowledge: Breaking the Monopoly with Participatory Action-Research.* New York: The Apex Press (pp. 121-131).

Giroux, H. 1985. Introduction. In: P. Freire (Ed.). *The Politics of Education.* New York: Bergin & Garvey Publishers.

Griffin, V. R. 1988. Holistic learning/teaching in adult education: Would you play a one-string guitar? In: T. Barer-Stein and J.A. Draper (Eds.) *The Craft of Teaching Adults.* Toronto: Culture Concepts (pp. 105-131).

Guba, E. and Lincoln, Y. S. 1994. Competing paradigms in quali-
    tative research. In: N.K. Denzin and Y. S. Lincoln (Eds.)
    Handbook of Qualitative Research. Thousand Oaks, California:
    Sage Publications (pp. 105-117).

Habermas, J. 1971. *Toward a Rational Society*. Tr. J. . Shapiro. Lon-
    don: Heineman.

Hall, B. 1975. Participatory research: An approach for change.
    Convergence 8(2): 24-32.

_____. 1981. Participatory research, popular education and
    power: A personal reflection. *Convergence* XIV(3): 6-19.

_____. 1992. From margins to center? The development
    and purpose of participatory research. *The American Sociolo-
    gist* 26(1): 15-27.

Hall, B., Gillette, A., and Tandon, R. (Eds.). 1982. *Creating Knowl-
    edge: A Monopoly?* New Delhi: Society for Participatory Re-
    search in Asia.

Harman, W. 1988. The transpersonal challenge to the scientific
    paradigm. *Revision* 11(2): 13-21.

Heron, J. 1992. *Feeling and Personhood: Psychology in Another Key*.
    Newbury Park, California: Sage Publications.

Hope, A., and Timmel, S., and Hodzi, C. 1984, 1988. *Training for
    Transformation: A Handbook for Community Workers*. vols. 1, 2.
    Gweru, Zimbabwe: Mambo Press.

Huberman, A. and Miles, M. 1994. Data management and
    analysis methods. In: N.K. Denzin and Y.S. Lincoln (Eds.)
    Handbook of Qualitative Research. Thousand Oaks, California:
    Sage Publications (pp. 428-444).

Kemmis, S. 1991. Critical education research. *The Canadian Journal for the Study of Adult Education* V. Special issue (pp. 94-119).

Lather, P. 1991. *Getting Smart: Feminist Research and Pedagogy within the Postmodern.* New York: Routledge, Chapman & Hall.

_____. 1986. Issues of validity in openly ideological research: Between a rock and a soft place. *Interchange* 17(4): 63-84.

Lincoln, Y.S. and Denzin, N.K. 1994. The fifth moment. In: Denzin and Lincoln (Eds.) *Handbook of Qualitative Research.* Thousand Oaks, California: Sage Publications (pp. 575-586).

Macpherson-Smith, M., 1994. Sick society syndrome: Community and social ecology. *Humane Medicine* 10(2): 96-102.

Maguire, P. 1987. *Doing Participatory Research: A Feminist Approach.* Amherst: Center for International Education, University of Massachusetts.

Max-Neef, M.A. 1991. *Human Scale Development.* New York: The Apex Press.

Merriam, S.B. 1988. *Case Study Research in Education.* San Francisco: Jossey-Bass Publishers.

Park, P. 1993. What is participatory research? A theoretical and methodological perspective. In: P. Park, M. Brydon-Miller, B. Hall, and T. Jackson (Eds.) *Voices of Change: Participatory Research in the United States and Canada.* Toronto: OISE Press (pp. 1-19).

Park, P., Brydon-Miller, M., Hall, B., and Jackson, T. (Eds.). 1993. *Voices of Change: Participatory Research in the United States and*

Canada. Toronto: OISE Press.

Rahman, M.A. 1991. The theoretical standpoint of PAR. In: O. Fals-Borda and M. Rahman (Eds.) *Action and Knowledge: Breaking the Monopoly with Participatory Action-Research.* New York: The Apex Press (pp.13-23).

_____. 1993. *People's Self Development Perspectives on Participatory Action Research.* London: Zed Books.

Reason, P. 1994. Three approaches to participative inquiry. In: N.K. Denzin and Y.S. Lincoln (Eds.). *Handbook of Qualitative Research.* Thousand Oaks, California: Sage Publications (pp. 324-339).

Schapiro, R. 1995. Liberatory pedagogy and the development paradox. *Convergence* XXVIII(2): 28-45.

Schumacher, E.F. 1977. *A Guide for the Perplexed.* London: Abacus.

Shor, I. 1992. *Empowering Education Critical Teaching for Social Change.* Chicago: The University of Chicago Press.

Smith, W.A. 1976. *The Meaning of Conscientizacao: The Goal of Paulo Freire's Pedagogy.* Amherst: Center for International Education, University of Massachusetts.

Srinivasan, L. 1992. *Options for Educators: A Monograph for Decision Makers on Alternative Participatory Strategies.* New York: PACT/CDS.

Starhawk. 1987. *Truth or Dare: Encounters with Power, Authority and Mystery.* New York: HarperCollins Publishers.

Tandon, R. 1981. Participatory research in the empowerment of people. *Convergence* 14(3): 20-27.

Tilakaratna, S. 1991. Stimulation of self-reliant initiatives by sensitized agents: Lessons from practice. In: O. Fals-Borda and M.A. Rahman (Eds.) *Action and Knowledge: Breaking the Monopoly with Participatory Action-Research.* New York: The Apex Press (pp. 135-145).

Wallerstein, N. and Bernstein, E. 1988. Empowerment education: Freire's ideas adapted to health education. *Health Education Quarterly* 15(4): 379-394.

Zachariah, M. 1986. *Revolution Through Reform: A Comparison of Sarvodaya and Conscientization.* New Delhi: Vistaar Publications.

About the Contributors

MARIA-INES ARRATIA

Born and raised in Vina del Mar, Chile, Maria-Ines Arratia arrived in Canada in 1971. After taking a number of courses at the University of Western Ontario (London), she discovered anthropology and decided to leave her job of ten years as a medical administrative assistant. Maria-Ines worked with immigrant women in London until moving to Toronto in 1987 to pursue doctoral studies. She began working with the Aymara in 1989 as part of her doctoral fieldwork and returned for a post-doctoral period in Northern Chile from November 1991 to June 1993. In 1992, she designed a distance learning course in anthropology for Chilean rural school teachers, which received the approval of the Chilean Ministry of Education. Maria-Ines was recently awarded a SSHRCC (Social Sciences and Humanities Research Council of Canada) Research Grant to continue her work in formal education for rural Aymara children. She is currently a Research Fellow with the Centre for Research on Latin America and the Caribbean (CERLAC) at York University in Toronto, Ontario, Canada, and teaches at the Universidad de Tarapaca in Arica, Chile.

GERALD DEBBINK

Growing up on a dairy farm in central Alberta, Gerald Debbink became a dairy farmer himself in 1976. Gerald feels he is gaining a truer sense of self and security, learning from his work in rural Mexico and Canada. In 1993, Gerald and others founded an experiential two-week program called "Caminamos Juntos/Walking Together: A *Pasantia* Experience." The program brings together people seeking social justice and holistic human development. He and his family have recently returned to Mexico to continue working with *campesinos* and the Caminamos Juntos program on the outskirts of Cuernavaca.

ISABEL DE LA MAZA
Born and raised in Santiago, Chile, Isabel obtained her university degree and travelled in Europe before settling in Arica where she initially taught school. She has been involved with TEA since 1985. She started with the Women's Project and is presently Director of the Social Education Area. In 1990, she participated as a case presenter at the Participatory Development Workshop at Regina Mundi in Ontario, Canada. Isabel is actively involved in an organization of women working in NGOs in Arica. She is also active in the Parents' Committee at the school of her three children.

NANCY ARBUTHNOT JOHNSON
Nancy is a researcher with experience in qualitative methods and an interest in PAR. She is also an editor, writer, and mother of two small boys, Malcolm and Mitchell. During the quiet times in her busy days, she enjoys puttering in her garden and shortening the stack of great books waiting to be read.

MARY LAW
Mary Law is an occupational therapist who has worked with children and families for many years. She is an Associate Professor in the School of Rehabilitation Science at McMaster University, and Director of the Neurodevelopmental Clinical Research Unit at McMaster University. She has a longstanding interest in examining environmental constraints that affect the daily activities of children with disabilities and working in partnership with parents to change disabling environments.

JANETTE NAKUTI

Janette Nakuti is a Mugusu woman from Mbale in the Mount Elgon region of Eastern Uganda. She has an undergraduate degree in social sciences from Makerere University, Kampala, Uganda. Having been with the project, "Talking About AIDS," since its inception in February of 1993, Janette's work has been critical to the research team's understanding of risk from a woman-centred perspective.

ARTURO ORNELAS

Arturo Ornelas, a Mexican educator and community activist, is well experienced in processes of social participation and participatory action-research. Arturo has worked with people in many countries of Latin America and Africa since 1975. Currently, he is supporting the development of the Caminamos Juntos program and establishing the Centro de Investigacion Popular en Plantas Medicinales y Microdoses (Centre for Popular Research in Medicinal Plants and Microdoses) in Cuernavaca, Mexico.

NELSON SEWANKAMBO

Nelson Sewankambo graduated as a medical doctor and later studied clinical epidemiology at McMaster University, Canada. With extensive HIV/AIDS biomedical and epidemiological research experience in urban and rural settings in Uganda, he has since developed a growing interest in anthropological and participatory research methods. This combination of research experiences has enriched his career and given him new insights in the development of HIV/AIDS interventions. At present, he is a Senior Lecturer, Director of the Clinical Epidemiology Unit, and Associate Dean of the Medical School at Makerere University, Kampala, Uganda.

PATRICIA SEYMOUR

Born in the Netherlands, Patricia lived and travelled all over the world with her family until settling in Ottawa where she completed high school. She studied medicine at the University

of Western Ontario and went on to do Family Medicine at
McMaster University. She now practises as a family doctor in
Hamilton, Ontario.

SUSAN SMITH

Susan Smith, a nurse, educator, and writer, is self-employed
with Luz de Luna Internacional, a community-based research
and development for health initiative. She holds an assistant
clinical professorship at McMaster University, Hamilton,
Ontario, Canada.

Susan graduated with a B.N. from the Faculty of Nursing
(University of Calgary) in 1975, and later pursued a Master of
Public Health degree from the University of Hawaii. She recently completed her Ph.D. in the Faculty of Education at the
University of Calgary. Zaina, her nine-year-old son, patiently
tolerates seemingly endless meetings, phone calls, and computer work, while adding zest and meaning to daily life.

PATRICIA SPITTAL

In the fall of 1995, Patricia Spittal completed her doctorate
in anthropology from McMaster University, Ontario, Canada.
Her dissertation entitled, *Deadly Choices: Women's Risk for HIV
Infection in Rural SW Uganda*, was based largely on her collaboration with the research team from "Talking About AIDS."
While working on the dissertation, Patricia lived and worked
in Uganda for 17 months. Together, she and Janette have tried
to capture the life experiences of women, who as caretakers and
victims, live with AIDS every single day.

DENNIS WILLMS

Dennis Willms graduated in 1984 with a Ph.D. in Social-
Cultural Anthropology from the University of British Columbia. Building on his initial fieldwork on sustainable models of
community-based health care in Kenya, his present ethnographic and participatory research is conducted in collaboration with researchers in Uganda and Zimbabwe. This research
is principally in the area of the design, dissemination, and

evaluation of culturally compelling HIV/AIDS interventions. At present, he is an Associate Professor in the Department of Anthropology, McMaster University, with a cross-appointment in the Department of Clinical Epidemiology and Biostatistics. He is the founding director of the Salama Shield Foundation based in Canada, which supports PAR activities internationally. Dennis lives in Kitchener, Ontario, Canada, with his wife Rita and their two sons, Luke and Mark.

Index

Abuse, 4, 189
Action and Knowledge, 225, 235
Action-reflection, 19-20, 156-57,
    177, 183, 239, 256
    cycles of, 246, 249
    dialectic of, 205
    facilitating, 238
Actions, 184-88, 191-97, 208-11,
    224-27, 231-34, 239-42,
    250-57. *See also* Taking
    Action.
    collective, 256
    commitment to, 52
    component of, 46
    consequences of, 248
    humanized, 144
    practical, 40, 157, 169,
    social, 112, 121, 126, 129,
    132, 181,
    testing, 127, 201
Agents. *See* Catalytic; External;
    Insiders; Outsiders.
Akhri, 70-75, 78, 80, 83-85, 233
Alberta, Canada, 16, 28
    dairy farmers in, 7, 14, 21-
    22, 28, 202, 207, 216
Alcohol sellers, 88-91, 100, 103,
    106
Alienation, 11, 15, 156, 171-75,
    200, 221

Analysis, 161, 169, 184, 205-06,
    244-45, 250
    critical, 150, 185, 225, 228,
    251-52
    of situation, 230, 238
Arica, 114, 116, 118-19, 124, 128,
    210
    women's cooperative based
    in, 125
Assumptions, 179, 204, 232,
    245-47
Autonomy, 3, 128, 175, 194
Auxiliary nurse midwives
    (ANMs), 61, 64-65, 68-
    69, 75-79
Awakening, 183, 197, 216, 218,
    251
    of imagination, 229
    moments of, 195
Awareness, 29, 185, 192-95, 202,
    208, 221, 227, 236
    conscious, 249
    critical, 11,
    gaining, 51
Aymara of Bolivia, 115
Aymara of Cariquima, 116
Aymara of Chile, 113-19, 123-
    27, 129, 199, 203, 210,
    237
    ability of to remain rural,
    130

and lack of "legal" docu-
     ments, 124-25, 208
migration of to urban
     centres, 115-16, 118,
     124, 129-30, 234
women of, 119-22, 125, 133,
     200, 210
Aymara (language), 127
losing ground in favor of
     Spanish, 122
Azapa, valley of, 124

Bahu (daughter-in-law), 62, 74
Banaras, 60, 62-68, 70, 73-77,
     230
Banaras Hindu University
     (B.H.U.), 61, 63, 75
Basawo basilimu (AIDS doctors),
     95, 98
Basti, Harijan and Rajbhar, 77-
     78
Boal, A., 220, 222-23
Bohm, D., 227
Bojpouri (dialect), 72
Bolivian highlands, Aymara's
     migration from, 115
Brazil, 113, 175, 228
"Bridge activity," 237
Bureaucracies, 8, 132, 171

Calama, 116
Cambridge, Ontario, 9, 38-39,
     47, 50
establishing parent support
     group in, 45
Campesinos, Honduran, 142-43,
     146, 150, 164, 171
Campesinos, Mexican, 13-16, 20-
     23, 25-30, 200-01, 203,
     207-10, 213, 234
Canada, 21, 24, 131
Canadian International Devel-
     opment Agency

(CIDA), 61, 63, 232
Carr, N., 248-49
Caste conflict, 66, 71, 80, 240
Catalytic agents, 233, 235, 238
Ccanthati (dawn), 125, 210
Centre for Research in the
     North (CREAR), 114-16,
     118
Centre for Women's Studies
     and Development
     (Banaras), 61, 63, 65
CEPI (government develop-
     ment agency), 128
Cesar and *cesamo* communities,
     153
Change, 184-87, 195, 200, 232-
     34
of barriers, 53
for children, 15, 199
constructive, 129
creation of, 253
critical point for, 172
economic, 176
facilitating, 38, 50, 52-53,
     215
initiating, 84, 223
internal, 30, 213, 215
means for, 50, 188
positive, 195
process of, 84, 178, 233
of reality, 194, 221, 257
resisting, 223
social, 6, 9-11, 130, 139-40,
     168, 176, 204, 213, 234
social activities, undertak-
     ing, 113
in social structures, 250
suggestions for, 41
sustainable, 156
willingness for, 249
working for, 209, 217
of views, 245
Charity, 27, 136, 169, 216

"Chi," 224. *See also* Energy.
Chile, 9-10, 112-16, 122-24, 128-
    32, 197, 218
    authoritarian government
        of, 119
Chisholm, L., 223-24
"Choiceless choice," 98, 106
Christian Farmers Federation of
    Alberta, 14-15
Class tension, 133, 161. *See also*
    Caste conflict.
Clinical studies, inadequacy of,
    95
Colchane district, 120
Commercialism, transient, 92,
    101
Communitarian hospital, 139,
    151
    reaction of La Esperanza
        hospital to, 153
Community, 29-30, 211-13, 175
    development project, 125,
        128, 208
    facilitating change in, 53
    participating in, 51
    reconstructing, 130
    sense of, 3, 8, 15, 17, 183,
        201, 215
    shared needs for, 196
    survival of, 203
    sustaining development of,
        61
"Compassionate conscious-
    ness," 250
Confidence, 189, 194, 229, 239,
    244, 251-52
Conformity, 2, 194
Connections, 190, 192, 225, 237
    creating, 28
    essential, 152
    people-to-people, 200
    with like-minded people,
        31

with other communities,
    51, 139
seeking, 131, 183, 197, 200
Conscientizacao, 193
Conscientization, 150-51, 193-
    97, 215, 221, 229
    gaining, 156
    experiencing, 214
Consciousness, 150-51, 171-72,
    181, 193, 214, 224
    alienated, 156
    changing, 195
    critical, 177, 185, 193-95,
        215, 221, 250, 257
    deepened, 221, 227
    development of, 177, 185,
        194
    inner, 249
    naive, 193-94, 221
    personal, 249-50
    raising, 124, 129
    shared, 214, 227
    social, 27
Constructivism, 179
Consumerism, 3, 174-75
Contraceptives, 65, 74, 81-82,
    92, 102, 105-06
Control, 2, 25, 56, 182, 189, 193,
    220-21, 225-26
    authoritarian, 187
    of development, 61
    greater, assuming, 240
    lack of, 182, 230
    loss of researcher, 231
    need for, 236
    personal, 51-52
    sharing, 205
"Cops in the head," 220
Critical eye, 157, 162, 205
Cuernavaca Centre for Inter-
    cultural Dialogue on
    Development (CCIDD),
    14

"Culturally appropriate intervention," 94, 99

Dais (traditional village birth
attendants), 61, 64-65,
68, 71, 75-76, 79
Data, 108, 211-12, 241-45, 248-
49
analysis, 41-42, 206, 235,
256
collection, 7, 42, 53, 107,
169, 248
extraction, ethnographic
process of, 99
gathering, 256
interpretation of, 7, 242
management, 236
organizing, 212
qualitative, 181
sorting through, 84, 218
trustworthiness of, 44, 242
verification of, 232
de Bono, E., 222
Democratization, 24, 199, 215
Denzin, N.K., 249
Dependence, 109, 178, 192
de Tocqueville, Alexis, 175
Development, 3, 6, 27, 160, 205,
220, 250-52
activities in rural Chile, 116,
120
from broader perspective,
130
child, 61
of coding themes, 41-42
community, 113, 118, 129,
131, 168-70, 176, 208
community-based, 109, 147
group, 255
holistic, 245
inner, 170
international, 60, 62
ongoing, 239

participatory, 10, 119, 126,
129, 240
social, 119, 245
sustainable, 61, 251
work, 84
Dialectic, 185-86, 192, 196, 219,
249
Dialogue, 19, 122, 170, 184, 203,
226-28, 256
creation of, 183
culture of, 205
documenting, 248
dynamics of, 132
needs, about, 239
ongoing, 185, 237
outsider's use of, 255
probing, 195
Disabled children, and parents
of, 7-10, 36-40, 44-46,
51-56, 215-17, 240
activities, day-to-day of,
4, 7, 36-41, 45, 53, 203
changing to fit environ-
ment, 188, 199
physical barriers of, 206
Doing Participatory Research, 243
Domination, 20, 174-78, 192-95,
224, 248
relationships based on, 189,
221, 225
Dreams, 224, 248-49, 252

Ecuador, 171
Ekins, Paul, 2, 5
Emotions, 223-24, 227-29, 246
expressions of, 248
reshaping, 9
Empowerment, 8, 44, 51-52,
108, 120, 125-29, 244
of community, 61
"Enabling resources," 94, 103,
109
Energy, 215-16, 224-26, 231,

236, 250
action, leading to, 229
interconnected, 190
points, 203, 228, 237
potential, 201
stimulating, 228
Environment
connections with, 188, 190
degradation of, 5
disabling, 36-37, 52
factors of, 41. *See also* "Sorts
of things."
Equity, 4, 177
"External change agent," 256

Fals-Borda, O., 112, 176-78, 192,
195, 197, 225, 235
Fatalism, ethos of, 204
Fear, 3-10, 97, 99, 158, 189-192,
202, 223
bringing out, 151
of confrontation, 24-25, 215,
252
notions of, 106
loss of, 25, 150, 208-09, 228
of unknown, 161, 172
Fernandes, A.W., 253, 255, 257
Freedom, 183, 194, 203, 221-22,
245
Freire, Paulo, 113, 125, 178, 193-
94, 199, 205, 219, 221-22
and understanding of
disadvantaged, 113, 199
Fulfillment, 11, 145, 205, 219

Galbraith, A., 227
Gaventa, John, 177, 245
"Generative term," 125, 208,
228
Generative themes, 228-29
Geneva, 170-72
Ghandi, Rajeev, 83
Goals, 202-04, 206, 210

common, 15, 143, 166, 174-
75, 178, 228
of justice, social, 216
proposed, 184
revising, 65
Good, Byron, 106
Griffin, V.R., 222-23, 225
Growth, 30-31, 160, 182
personal, 113, 229, 252
processes of, 123
strategy, 229, 246
Guba, E., 179

Habermas, J., 178
Harman, W., 249-50, 252
Heart, 223-24, 227, 249
Heron, J., 248
Hindi, 66, 79, 82
Holism, 11, 31, 132, 243
Honduras, 7, 9, 11, 139-42, 197
Humanization, 24, 215, 252

Identity, 172, 188, 192, 203, 220
Ignorance, 29, 145, 168, 202,
208,
India, 60-62, 76, 81-82, 85, 197,
204, 218
marginalized people in, 175
rural, village women in, 60-
62, 65, 68, 70, 74-75, 80,
83, 240
Individualism, 101, 174-75, 189,
204
Industrialized world, 3, 174-75,
189, 219
Inequity, 9, 101, 182
Infant Development Program,
50
Information, 5, 178-79, 212-213,
222, 232-33
analysis of, 235, 238, 255
classification, 255
correct, obtaining, 250

cross-checking, 242
flow of, 240
gathering, 210, 212, 222,
    224, 226, 238, 255
giving, 226, 228
necessary, 199, 236, 239
new, 207, 238
sharing, 210
Injustice, 150, 181, 214
    social, 29, 30, 172, 177, 208,
        214, 219
Inquiry, 176, 179-83, 191, 206,
    221, 241-42, 250
    critical, 229, 246
    joint-process, 253, 255
    nature of, 7
    notes, making, 248
    participatory, 246
    self-, 194
    sustaining, 244
    understanding, 7
    validity of, 246
    whole-spirited, 244, 249
Insecurity, 3, 31, 189, 199, 219-
    20
Insiders, 72, 177, 192, 235, 255
"Intentional nudging," 45, 52,
    212
Interconnections, 150, 152, 158,
    191. *See also* Connec-
    tions.
    between negative and
        positive components,
        156-57
International Development
    Research Centre
    (IDRC), 93, 110, 137
Interpretation, 238, 249
    with action, coherent, 245
    art of, 247
    of data, 242
    deepening, 227
    dreams as a key to, 224

of problems, 255
various, 252
"Intervention," 94-95, 101, 109
Iquique, 114-16, 118, 128
Isolation, 3, 172, 174, 216
    breaking, 161, 200
    loss of, 50

Justice, 150, 251
    social, 28, 132, 156, 183, 198,
        214, 216
    social, sense of, 135

Kenmis, S., 178, 248-49
Knowing, ways of, 222-25, 227
Knowledge, 19, 69, 133, 172,
    177-78, 181-87, 191-93,
    242-48
    alternative, 112, 212
    body of, building, 145-46
    of circumstances, complex,
        204
    clear, 221
    of context, 231
    creation of, 175, 253
    critical, 245, 256
    definition of, 5, 176
    democratization of, 3
    factual, 256
    gaining, 161, 166
    of human suffering, in-
        creased, 99
    individual, 215
    interpersonal, 256
    new, 207, 213, 243, 249
    outsiders, brought by, 231
    of place, 201
    popular, 184, 245
    practical, 122, 187, 248
    production of, 6-10, 145,
        161, 166-68, 176-181,
        191, 196
    reconstructing, 226

of self, 197-98
social, 176, 215, 243
theoretical, 171
uses of, 112
validation of, 213, 245, 249
work as a source of, 17
Knowledge, Attitude and
Practice (KAP), 95
Krishnamurti, 222

La Esparanza ("the Hope"), 11,
140-42, 146, 164, 202
Lather, Patti, 177, 242-43
Latin America, 14-15, 145, 150,
164, 171, 199
and Church, 142
cultures indigenous to, 119
doctors in, 139
La Vara Alta de Moises (The
Staff of Moses), 142
Liberation, 8, 11, 170-75, 183
act of, 223
of oppressed, 177
situations of, 250
Lincoln, Y.S., 179
Linkages, 149-51, 160, 200
"Links," 146, 206, 241. *See also*
Relationships.
Lord, J., 51

Maguire, P., 178-79, 181, 243,
253, 255, 257
Martinic, 255
Maternal and Child Health
(MCH), 64, 73, 76, 79
Max-Neef, M.A., 203
McMaster University, 60-61
Menlo, 223
Mexico, 14-18, 21-24, 28-31, 200,
207, 215-16
people of, 202
traditional medicine,
practice of in, 164

Millet, Alberta, 14
Mind, 222-27
Ministry of Agriculture (Honduras), 166
Ministry of Agriculture
(Mexico), 24-25, 207
Ministry of Health (Honduras),
139-40, 144, 151, 160,
164, 166
Ministry of Health (Mexico), 29,
210
Mothers' Centres, 120
Movement, 30, 188, 197, 226,
229, 249-50
creation of, 181, 188, 214,
234
developing, 219
liberating, 222
social, 234

Nahuatl, 26
Needs, 146-49, 160, 169, 184-89,
195-99, 201-07, 234-39
community-based, 94, 152
defining, 54
economic, 127, 203
PAR and, 8, 23, 136, 181
of poor people, 140
recognizing, 19
specific, 157
urgent, 126, 128
women's health, 79
New World Order, 2-3
Non-governmental organizations (NGOs), 10, 100,
113, 116, 158, 168

Objectivity, 181-82, 212, 218,
235
Objectivization, 255
Ontario, Canada, 9, 39, 52, 84
Oppressed, the, 143, 202, 220,
225

liberation of, 177
Oppression, 174, 193-94, 221-22
    domestic, 62
    fighting, 169
    internal, understanding,
        214
    overcoming, 256
    silent, 234
    social, 29, 62, 208, 214
    structures of, 249
    understanding, 150
Oppressor, 143, 194, 202, 220,
        225
    invisible, 220-21, 225
Outsiders, 17-18, 27, 107, 169,
        177, 192-97, 223, 230-37
    disengagement, eventual
        of, 240
    lack of control of, 182
    problem-posing techniques,
        use of, 255
    trust of, 143, 201
    urban, 149

Pan American Health Organi-
        zation (PAHO), 140,
        166
Papua New Guinea, 61
Park, P., 225, 234, 245, 256-57
Participants, external and
        internal. See Outsiders;
        Insiders.
Participating Families–Cam-
        bridge (PF–Cam-
        bridge), 49-52, 210, 217,
        240
Participating Families–Ontario
        (PF–Ontario), 49, 51,
        208, 217
Pasantía (passing through), 11,
        145-46, 151, 153, 156-58,
        162, 166-68, 205, 213

Pascal, 255
"People bridges," 28, 207
Perception, 190-91, 214, 249
    alternative, value of, 236
    analysis of, 238
    capacity, human for, 150
    challenging, 246
    ecocentric, 3
    personal, 181, 231, 240-41
    of reality, 168, 181, 205
    shifting, 196
Perspective, 37, 54, 228, 246
    bureaucratized, 171
    critical, 181
    different, 196
    global, 3
    multiple, 248
    new, gaining, 195
    various, considering, 252
Pinochet, Ugarte, 113
Poor, the, 5, 105, 139, 156, 220,
        234
    life of, 208
    violence among, 169
    working with, 172, 219
Posada (procession), 22-23
Positivism, 179, 181, 191, 218
    rejection of, 182
Postpositivism, 179
Poverty, 2-5, 18-19, 29, 91, 101,
        107, 132, 142
    extreme, 233
    and guilt, 28
    and ignorance, 169
    and illness, 164
    meaning of, 208
    of spirit, 4, 164
Power, 181-82, 188-94, 205, 221,
        224
    complexities of, 219
    decision-making, 27, 202
    distribution of, 178
    gaining, 196

inner, 190, 193-94, 216, 251
keeping, 214
political, 208, 239
retaking, 8, 23-25
sharing, 24, 26, 190, 193-94,
  214, 216
summoning forth, 229
taking, 25, 209, 215
Power-from-within, 189-90, 192
Powerlessness, 3, 234
Power-over, 189, 192, 194
Power-with, 189-90, 192
Praxiology, 193, 197-98, 257
Praxis, 186-88, 192, 209, 211-12,
  225, 245, 252
  beginning, 197, 204
  engaging in, 229
  ongoing, 204
  people in, 252
Problems, 4, 193-94, 206, 228,
  238-40, 248, 255-56
  analysis of, 153, 157, 230
  in childbirth, 164
  economic, 4, 103
  family, 94
  focussing on, 207
  serious, systematic, 195, 218
  solutions to, facilitating, 54
  solving, 152, 157, 184, 230,
    255
  time as, 204
"Problematization," 205, 255
Production, 5, 31, 199
Prostitution, 93, 100-02, 106-07
Purpose, meaningful, 190, 252
  lack of, 174, 199

Rahman, M.A., 195, 197, 225
Rakai district, 92
Rakai AIDS Information
  Network (RAIN), 100
Reason, Peter, 236, 243, 246, 249
Reflection, 28-29, 160, 186-87,

191, 194-95, 216-17, 224
building upon, 147
critical, 249
dimensions of, 169
on knowledge, 248
personal, 11
on reality, 8, 187, 226
representation of, 247
silent, 229
texts, validity of, in terms
  of, 242
on values, 226
Reflection-action. *See* Action-
  reflection.
Relations, 188-89, 191-93, 195-
  96
  interpersonal, 234
  power, 181, 189, 192, 224
  understanding, 231
Relationships, 3, 161, 171, 188-
  96, 215, 221, 225
  asymmetrical, 178
  breaking, 25
  changes in, 250
  complexities of, 219
  creating, 104, 146, 201, 206,
    235
  dialectical, 10, 157, 219
  equitable, 168, 190
  human, 229
  identifying, 212
  maintaining, 170
  maladaptive, 94
  multiple, 248
  notions, indigenous of, 106
  risky, 202
  "subject-subject," 178
  testing, 201
  of trust, 227, 253
Research, 6, 11, 27, 140, 175-83,
  208
  attitudes towards, 244
  bias, 241

conventional, 8, 178, 183,
    235-36, 257
design, 256
emancipatory, 242
"emotional collisions" in,
    223
and emotions, 224
ethnographic, 93-95, 98, 100
experimental, 56
nature, collective of, 253
other, 49-52, 55, 179, 196,
    200, 231, 257
prevention of, 234
products of, 255
qualitative, 38, 95
questions, 211
rediscovering, 7
Research process, 8, 40, 69, 178,
    200, 215, 255
change, facilitating, 50
control over, 53, 212, 231
and discussion, 247
manipulation of, 241
participation in, prevention
    of, 195
Resources, 5, 8, 15, 27, 177, 225-
    26
common, using, 174
compiling, 166
financial, 108
shifting, 196
sufficient, obtaining, 251

Santiago, Chile, 119
Security, 30-31, 199
dependent, 143, 202
emotional, 213
false, 219-20
Self, 166, 185, 194-98, 212-13,
    220-22, 227
development within, 188
identification of, 225
inner, 6, 188, 195

questioning, 244
reconnecting with others,
    218
redirection of, 11
reliance, 5-6, 194
researching, 170
sense of, 31, 198, 216, 221,
    250
Self-esteem, 6, 25, 144, 189, 223,
    229, 251
Schapiro, R., 243
Shor, I., 226
Silimu (AIDS), 93, 97
Social Education Area (SEA),
    128-29
Society, 181, 183
collective, 175
hierarchial, 62, 71, 156
industrialized, 189
mass, 219
nature of, 179
redirection of, 11, 139
structure of, 24, 215
Solidarity, 10, 24, 26, 28-29, 75,
    171, 215
act of, 216
breaking, 214
building, 200
community, lack of, 101
comprehending, 150
farmer-to-farmer, 14
freedom of, 222
meaning of, 169
symbol of, 161
"Sorts of things," 40-41, 53, 203
Spirit, 224-25, 250-51
poverty of, 4, 164, 249
Spirituality, 225
Srinivasan, L., 229-30
Starhawk, 189-90
Status quo, 8, 55, 161, 177
Study, pilot, 65-69, 73
Subjectivity, 181-82, 212, 243

Survival, 2-3, 98, 144, 172
  of community, 118, 121, 203
  physical, 194
  understanding, dependent
    on, 124
Synergism, 160, 210, 219, 252
System, the, 48, 194, 206

Taking action, 6, 11, 19, 27, 191-
    97, 208-11, 221
  political, 177-78, 225-26
Taller de Estudios Aymara
    (TEA), 10, 114-31, 203,
    206, 208, 218, 239
Taller de Estudios Regionales
    (TER), 114-15, 128
Tandon, R., 178, 245, 253, 255,
    257
Tapia, 255
Tarapaca, region of, 116
Technology, 4-5, 142, 144
  appropriate, 252
  development of healthy,
    244
  domination of, 193
Tepoztlan, municipality of, 14,
    21
Tilakaratna, S., 195, 235, 238-40
Tractor, idle, 24-26, 207, 209,
    214-15
Triangulation, 241-42
Trust, 11, 157, 170, 201, 226-27,
    237, 245-46
  building, 84, 131, 135, 143,
    200, 217, 237
  gaining, 119
  lack of, 241
  mutual, 185, 227

of outsiders, 143, 201
  relationships based on, 253
Truth, 140, 153, 179, 191-93,
    214, 242, 247
  new, 191, 195
  pursuit of, 176
Truth or Dare, 189

Uganda, 10, 87, 92-93, 103, 197
Ugandan AIDS Support Orga-
    nization (TASO), 98
Uttar Pradesh, 60-62

Validation, 150, 222, 240, 246
  four methods of, 242
  of knowledge, 213, 245, 249
  social, 212
Validity, 241-47
  obtaining, 239
  silence about, 242-43
Village assemblies, 124, 128,
    206, 239
Village leader (Chile), 123-24,
    126, 130
Village leader (Mexico), 24-26,
    207, 214
Vio Grossi, 255, 257
Violence, 3-4, 189, 220-22
Vivencia, 195-96, 245, 257
Voices of Change, 225

Waragi (raw gin), 89-90
Washington, D.C., 171
Waterloo, Regional Municipal-
    ity of, 39
  Health and Social Services
    Committee in, 50